Connie's Violin Page

Internet resources for string players, teachers, parents and students

by

C.M. Sunday

Publish date August 14, 2009 by createspace, an Amazon.com company. ISBN: 144867333X Category: Music/Music Instruments/ Strings. Title ID: 3395021 EAN-13: 9781448673339 Cover graphic HC7000 by Howard Core Company, LLC. Used with permission.

To Kyra and Alexandra

Contents

FAQ: Auditions & Gigs

III. Guides

IV. Music Education Resources

V. String Teachers Questionnaire

Acknowledgments

This book would not exist without the insights of many, many musicians, teachers, parents and students over many years, found on string-related forums such as Suzuki Xchange, Maestronet, Fiddle-L, rec.music.makers.bowed-strings, rec.music.early, and YahooGroups forums such as bavs, string_teacher_support, Viola list, OrchestraList, and a host of others. If relationships have not always been cordial, they have at least been fruitful, and I am very grateful.

When graphic interface was new, and the personal homepage was just beginning to be seen–nearly 20 years ago–there was nothing like the information available now, specifically on violin and string pedagogy. There were only five sites on violin, online: my own, and that of John Krakenberger, Cheniston Roland, Shiela Helser and José Sánchez-Penzo. If I remember correctly, the latter three preceded John and me, and I'm happy to say, all five sites are still alive on the net. John and I are still friends; his amazing intellect and vitality are an inspiration.

I would be remiss if I did not personally thank a number of people individually: Jon and Rolland on the USENET group (to name two); Carolyn, list ma and manager on bavs and friend of 10 years; and so many others who have taken many valuable hours of their lives to express their views and share their knowledge. Mary, who encouraged me to write this material out in book form. Theresa, who reminds me of myself, so much, when I was very young and trying to find my way as a musician and a teacher.

I want to thank every teacher who contributed their comments to the survey, and especially all the students I've been privileged to teach over the years. My hope has always been that by organizing these materials, other teachers and musicians will find help and resources, so they do not have to learn everything by painful trial and error, as I had to do. If I have succeeded in this only a little, it will all have been worthwhile.

C.M. Sunday
Lubbock, TX
August 6, 2009

E-mail: cmsunday@alumni.rice.edu

ESSAYS

Early History of the Violin
(1520-1650)

Relatively little is known about the violin before 1600, though the true violin was popular at village fetes, taverns, in homes, and at aristocratic court functions such as the French ballet, English masque, and Italian intermedio. Its power of rhythmic articulation and penetrating tone was used extensively for dance music. Instrumental music was modeled on forms derived from vocal models not idiomatic to the violin, which was also used to double or accompany vocal parts. The real potential of the violin was not exploited until the 17th century when the Italians wrote sonatas. With the possible exception of Orlando di Lasso, no great composers wrote for violins until Gabrielli and Monteverdi. The two uses of violins contrast sharply; on the one hand, the undignified and festive use of violins for dancing, (jamming), with no music in sight; and on the other, the serious use of violins for religious or semi-religious purposes, in church, say, with instruments held at the neck and longer bows. The unwritten tradition of improvisation is comparable to the early history of jazz, the violinist being much like the sax player. In the area of dancing, the violins gradually drove the rebecs from court. (See: *The Rebec Project*: http://www.crab.rutgers.edu/~pbutler/rebec.html)

Violin playing was not considered a lady-like or gentlemanly pursuit; violinists were considered to be a species of servant, and the violin had little social or musical prestige. It was considered a lowly instrument played mostly by professionals. In time, however, it spread through every class. The formation of the "24 Violins of the King," in France, symbolized increased social prestige.

"Virtuous" people (aristocratic amateurs), according to Jambe de Fer (see below) passed their time playing the viol, a family of instruments unrelated to the violins which persisted for 150 years after the violins came into being, and fell into neglect when polyphonic music went out of style. All viols (lira da gamba) were played held downward, larger ones between the legs and smaller ones on the knees, and the bow was held underhand. The violins developed independently.

Though hybrid instruments continued to exist some time after the emergence of the violin, its origins are said to have been the rebec, the Renaissance fiddle, and the lira da braccio. The rebec dates back to the 13th century and consisted of a family of treble (discant), alto-tenor, and bass instruments. It was pear-shaped, and without a soundpost; the neck and pegbox were integral parts of the instrument. There were no overhanging edges, no frets, and the three strings were tuned in fifths. The sound of this instrument is said to have been smaller than the violins, with a nasal, oboelike quality. The bow was held overhand. The Renaissance fiddle, c. 1500, had five strings, (one a drone), and frets. Shaped like the violin, it had a top and back with connecting ribs, a separate neck and fingerboard, and it was in the soprano register. Close to the violin body outline, the lira da braccio was designed in several sizes; its bouts made it easier to bow then the rebec. Like the violin, it had an arched back and top, overlapping edges, ribs, a sound post, and f or c-shaped sound holes. It had seven strings, two of which were drones.

By a kind of organic, triangulative process between craftsmen, players, and composers, early violins came into existence around 1520 in northern Italy. The four-stringed "true" violin family was complete in its basic structural features - though not standardized - around 1550. (Jambe de Fer described them explicitly in his *Epitome Musical*. Lyons, 1556.) The controversy over who invented the first violin is probably not answerable; Gasparo da Saló was a candidate, as were several Brescian craftsmen. It is now generally accepted that da Saló was not the inventor since he wasn't born until 1540. Better candidates are Giovan Giacoba dalla Corna and Zanetto de Michelis da Montichiaro, both born in the 1480s. It is, however, clear that Andrea Amati perfected the form. Similar instruments in France and Poland suggest the far-reaching influence of the Italian Renaissance. Native schools of violin-making existed in Cremona and Brescia, and also in Paris and Lyon; but this had to do with the trade routes (and the silk trade) from Venice to Paris. Changes in the violin after 1600 were largely decorative.

Early violins could be either 1/4" shorter or 1/2" longer than the modern 14" (35.5 cm) instrument. Pegboxes sometimes ended in carved heads instead of scroll. The neck is shorter, projects at right angles from the body, and the fingerboard is shorter (by 2 1/2"), with a wedge between neck and fingerboard. The bridge is both lower and rounder. Open strings were used when possible, and the more yielding hair of the old bow made it easier to sustain triple stops at forte. The modern chinrest was unknown, and the violin was held at the neck; perspiration marks on either side of the tailpiece indicate the chin held the instrument there. In dance music, the instrument was often or usually held lower.

While the Tourte bow rendered the older bows obsolete and of no commercial value (therefore none exist today), the older violins were carefully preserved, though apart from rare exceptions, usually opened and altered with modern fittings, including neck, fingerboard, bridge, bass-bar, sound-post, strings, chinrest and E tuner. Because of the lower tension, the old bass bar was shorter and lighter and the soundpost thinner. Early (convex) bows varied greatly in shape, and the modern frog was predated by various attempted solutions to holding the narrower ribbon of hair in place. The modern Tourte bow, with its logarithmic inward curvature, cannot be pressed too deeply in the middle, or the wood will be scraped by the strings. Baroque bows did not have this problem, though the degree of curvature began to decrease at the end of the 17th century.

Early in the 16th century the advantages of combining from its predecessors the greater sonority, the easier and more efficient playing and tuning, and the more sensible fingering were discovered. The new instruments were easier to carry at dances, weddings and mummeries (theatrical productions including masked figures), and their sound "carried well," which was important for dancing. Many musicians played both old and newer instruments, and technical practices were borrowed from the old.

Though the Baroque violin was considered "beaucoup plus rude en son" (Jambe de Fer, 1556), it was, by our standards, less intense, purer, reedier and more transparent. Gimping, or the practice of using gut strings overspun with fine copper or silver wire, was not practiced until the early 18th century. Strings were gut, (for this reason the G was unresponsive, and seldom used), and gauges were not known, though violin strings were stronger and thicker than viol strings.

Early Baroque violin music, (of which there is very little before the turn of the century, and that in the last 20 years, and not idiomatic), seldom ventures beyond the third position. (The first written music designated with a violin part is that of a Royal French wedding in 1581.) Therefore the usual range was d'-b" or c", (since the low G was seldom used)–the typical range of the soprano voice. Though lute players were encouraged to play "beyond the frets," the short, fat neck of the violin did not encourage playing in upper positions, and made it more difficult to use the fourth finger; the momentary robustness of open strings was not uncommon.

There were no accepted standards of pitch; string players were regularly told to tune their instruments up as high as they would go, (Agricola, 1528) and pitch varied from town to town and even from one organ to another within a church. Nor was there any equally tempered tuning system. There was probably a distinction between harmonic pairs of notes, but it worked opposite to what it is today. (For example, violinists today think of F#, say, as a sort of leading tone to G, and the F# is played higher than the upper enharmonic. The reverse was true in the Baroque.)

Nor was there any standardization in the way the bow of the violin was held. As mentioned above, the violin was held in a more relaxed position while dance music was played on the breast or arm, (hence, the distinction "lira da braccio,") and held at the neck for more serious music. The bow was held in two styles; that of the French – very different than the modern way – with the thumb under the hair and not between bow and stick, as in the second, or Italian way, which is said to be entirely similar to modern teaching, such as that of Carl Flesch.

The animated styles of dancing and the short bows were made for an articulated style, unlike the "endless bow" idea of modern practice. Vibrato was not continuous, but used as expressive ornamentation. (Our wide and continuous vibrato would have been disruptive.) No fingerings have been found before 1600 even for such simple music that exists. Playing in the higher positions seems unlikely, considering the way the instrument was held in dance music. (From the modern viewpoint, second position is excellent to use, particularly in sequential passages.) However, there was more to violin music than the extant pieces indicate. So much money was spent on fine instruments, and this is not compatible with the idea of primitive instruments and technique. Orchestral and chamber parts were not required to go above the third position, but virtuoso pieces were another matter. Some advance technique may have been lost because it was considered a professional secret.

After 1600, violin players built on the technical achievements of the viol players, and the practice advanced rapidly. Monteverdi's operatic writing included idiomatic sections with comparatively sophisticated technique. After 1610, the advent of the violin sonata, the formative period of violin practice ended and a new technical virtuosity came about in response to an age which produced Galileo, Kepler, Bacon, Descartes, Newton and Harvey. (And anticipated by da Vinci and manifested in the Reformation.) The rise of opera and instrumental forms not subordinate to the voice is analogous to the gradual subordination of religious to secular authority. Musicians were usually lower-middle class, and traditionally from long lines of musical families; socially, the lot of the musician varied from little better than beggar to that of the Royal musicians, who enjoyed fine clothes, salaries, and some measure of security. Even the ordinary musician was protected by unions in both France and England. During the early 17th century, the preeminence of violin making continued in Brescia and Cremona, and Biago Marini of Brescia (1597-1665) was the most important composer of violin music of the time; he and contemporaries such as Dario Castello, Salomone Rossi, Maurizio Cazzati, and Marco Uccellini experimented with purely instrumental forms. The sonata – most advanced of instrumental forms – came from the old practice of doubling vocal parts of a chanson, one of the principle Renaissance forms.

Marini's work is calculated in terms of the violin; the rapid passages fit the hand, particularly in descending or ascending sequences and arpeggios and broken chords involving playing back and forth across strings. Marini used the "stile concitato," predating Monteverdi, and experimented extensively in double - and triple-stops. (Capriccio per Sonare il Violino con tre corde a mondo di lira, Op. 8.) His scordatura was written at pitch, leaving the player to work out the fingerings. (Most later scordatura works were written in "hand-grip" notation.)

Other special affects of the Baroque were the use of pizzicati like that used in Monteverdi's operas (not called such), the mute, col legno, sul ponticello and sulla tastiera. Harmonics may or may not have been known, and the matter is not settled. Two types of ornaments were used; (a) those with specific names, such as the trill, mordent, vibrato and (b) those which constituted some improvised melodic formulae. The practice of adding passages to the written score was so common that sometimes composers felt it was necessary to add "come sta senza passaggi." Since the demands of dance music were chiefly rhythmic, it is not known if violin practice included ornamental elaboration like the diminutions and passaggi of Francesco RognIono.

All of these physical characteristics contributed to a sound which was altogether less assertive, less massive, and more edgy, pungent, and colorful. "Just as the painter imitates nature," (wrote Ganasssi, in "Regola Rubertina," the only detailed treatise on string playing in the 16th century; Ganassi was a professional viol player,) "so wind and string players should imitate the human voice." Vibrato on long notes must have been combined with dynamic nuance, and the *messa di voce* probably carried over into string practice.

Though if one sees a lot of dynamic markings in a Baroque piece, and it may be inferred that they were put there by the editor, they nevertheless existed from the start of the period and increased in frequency throughout. Performers considered them hints, however, and dynamics are properly used for structural shaping, to delineate the form by terraced fortes and pianos, and to mold the texture within the form. This may cause a built-in echo effect. Agogic accents were probably used for expression, but no mention is made of the audible shifting or portamento so usual in modern playing; the practice was that several shifts were preferred over one big one. Marini's greatest contribution lies in his purposeful adaptation of vocal style to idiomatic violin writing. Affetti Musicali, the title of Op. 1 (1617) may be said to indicate that the affections could be moved (that all-embracing Baroque ideal) by means of instruments alone.

The Baroque ideal is an arch of sound, appropriately well-sustained and well-proportioned. For Baroque music to get airborne, the line must soar. The bow is like the breath of a singer. To quote Donington (p. 88): "Phrases generally go to a peak note, which is often though not always the highest note, and then relax to a note given away at the end. There is the unit; that much, and no less nor more, is the phrase; and it is for our own musicianship to recognize the fact. Nothing in the notation and nothing in the historical evidence, is going to show us the pattern if our own musicianship does not." To achieve this, the modern violinist (with modern instrument) would have to slow down the bow, use less of it, and play into the string with the hair a little flatter and near the bridge. Donnington remarks: it can be done.

Bibliography

Baroque Music, Claude V. Palisca. 2nd Edition. Prentice-Hall. N.J. 1981, pp. 145-6.

The Concise Oxford Dictionary of Music, Michael Kennedy. 3rd Edition. Oxford University Press. London. 1980. pp. 608.

Historical Anthology of Music, Archibald T. Davidson and Will Apel. Harvard University Press. Cambridge, Mass. 1950. pp. 30 and 281.

A History of Western Music, Donald Jay Grout. [3rd Edition with Claude V. Palisca.] W. W. Norton & Co., Inc. New York. 1973. pp. 293-40, 334-5. Newest ed. of the Grout, 7th ed., Burkholder

The History of Violin Playing from its Origins to 1761 and its Relationship to the Violin and Violin Music, David D. Boyden. Oxford University Press. 1965. pp. 2-189.

The Grove Dictionary of Musical Instruments, edited by Stanley Saide. MacMillan Press, Ltd. London. 1984. Vol. 3, pp. 767-773.

The Oxford History of Music, Vol. III. "The Music of the 17th Century," C. Hubert H. Parry. Oxford. 1902. p. 308.

Sonata Per Due Violini Und Basso Continuo (1665). Hortus Musicus 143.1 BÃƒÂ¤renreiter-Verlag Kassel und Basel. Germany. 1957.

Sonate D-Moll für Violine, Streichbass (Gambe oder Violincello) Und Basso Continuo, Biagio Marini. Hortus Musicus 129. Barenreiter-Verlag Kassel und Basel. Germany. 1955.

String Playing in Baroque Music, Robert Donington. Charles Scribner's & Sons. New York. 1977.

Ornamentation in Giuseppe Tartini's
Traité des Agréments

Ornamentation, Part I : Single Note Ornamentation

In examining 18th century ornaments, a number of questions come to mind: Is the ornament diatonic, or does it require an accidental? Does it precede the main note or fall on the beat? Is it fast or slow? If slow, what proportion of the main note does the ornament require? Does the stress lie more on the ornament or the main note? The questions are complicated, since instructions in various treatises are often contradictory and stenographic indications are not consistent. Methods of execution were dependent upon tradition and musicians have always tended to deviate from accepted practice. In addition, writers may have put more effort into disclosing what they consider bad practice as opposed to what they accept as correct. Since up until the time of Beethoven so much was left to the discretion of the player or singer, an executant two centuries later is often left with a series of puzzles. In Tartini's treatise, as Frederick Neuman points out several times, much of the material is unclear or ambiguous, and there are opinions stated which are given without any specific compelling reasons.

The Appoggiatura, Trill and Mordent

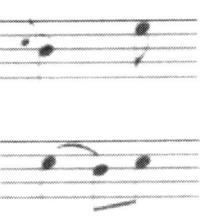

Frederick Neuman categorizes two primary sorts of Vorslage[1] in Tartini's ornaments: (1) The long or sustained (appoggiature lunga ossia sostentatat) and (2) the short or passing type (appoggiature breve ossia di passaggio). The first, which Tartini limits to the heavy beat and generally to pieces in slow tempo, is said to take half the value of the printed note, and 2/3 the value of the dotted note. The reason that composers do not write this material out directly is because of the difference in execution; normally, the first eighth note would need a short trill to further underline it, but as an appoggiature, it should begin softly and swell and diminish before it falls on the eighth note. Since dissonance "ought" to be resolved downward, Tartini dislikes a long ascending appoggiature that creates a dissonance. The second type is an anticipated gracenote, a fleeting expression with the accent on the primary note.

Tartini's advice to singers and string players about the use of the trill is unique and sensible. The trill was the most usual and important of ornaments during this style period, and currently the most controversial, in respect to the conflict over the upper note start. Despite Neumann's "intuitive misgivings about prevailing theories of baroque ornamentation,"[2] the upper note start of the trill was given with monotonous regularity from the middle of the 17th century; it is to be found in the works of Playford, d'Angelbert, Muffat, Purcell, Hottenterre, Couperin, Tosi, Rameau, Quantz, C.P.E. Bach, Marpurg, and Türk. However, Leopold Mozart mentions no rule about starting trills with an upper note, and in two long chapters on the trill, Tartini never mentions the need to start on the upper note, though patterns in the Treatise do show upper-note start and anchor.[3]

The trill, according to Tartini, is like salt in cooking, which must not be used too much or too little. Different speeds of trills suit different moods of music, and a good player must master all speeds. Trills may be started from above or below and there are several forms of ending trills, the bad sort being "abhorrent to nature."[4]

Tartini mentions two ways for a violinist to produce a trill. One is by pressing hard on the lower note and striking the trill; the other is the "ripped" not "struck" affect created not by raising the finger but by using the wrist to carry the hand in a rippling motion. This is not the same as Carl Flesch's Bochstriller which is created with the arm in the higher positions. [5] In the letter to Signora Lombardini,[6] the composer recommends that the student learn the shake by increasing the speed by gradation, beginning first with the open string and first finger:

This exercise is also given in the Treatise with the addition of passing by gradation from piano to forte:

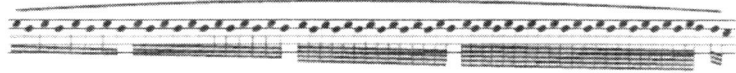

Tartini's mordente is often a prebeat turn; in his treatise he introduces two sorts of grace notes which he calls mordente: (1) a melodic form of a turn; and (2) a genuine mordent with one to three alternations. The melodic form, consisting of scalewise notes centering on and preceding the primary note, is of two types, but the falling appoggiatura sounded better to his ears.

His instructions are that these graces are to be performed as quickly as possible, and not be heard individually but as part of a total affect which is vivacious and spirited. The accent falls on the primary note and not on the graces. In the case of the genuine mordent with the alternation, the primary note still has the accent and the ornaments are to be done piano and very quickly. The French translation of the Treatise gives an incorrect account of the two types of turns, revealing a rhythmic ambivalence not out of keeping with other difficulties in the Treatise. Tartini's mordents are anticipated turns from either above or below; they are not to be placed on notes where any accent is not appropriate. The genuine mordent is identical to our presentday mordent; at first glance it looks like a shorter trill, but falls, instead, to the note below instead of rising. It may consist of four or six notes, depending on finger speed.[7] The Italians have no written symbol for the mordent.

Vibrato
Tasteful vibrato (tremolo) was applied not continually, but as an occasional ornament.[8] To Tartini, this ornament was an affect

produced by the imitation, on stringed instruments, of a wave motion in the air, which is naturally left behind by harpsichord strings, bells or the open string of any good bowed instrument. He disparaged its use on half-steps, but felt it sounded well on final notes of phrases, long notes in singing passages, and double steps on long notes. The modern arm vibrato was unknown in the eighteenth century, and would have been impossible to produce, given the absence of a modern chin-rest. Vibrato was produced with the left wrist, more enabling one to control the speed: fast, slow, or accelerating on one note. The hand undulated toward the bridge, rather than the scroll, and the left hand held the instrument differently than it is held today; changes in the form of the bow, and tension in the hair and string, also contribute to the difference between 18th and 20th century violin sound.

Ornamentation, Part II: Compound Ornaments

The second part of the Treatise deals with natural and artificial modes, by which Tartini meant not keys (as meant in French) but the manner of placing ornamental figures, similar to the "divisions" of Elizabethan music. [9] Regarding natural figures; in the course of treating a bass line, certain cadential points lend themselves to figurations, whether a full stop is made or the melody is unfinished. Tartini compares these cadential points with punctuation in writing. Cadential formulae are given at length, but composite figures may occur naturally, as the primary cells are simple and few in number. In contrast, artificial figurations are very many in number and it would be necessary to treat all the possible permutations; they have to do with compositons, and good taste is the rule. One can generate ideas about these cadences by examining the possible thorough-bass progressions.

Natural cadences are those phrase endings on which the melody stops. An artificial cadence indicates a final cadence, with a fermata sign, that the signer or player may draw out as long as he or she wishes. This free cadenza was very much in the spirit of the time, though the freedom to embellish was much more limited in Tartini's day than it later came to be. As time passed, composers increasingly gave more explicit instructions, and performers tended more and more to concentrate their improvisitory impulses on the cadenza. Initially, Tartini gives nineteen of the simplest examples of these, cautioning that one must be sure to avoid consecutive fifths and octaves. Numerous examples follow with increasing complexity. While the examples are in major, they could just as easily be used in minor, though Tartini states that they would not sound as well, due to the irregularities in the minor mode.

Background of the Treatise

The Composer

Giusippe Tartini is the link between the old style of Vivaldi and the "new" classicism of Viotti. His style changed gradually from baroque to *style galant* and was a synthesis of *galant* and *empfindsam* qualities during the mid-eighteenth century. His fame was based on a rare combination of talents; his virtuosic playing, his compositions, (consisting of over 400 works written within the space of four decades between 1720 and 1760, [10]), and on his scholarship and teaching. Quantz criticized Tartini's excess of virtuosity, perhaps reflecting the prejudice against the Italian style in music, while praising his beautiful, sweet tone aimed more at expression than power, and his mastery of the great difficulties involved in trills, double trills, double stops and high positions.

Considering that he was the greatest violin master of his time, and was known all over Europe during the mid-eighteenth century, Tartini's life was relatively sedentary and uneventful.[11] He was known for his well-bred and unassuming manner, warmth, sensitivity and paternal interest in his students. He was given to visionary mysticism, and wrote mottoes in secret code on many of his compositions. He was an eighteenth century genius who was not only a composer and pedagogue, but an inventor who took contemporary criticism of his scientific work quite seriously.[12].

Tartini's music disappeared from active concert repertory, but continued to be used as study material. A change in musical taste is reflected in Burney's two published opinions of the composer; the one expressed in 1788 was less favorable than the first from 1770; during the interim Tartini's ornate style had begun to seem stilted and out of fashion. Eighteenth century audiences were not historically minded; Tartini's work was apparently not referred to in other treatises after its publication, and by the time of its publication in France, had begun to be outmoded.

The School

Tartini's academy for violinists, founded in 1727 or 1728, was the composer's main source of income; he gave daily lessons, working ten hours a day. The school existed for more than forty years, and the students there comprised most of the great European violinists.[13]. The Treatise was compiled by his students from lessons; it was unique in being the first pedagogical work exclusively to detail the reason for and applications of ornamentation, providing information continued in no other books of the period; Tartini's Treatise takes its place among the most significant contributions during the first part of the 18th century, including those of C.P.E. Bach, Quantz, Agricola, Tosi and Leopold Mozart. [14]. It was never published in Italy. It must have existed by 1750, since Leopold Mozart used it in 1756, but could have originated any time between 1728 (the year Tartini founded his school) and c. 1754 (when Mozart began his Violinschule).[15] The original manuscript, which was thought to be lost, was discovered in two independent copies, one at Berkeley and one in Venice.[16].

Conclusion

Eighteenth-century Italians were more interested in art and music than the philosophy and politics that consumed the rest of Europe and England. It was a time of growing popularity of the violin and its virtuosi, and in this Tartini's importance is secure; he was the teacher of Pugnani who taught Viotti, and the teacher of Leclair who taught Gavin's.

Examining the master's work today, one can only conclude that the rise of the super virtuosi in music has come full circle, and the return to the original intentions of the composers has become necessary for educated musicians. In this way the accumulated miscellany of two centuries may be removed and the purity of the originally intentioned sounds may be recreated or approximated.

In the preface to the Moeck edition, Erwin Jacobi states:

> Whoever has heard Italian string music of that period (particularly slow movements) played without our permanent vibrato by good musicians will realize that aesthetic appreciation has in the meantime changed less than one might have supposed; stylistically faithful performance still remains an inseparable part of true artistry.[17]

Endnotes

1. The German term is substituted for the Italianate "appoggiature" in order to avoid the questionable connotation of "leaning."

2. In Neumann's book, lesser-known documents that illustrate the main-note trill include those of Vincenzo Panerai, Carl Testore, Vincenzo Manfredini, Signorelli, Lorenzone, and Antonio Borghese. [Frederick Neumann, *Ornamentation in Baroque and Post-Baroque Music with Special Emphasis on J.S. Bach* (New Jersey: Princeton University Press), 1978, vi.]

3. Neumann's complaint about the rigidifying effect of certain assumptions in baroque performance practice is keyed on two areas: (1) that all primary small grace notes (such as the slide, appoggiature or mordent) must necessarily start precisely on the beat and take their values from the following note: and (2) all trills must necessarily start with the upper auxiliary. Neumann's scheme of organization consists of divisions of types.

Neumann's Division of Types

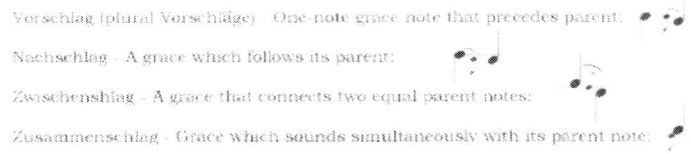

Vorschlag (plural Vorschläge) - One-note grace note that precedes parent:

Nachschlag - A grace which follows its parent:

Zwischenshlag - A grace that connects two equal parent notes:

Zusammenschlag - Grace which sounds simultaneously with its parent note:

4. What Tartini means by "natural" has not to do with the ideas associated with Voltaire, Rousseau and the Age of Reason, but something more concrete and literal; that is, the "naturally" ornamented singing of the people with whom he associated as he grew up, in Pirano on the Istrian coast. [Giuseppe Tartini, *Traité des Agréments de la musique*. French translation, P. Denis, Paris (1771), ed. Erwin R. Jacobi, with English translation, C. Girdlestone, and facsimile of original Italian text (Cell and New York: Herman Moeck Verlag), 1961, 77.)]

5. *Ibid.*, 79.

6. The Letter to Madalene Lombardini (with an English translation by Charles Burney) is more than half concerned with the use of the bow. The pupil was told to practice short strokes at the point, upper middle,

middle, and lower middle, and, in general, to make herself "mistress of" every section of the bow and every species of bowing. The notion that to play well, one must sing well, is insisted upon. Bow articulation, strong left hand technique in double stops, and fluent runs are recommended. He had what were once considered to be peculiar notions about practicing in various positions and was meticulous about intonation. The autograph copy of this letter, dating form 1760, is lost; the one often cited in the Municipal Museum in Pirano, Tartini's birthplace, is not in the composer's handwriting and contains mistakes in the musical examples.

7. Tartini's mordents are not to be confused with Tosi's trillo mordente (miniature trill). Agricola also complained that the Pralltriller (upper mordent) was confused with the mordent. In German, mordent means only the lower mordent.

8. Today the practice is the opposite: if a composer does not wish to use vibrato, they must indicate so. (Ex: Stravinsky's *Firebird* or Bartók's Fourth String Quartet, third movement)

9. "Divisions" is an obsolete term, and refers to a preclassical technique of extemporization, common in viol playing, consisting of splitting up the notes of a tune into shorter notes, i.e., a form of variation.

10. A thematic catalog, *Le opera di Giuseppe Tartini*, was edited by Farina and Scimone and published in Milan in 1975. A complete catalog of Tartini's concertos was created in 1935 by Minos Dounias; hence the "D" numbers. Paul Brainard published a thematic catalog of Tartini's sonatas (1975) which includes 191 works, some incomplete or spurious. The twelve sonatas of Op. 1 and the twelve of Op. 2 were the only publications authorized by the composer. Op. 4, 5, 6, 7, and 9 are suspect, as handwritten copies were often used by unscrupulous publishes. Vieuxtemps, Wieniawski and Joachim admired and performed his sonatas. Tartini was the most important composer of violin concertos between Vivaldi and Viotti: his violin concertos were models for violinists and harpsichordists.

11. The primary source for information about the composer's early life is material compiled at the time of his death by an old friend and colleague, Vandini. Documents prior to 1721 are rare and not very reliable. There are unverified reports about his early years; it is thought that his parents intended for him to be a priest and that Tartini learned the violin as a child, continuing to pursue music seriously against parental wishes. Despite his clerical status, Tartini came into conflict

with the church, and more particularly, with the bishop of Padua, Cardinal Cornaro: when Tartini was 19 he married 21-year-old Elisabetta Premazore (described later as Xantippe-like), the Cardinal's protégée. Tartini was charged with abduction and subsequently took refuge in the Franciscan monastery at Assisi. In 1709 his name appears, oddly enough, among the law students at the University of Padua. By 1714 he was spending time in both Assisi and Ancona, where he played in the opera orchestra, and where he pursued his acoustic studies. In 1715 he obtained pardon from the Paduan authorities and was reunited with his wife.

12. Tartini experimented with bow sticks and thicker strings and studied acoustics; he published his acoustical findings in *Trattato di musica*, Padova, 1754. He "discovered" resultant tones: difference and summation tones. Mozart has a whole section of these tones in his work, but both writers heard the tones in the wrong octave and the minor sixth is given incorrectly by both. Herman Helmholtz, a German authority on acoustics, medical man and professor of physiology, explained this phenomena, formulating it correctly in *Sensations of Tone*, 1862.

13. Tartini, the "Master of Nations," had more than 70 important students, including: Alberghi, Bini, Fracasini, J.G. Graun, Helendaal, La Housaye, Leclair, Meneghini (Tartini's successor at the school), Nardidni, J.G. Naumann, Nicolai (who took the Treatise to Paris), Pagin, Puganelli, Pugnani.

14. Leopold Mozart lifted wholesale many ideas and specific examples of Tartini's work (especially the trill and vibrato), being careful only to transpose the examples, and gave no acknowledgment except to mention that "a great Italian Master teaches his pupils thus" (in reference to Tartini's example of the augmented second trill). [Leopold Mozart, *Versuch einer grundlichen Violinschule* (1756), translated and edited by Editha Knocker as *A Treatise on the Fundamental Principles of Violin Playing* (London: Oxford University Press, 1948), 187.] Wolfgang Mozart's early compositions were strongly influenced by Tartini.

15. Probably nearer the later date, because of such practices as 6-4 chord preparations of cadenzas, a relatively late development. In his *Biographic Universelle*, Francois-Joseph Fétis gives the date as 1782, which was an error.

16. After two centuries of obscurity, a very unusual coincidence

occurred; printing of the Moeck Edition was about to begin when an Italian version was discovered at Berkeley and, at about the same time, a more complete version was found at Venice at Pierluig. Petrobelli, in an Addendum to the Preface, discusses the new sources. There is very evident mutual cooperation and generosity among the several actors in this expensive process of adjustment.

The Venice MS (V) is an excellent condition and contains an abundance of new examples, including 36 cadences, grouped by keys. It was lovingly and painstakingly copied by Nicolai, a Tartini pupil and leading violinist in Rome. The Berkeley copy (B) has more dialect and abbreviations. Accents, capitalizations and punctuation are carried out more carefully in V than in B. The Italian MS is more constant in terminology and certain examples are more accurate than the French edition, perhaps reflecting the devotion of Nicolai. Also, the essence of the material not included in the French edition turned up in Leopold Mozart's work. La Houssaye, one of Tartini's favorite pupils, brought the MS to Paris and arranged to have it translated by P. Denis; this translation from Paris is designated as P.

The collection at UC Berkeley, in which the Tartini MS was found, consists of over 1,000 works for small string ensembles dated from c. 1750-1800. Over 80 composers are represented, around 23 unknown. The collation was probably designed for use in a petty Italian court or wealthy family and was located at Sacile (near Pirano, Tartini's birthplace) before being purchased by Berkeley. Some parts of the collection had been preserved for two centuries, according to dated MSS. The initial impulse for acquisition came from Vincent Duckles and Paul Brainard; the later came across the material while he was doing his dissertation research on Tartini; he mentioned his discovery to Duckles (head of the music library at UCB and a Fullbright research fellow) who quickly relayed this information to Berkeley.

17. Giuseppe Tartini, *Traité des Agréments de la musique*, French translation, P. Denis, Paris (1771) ed. Erwin R. Jacobi, with English translation, C. Girdlestone, and facsimile of original Italian text (Celle and New York: Herman Moeck Verlag), 1961, 43.

Francesco Geminiani:
The Art of Playing the Violin

Three primary 18th century violin treatises (Geminiani, Leopold Mozart and L'Abbé Fils - the Italian, the German and the French) were all created within the space of the decade 1751-1761 and summarize the traditions they represent. A paradox exists, however, in that both too few and too many details of violin playing are known. Certain questions cannot be answered with assurance; the bewildering array of answers within the boundaries of accepted practice leads to the conclusion that there is not one but a variety of 18th century styles.

Geminiani, whose works provide a vital link between the Italian tradition from Corelli to Tartini, was a student of Corelli in Rome and Scarlatti in Naples, and came to England in 1714 (15?) shortly after the death of Corelli, never returning to Italy. He enjoyed a fantastic success as a virtuoso in England, playing for King George with Handle as accompanist (1715). He later had immense prestige as a composer, teacher and theorist. Burney is said to have a malicious prejudice against Geminiani; in Naples Burney said Geminiani was discharged from the opera orchestra in Lucca for "frequent absences." [1] Geminiani wrote a substantial amount of music for his treatises, including twelve compositions for *The Art of Playing the Violin*. Donington characterizes Geminiani as being only a "moderately good composer," [2] but Boyden clarifies this consideration of the value of the composer's works by stating that they are undervalued and unfortunately overshadowed by Vivaldi. Geminiani nevertheless had an illustrious reputation as a teacher, influenced a large circle of pupils and was one of the most deeply respected, influential and celebrated violin virtuoso of his time. He was also a financial success in London and Dublin, and known for his vigorous and elegant English prose style.

Geminiani was on good terms with leading figures such as the Earl of Essex (who rescued him from debtor's prison due to the composer's predilection for acquiring paintings). His contemporaries considered him superior as a player even to Veracini. Tartini characterized him as "the violent one" [3] and Burney noted his "overwhelming technical audacity." [4]

Reprints, translations and imitations of his works indicate that the composer was widely read by the musical public of the 18th century. It was at one time thought that *The Art of Playing the Violin* was a reprint of an anonymous violin method, *Volens Nolens*, published in London in 1695. All of this is cleared up in Boyden's article Acta Musicologica, February, 1960. A simplified version of Geminiani's work was printed after his death by Stephen Philpot (pupil of Festing) and an abbreviated version was printed in Boston by John Boyles. After the composer's death a number of merely imitative violin tutors for amateurs were published, exploiting the composer's name when he was no longer able to defend himself.

Though *The Art of Playing the Violin* is said by Boyden to be merely of archeological use if considered apart from the original instrument, it has significant historical importance and much of the material is still applicable to contemporary technique. The treatise was written during the last period of the composer's life, and was the most successful of his works. Though certainly not the first violin method, it was the first mature exposition of this kind of material and covered very adequately the technical groundwork necessary to cope with almost any violinistic problems of the time, aside from exceptionally virtuosic pieces such as the Locatelli *Caprices*. It was the first violin treatise addressed to professional violinists, reflecting their practices, particularly those in the Italian tradition of Corelli and his pupils. The work is based on long-established traditions which had dominated Europe for two centuries. Instruction of this sort was fundamental to the education of the post-Corelli generation; Locatelli, Veracini and Geminiani himself. All the pieces in both works are based on English, Scottish and Irish folksongs, reflecting the composer's absorption of his adopted environment.

A Treatise of Good Taste in the Art of Music is a brief, interesting, second part of Geminiani's writing on the subject of "good taste," a technical phrase which during those days denoted the ability to use ornamentation in the refined and cultured manner; both works have tables of ornaments carefully described, and even have some part of the text in common. Artists at that time were expected to use their imaginations and the music that one undoubtedly heard was submerged beneath the bare surface of the score, as for examples in Corelli's Adagios, which are written very plainly but are reputed to have been performed by Corelli in a very ornate fashion. Geminiani's belief was that technique was inseparable from emotional expression; an expressive performance was required by means of dynamic swells, ornaments and vibrato. The composer meant expression in a general sense, not in the descriptive, as in the French bird-calls he so detested.

Geminiani was furiously impatient with the French predilection for dance music (versus the abstract Italian sonata) with its "wretched Rule" [5] of the down-bow. He opposed the idea of imitating bird calls, whistles, etc. [Not until 1750 did French aestheticians concede that music need not represent anything concretely.] Geminiani's notion that the singing voice is the most appropriate model for violin sound is still very much useful.

Geminiani's work looks to the future with respect to chromatic fingering, extensions and contrations of fingerings and the continuous vibrato. However, compared to Mozart's work (1756), Geminiani's looks primarily to the past. His way of holding the instrument is relatively old-fashioned (though the frontspiece shows a different hold than that mentioned in the text, and one more likely suitable to his fingerings). Unlike Mozart, Geminiani mentioned nothing about certain matters which relate to the technical equipment of later violinists (consecutive trills, trills in thirds and sixths), and he mentions nothing about harmonics and the technique of using higher positions to preserve the same tone color within a passage. A primarily difference with Mozart is Geminiai's use of what amounts to a continuous vibrato. Mozart recommends that vibrato be restricted to a closing note or any sustained tone: "Performers there are who tremble consistently on each note as if they had palsy." [6]

Organization of the Treatise

I. Subject area:
1. Position violin is held: general controversy over collarbone or chin hold, and where chin is held; middle, right or left?
2. Position bow is held; implied bow grip above the nut.
3. Fingerings

   a. Chromatic fingering; one finger per note, rediscovered in 20th century
   b. Extension and contraction; a speciality of Geminiani
   c. Frequent shifts. Burney states that Geminiani claims invention of the half-shift but the composer's claim, if accurate, is doubtful. Geminiani favors larger shifts to reduce the number of shifts.

4. Vibrato; continuous, not just an ornament
5. Seven positions ("orders")
6. Multiple stops; unisons to octaves
7. Dynamics
8. Bowing; detests the "rule of the down-bow"
9. Tempo Rubato: notorious for, mentions nothing of.
10. *Notes inégales*; forbids these saying they "alter and spoil the piece."

II. Ornaments

1. Plain Shake
2. Turned Shake
3. Superior appoggiatura
4. Holding a Note
5. Staccato
6. Swelling Sound
7. Falling Sound
8. Piano
9. Forte
10. Anticipation
11. Separation
12. Of the Beat; mordent
13. Close Shake (Vibrato)

Bibliography

1. *The New Grove Dictionary of Music and Musicians* , ed. Stanley Sadie. London: MacMillan Publishers; 1980, 224

2. *A Treatise of Good Taste in the Art of Music* (1749), facs. ed. by Robert Donington. New York: Da Capo, 1969, vi.

3. Groves, *Ibid.*

4. *Ibid.*

5. *The Art of Playing the Violin*, Francesco Geminiani. London; Oxford University Press, 1952, 4.

6. *The History of Violin Playing from Its Origins to 1761 and Its Relationship to the Violin and Violin Music.* London: Oxford University Press; 1965, 387.

The Beethoven Violin Concerto in D Major, Op. 61: Some 20th Century Viewpoints

For scores, parts, piano reductions and cadenzas, please see:
http://beststudentviolins.com/beethoven.html

In 1806 Beethoven was persuaded to write his monumental violin concerto in D Major, Opus 61, for Franz Clement, leader of the theater orchestra at Wien. Clement had been a child prodigy, and was considered to be a remarkable violinist with a prodigious memory, but was, as well, something of a charlatan in that some of his public performances were said to be circus-like. He performed the Beethoven Concerto by sight-reading (though there is some dispute about this) with an unrehearsed orchestra, and he divided the work up, inserting a sonata of his own after the first movement, playing his sonata with the violin up-side-down, and on one string. The first performance was a benefit concert for Clement, but it is not known whether Beethoven consulted Clement about the violin part. The piece, written in haste, was not met with very enthusiastic reviews (Möser wrote that the thematic material was commonplace, confused, wearisome and too repetitious) and the work had only three performances between 1806 and 1844.

Piano concertos were more popular during that time, and Beethoven was persuaded to write a piano version, which was published the following year, a year before the composer subjected the violin concerto to a final revision. There was no known exchange between the composer and the performer after the initial performance. No violin cadenzas were written by Beethoven, though he wrote cadenzas for the piano version, and violin cadenzas were subsequently written by Joachim, David, Kreisler and many other celebrated violinists. One can really better understand why there is no definite edition of the work, considering the composer's indecision and haste and how improvised the première of the work was.

In 1828 Pierre Baillot played the nearly forgotten violin concerto of Beethoven, which, since its première in 1806, had received only one performance, in Berlin, in 1812. The fourteen-year-old Henri Vieuxtemps played it in Vienna in 1834. However, it did not begin to find its first interpreters and admirers until Joseph Joachim performed it in London in 1844 under the direction of Mendelssohn; both artists were vitally interested in stimulating appreciation of the classical masters. As late as 1855, Louis Spohr (who rejected the late works of

Beethoven), said to Joachim after a performance of the Beethoven Concerto that he supposed it was fine in its own way, but he would rather hear Joachim play a "real" violin piece. [1]

This negative judgment was conditioned by the artificial bravura practices of the early 19th century; concertos were written for the purpose of displaying the player's pyrotechniques, sometimes leading to music which was bizarre, sentimental and eclectic. Spohr wrote his first five violin concertos before Beethoven completed his, and neither Spohr nor his contemporaries gave attention to the merits of Beethoven's Concerto. The Beethoven Concerto was not a display piece, and found slow acceptance by virtuosi, who had, during that era, their own concerti primarily in mind, with the desire to showcase their particular virtuosic strengths. Beethoven's towering musical concepts, mirroring the spirit of reform, democracy and revolution, and his idiomatic treatment of the violin and pianistic thinking, had to wait for a later era to be appreciated.

Beethoven was aware of the conflict between his vision and the performance practices of contemporary violinists, and assigned four staves to the violin solo, in order to leave room for alterations; in many places the four staves are filled. Beethoven had studied the concerti of his contemporaries and predecessors; while Rode's technical propensities were too intricately violinistic to appeal to Beethoven, the influence of Viotti's characteristic use of broken octaves and Kreutzer's elaborating of a melodic line in triplet passages were put to good use in the concerto.

Joachim was the most widely accepted interpreter of the Beethoven Concerto, and his cadenzas are still played. The interpretations of Vieuxtemps and Sarasate were compared unfavorably to Joachim's. Vieuxtemps was said to slide up and down the strings à la Paganini, and Sarasate's elegant and immaculate style was not suitable, according to Flesch, for such a large scale composition. The interpretations of Ysaÿe (the last eminent violinist in the tradition of the Liszt-Rubinstein interpreter) were also characterized by the attitude of his generation that textual fidelity should be secondary to expansiveness of feeling and that it was acceptable to take liberties if doing so brought life to the music.

Violin technique developed through time, however, and interpretation began to be discussed more fully as traditional habits began to outlive their usefulness; developments in left and right hand technique and tone production kept place with a more systematic approach to the violin, parallel to advancements in science and political thought. Included in the developments over the past two centuries would be a greater left-hand mobility, the preservation of uniform tone color within a phrase, and the use of positions not for convenience but with a view to expression and evenness of tone. Sequences are given matching fingerings, bowing and string changes, and the stark tonal contrast between open and stopped strings is avoided, as well as an attempt made always to veil the differences in timbre between strings. These adjustments were all the more necessary because with the introduction of metal covered strings the sounds of the strings became harder still.

The complex of new technical devices included simplifications connected with the elimination of unnecessary movements of the left hand, use of even numbered positions, and rational fingerings. The combined use of the pronation of the hand, with hand, finger and wrist pressures, evolved from the necessity of producing larger sounds to fill the larger halls. Isaac Stern writes of the circle of pressure created by the opposition of thumb and second finger, which is a very different thing from the isolated index-finger, or wrist, or thumb pressure which was taught in the last century. In addition, older halls generally had more reverberations and, therefore, if tempos are sometimes faster today, it may be because a too fast tempo in an older hall would have been blurred for acoustical reasons. Bow speed and pressure, which is responsible for dynamic shading, was not treated in as much depth by 18th century writers as it was by their 19th century successors. Bow management relative to the Tourte bow only began to be formulated in detail in Capet's school, and in the Methode by Rode and his contemporaries during the period 1800-1840.

By the last decade of the 20th century, issues such as tempo markings in Beethoven's work, and the inevitable conflict over upper note start of trills [2] have been thoroughly explored by musicologists. Nonsensical adjectives (when applied to music), such as "masculine" and "virile," have fallen completely out of fashion, though they were used and applied liberally not so very long ago. Additionally, the autocracy of the bar line has been subjected to less dogmatic interpretation, and new concepts of dissonance have widened perceptions. A regard for psychological effect and a focus on musical and aesthetic content have become central to interpretation. Beethoven's concerto may be thought of as a portal through which we may view the artistic and intellectual climate of the previous two centuries.

The following table lists examples taken from 20th century pedagogical literature which illustrate the refinements of technique which have evolved since the first performance and represent the most modern concerns about this work. These illustrations may assist in correcting the prevailing type of study which was widespread from the second half of the 19th century, and which had a one-sided fixation on isolated technical points and purely mechanical and gymnastic training. Choices of bowing and fingering are vital factors in artistic playing, and creatively serve and enrich the expressiveness of the instrument, allowing its full possibilities to come to fruition.

Table of Examples
Graphics by Catherine Schmidt-Jones

Example 1: Fingering of Octaves - Gerle
Example 2: Fingered Octaves - Szigeti
Example 3: Traditional and fingered Octaves - Yampolsky
Example 4: Avoidance of Slides - Galamian
Example 5: Finger Extensions - Yampolsky
Example 6: Use of Open Strings to Color Passages - Yampolsky
Example 7: Natural Harmonics for Tonal Contrast - Yampolsky
Example 8: Natural Point of Support - Yampolsky
Example 9: "Natural" vs. "Unnatural" - Szigeti
Example 10: Controversy of Articulation of Rondo Themes - Szigeti
Example 11: Suggestion by Wilhelmj of Rondo Themes - Szigeti
Example 12: Avoiding an unwelcome slide - Joachim and Sauret
Example 13: Theme according to Czerny

In terms of clarity of sound, a contribution toward performance practice may be found in a special technique for playing the octaves in the first movement of the Beethoven; Robert Gerle extrapolates from the rule of making a double-stop shift on pairs of strings by using the lower set of fingerings to move into the new position before placing the next shift:

Example 1 - Gerle, Fingered Octaves

(b) in Octaves with 1-4:

The same rules apply as for same-finger shifts.

Violin Concerto: first movement *Beethoven*

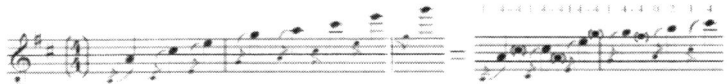

Joseph Szigeti is particularly interested in the question of fingered octaves, the use of which cannot help but contribute to technical security. He is astounded that not one of the many editions of the Beethoven Concerto has suggested a fingered octave solution until his 1963 (Curci, Milan) edition. One bar before the repetion of the theme in the third movement is an especially useful example of this sort of fingering:

Example 2- Szigeti, Fingered Octaves

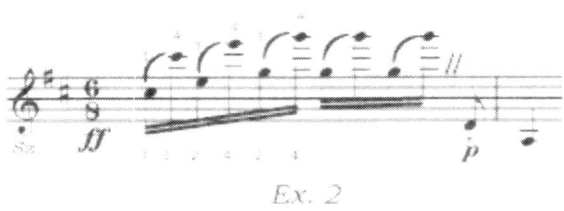

I.M. Yampolsky compares traditional and fingered octave choices:

Example 3 - Yampolsky, "Rational Fingerings"

Ivan Galamian quotes from the first movement of the Concerto to illustrate new devices for the elimination of slides. However, he cautions violinists that to go to extremes in trying to avoid all slides leaves the playing colorless, dry and cold. One should avoid unmusical slides, but fingering should be used to color the music, and to allow for an expressive gesture or for the sake of better vibrato and richer sound. Galamian taught the modern Franco-Belgium bow hold, which has entirely superseded that of the German style, characterized by a very high right wrist and low forearm. Two choices of fingering are given:

Example 4- Galamian, "Creeping Fingerings"

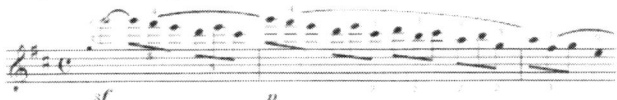

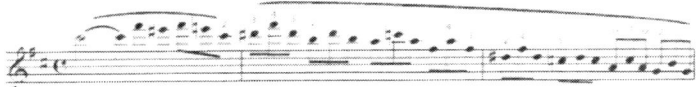

Example 27
Beethoven, *Concerto in D major*, Op 61
First movement (measures 4-7 of the solo)

Example 28
Beethoven *Concerto in D major* Op. 61
First movement (measures 304-306)

Yampolsky favors finger extensions for broken thirds.

Example 5 - Yampolsky, Broken Thirds

Examples of broken thirds :

The juxtaposition of stopped and open strings may strengthen the
expressive contrast of a passage (Yampolsky):

Example 6 - Yampolsky, Expressive Contrast

An effective contrast between a stopped string and a natural harmonic
on the same note (Yampolsky):

Example 7 - Yampolsky, Effective Tonal Contrast

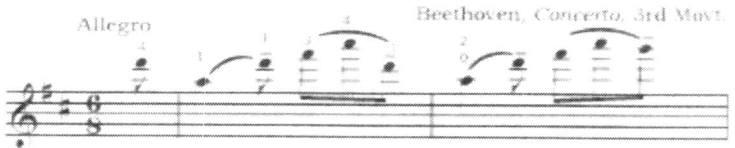

A greater security of intonation and an avoidance of unnecessary string
changes can be achieved by devising a special point of support on the
fingerboard (Yampolsky):

Example 8 Yampolsky, Point of Support

Fingering and Intonation

The purity of the violinist's intonation depends to a certain extent on his choice of fingering. A bad fingering is often the reason for uncertain and inexact intonation, even in technically easy passages. This is the result of the awkward movements of the hand and fingers which are required by such fingerings. For example:

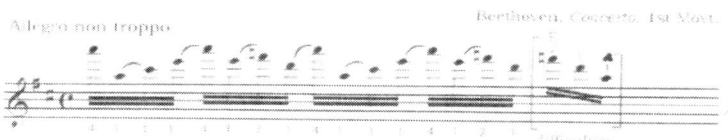

Allegro non troppo

Beethoven, Concerto, 1st Movt.

Difficulties

The fingering given above, which requires an extension of the second finger followed by the first finger crossing strings, gives the fingers no point of support, which is the reason for the uncertainty of intonation. The advantage of the following fingering:

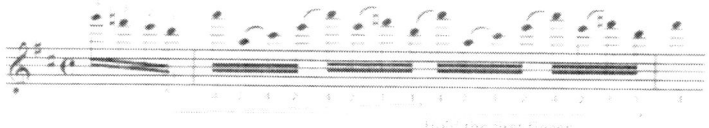

Hold the first finger

is that by doing away with the unnecessary string crossing of the first finger, it gives a natural point of support for the precise movements of the fingers in the given hand position and thus makes for more accurate intonation.

However, the causes of uncertain intonation are not only bad fingering. It is well known that violinists make the same mistakes in intonation when playing the same passages in certain works. This is explained by the fact that such passages are not only technically *difficult*, but *awkward* as well.

Szigeti is known for his scholarly approach to violin technique, and many of his suggestions are very useful for some violinists. In the first movement of the concerto he has examined what is "natural" versus what is "unnatural" and come up with some very interesting alternatives:

Example 9 - Szigeti, "Natural" versus "Unnatural"

who have tried the traditional 1 and 4 fingering! It is not only difficult passages like the above that can be made easier but simple ones like the following one from the first movement of the Beethoven Concerto that can gain in smoothness by adopting more rational fingerings than those of the past:

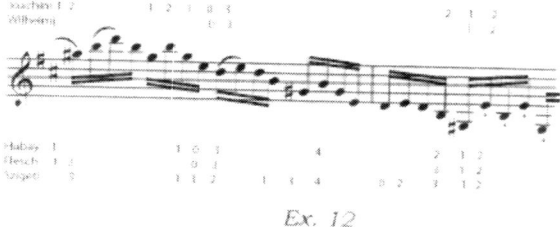

Ex. 12

It is the unison B (1st and 4th) and the use of the half position (second bar) that solve the problem. This smooth joining together of adjacent positions is at the very root of the problems posed by some contemporary works like the second Bartók Concerto or the Sonata No. 1 (1923). Once one has recognized the basic pattern, everything falls into place, but try and play these with traditional fingerings and they become forbidding.

To return to the question of 'natural' versus 'unnatural' stretched basic positions on our fingerboard - after these several digressions - it is interesting to find the so-called 'Geminiani grip'

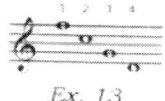

Ex. 13

Szigeti devotes several pages to the conflicting schools of thought regarding the articulation of the Rondo theme. It is unclear in the original score whether the mark above the D is a fingering or an elongated dot, and the manuscript can be made to support either reading. There is an unmistakable slur between the A and D, but it may be in different ink from that of the notes. Thus at least two interpretations of the theme may be considered:

Example 10 - Szigeti, Articulation

two 'schools of thought' in this question : the one favours a slur between
the A and the D of the theme (G string) :

Ex. 1

the other detaches (on one bow) the A from the D.

Ex. 1

If one chooses the slurred example, it is necessary to use the fingering
suggested by Wilhelmj in the old Peters edition:

Example 11 – Fingering

The slurred approach necessitates either the fingering suggested by
Wilhelmj in the already mentioned undependable old Peters edition:

Ex. 3

An unwelcome slide is produced if one takes the Joachim and Sauret
fingering, and it is a dangerous choice in terms of security of
performance:

Example 12 - Slide

Ex. 4

Carl Flesch chose Example 10(b), which allows the player to comfortably change position during the pause, and Hubay, who studied with Joachim, agrees with Flesch, as does Francescatti. There is even a fourth choice; Czerny gives the theme with the dots below the slur:

Example 13 - Articulation

Endnotes

1. Spohr augmented the orchestra, but did not exploit its possibilities for color or thematic participation. The solo violin dominated autocratically and the orchestra remained subservient. The cello and bass parts were almost always doubled, in the conservative tradition of Mozart and Haydn, and Spohr continued to use the antiquated clarino. His works lacked the spirit of modern polyphony and Beethoven's rhythmic and thematic brilliance.

2. Since Beethoven's fingerings in his piano music show alternate use of both main note and auxiliary note start of trills, the notion that all of Beethoven's trills are to begin on the main note is not absolutely secure; he never completely abandoned 18th century practice in this regard. Examples of upper-note starts can also be seen from measured trills in the Sixth Symphony (2nd movement, solo flute, bar 131) and in the Ninth Symphony (3rd movement, first violins, bar 129).

Bibliography

Bickley, Nora. *Letters from and to Joseph Joachim*

Flesch, Carl. *Art of Violin Playing*

Galamian, Ivan. *Principles of Violin Playing and Teaching*

Gerle, Robert:
The Art of Bowing Practice: The Expressive Bow Technique
Art of Practicing the Violin: With Useful Hints for All String Players

Grout, Donald and Claude V. Palisca. *A History of Western Music,* Sixth Edition. Newest ed. of the Grout, 7th ed., Burkholder

Szigeti, Joseph. *Szigeti on the Violin*

Szigeti, Joseph. *With Strings Attached: Reminiscences and Reflections*

Yampolsky, I.M. *Principles of Violin Fingering*

Common String Articulations

NOTE: Musicians can argue endlessly about these meanings; many definitions are dependant on the stylistic practices of any given era, or even a specific composer. This is by no means a complete list.

Please see Sound Files Library http://beststudentviolins.com/SoundFiles.html for audio examples.

Arco: Italian for bow. Written in after passages of pizzicato (plucked) notes. Means to return to playing with the bow.

Articulation: Shape of a note or phrase. Basically three marks (and combinations thereof). The dot (.) which is staccato (short); the line (-) which is tenuto (stretched); and the accent (>) which is like a little punch at the beginning of a note. (Accent marks are the chevron pointing to the right.) Sometimes in an otherwise more or less staccato passage, the articulation line (-) is meant to give the note full length, where it's equivalent to tenuto. Sometimes, in combination with a slur, it means the notes are detached although played without a change in bow direction. Sometimes the line implies that some sort of weight should be given to the note. Sometimes it's composer-defined.

Bariolage: A passage, often in Bach but in Brahms and elsewhere, where the fingers are held down over several strings and the bow oscillates between the several strings. The Bach E Major Partita is a notorious example. Very impressive sounding; not so hard once you get the trick of it.

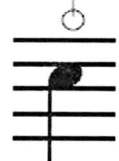

Bartók pizz: Also called snap pizz. Right hand pulls the string away from the fingerboard and releases, causing a snapping sound.

Bouncing bow: This is not just spiccato, which is an off-the-string, at-the-sounding-point technique of very small up and down bows, originating from the wrist, but a host of other definitions with very fine distinctions as to their meanings. [Worthy of further study are: saltando, saltante, saltato, saltellato, saltellando, sautellé.] .

Collé: "Chipped" bowing. Normally at the frog but may be articulated in any part of the bow. Created by setting the bow on the string and then playing a short stroke by springing the bow, about two inches from the string. Thumb and little finger should be curved, with the elbow as high as the top of the hand.

Col Legno: Passage where the sound is produced by striking the wood of the bow against the string(s). One should not use one's best bow in this type of passage, particularly if the bow is expensive. To end the passage in col legno, Kurt Stone's *Notation in the Twentieth Century* uses normale and ordinario (abbreviated norm. and ord.)

Con sordino: With mute. Passages with mute end with the phrase "senza sordino" which means to remove the mute. There are several varieties of violin mute. One is a "Sihon" or slide-on mute, often used by students, which slides up upon the bridge, from between the end of the tailpiece and the bridge. Costs about $2-$3US. There is the Tourte mute, which also can hang behind the bridge in that area. There is a Heifetz mute, which clips on rather snugly and has to be put on by hand. There is also the heavy practice mute of silver or gold plate, which is not used in orchestral performance, but to practice without disturbing neighbors or roommates.

Contact point: Also called sounding point, the explicit part of the bow hair which touches the string. In Suzuki parlance, related to the "Kreisler Highway," or the effort to play perfectly parallel between the end of the fingerboard and the bridge at the optimal spot which will produce the best sound.

Détaché: Impossible to define this, as there are so many varieties. Basically, up and down; a change of bowing direction with some articulation. Does not necessarily mean staccato (though sometimes defined as such); can be heavily accented or not.

Down bow: If the bow is on the sounding point in the middle of the bow, if you pull down toward the right, that is a down bow. Up bow is the opposite.

Flautando: Flute-like sound produced by deliberately playing over the fingerboard.

Harmonics: Bell-like tone created by lightly touching the string with the flat part of the left finger, which breaks the string into partials. The first harmonic learned by students is the one mid-way between the nut and the bridge, at about an inch or so above (towards the bridge) where the body of the violin begins. Indicated by a 4 and a 0 fingering. Used by composers for affect.

Jeté: Individually produced or "thrown" series of notes, produced at the same part of the bow.

Left hand pizzicato: pizzicato created by a sharp plucking of the string with the violin (left) hand. Common in Paganini.

Legato: Smooth, tied together. May be indicated by a slur mark.

Marcato: Unclear term. Accentuated in some fashion, as détaché or martelé.

Martelé: Staccato (short) with heavy accent.

Pizzicato: Usually written as "pizz" in the parts, and "arco" when the pizz section is meant to end. Plucking the string with the right hand. Technique may be done in several ways with respect to the holding of the bow in the right hand: (a) for very quick notes in pizz, the right index finger may be extended, and the pizz done without much changing the shape of the bow hold; (b) the bow may be grasped by the fist and the thumb balanced against the corner of the fingerboard with the index finger pizzing; and (c) the bow may be set down in the lap or on the stand for extended passages in pizz. There is also the virtuosic technique of left hand pizzicato, found, for example, in Paganini *Caprices*, where the left hand does the plucking of the strings in conjunction with or interspersed with bowing.

Ponticello: Orchestral technique of playing on the bridge (sul ponticello). "Dietro il ponticello" is playing behind the bridge. These and much more unorthodox techniques may be found in Penderecki's "Threnody to the Victims of Hiroshima." End of ponticello passage may be indicated by "ordinario," often written as "ord."

Portamento: An audible slide from one position to the next. As modern stringed instrument technique developed in the later part of the 20th century, players tended to be less and less "smaltzy," and portamento used more carefully. But in the performances of Yo-Yo Ma (for example) you will be surprised to discover a lot of portamenti, but they do not sound syrupy at all. This is a matter of "taste," that longed for but often hard to define characteristic of great string playing.

Richochet: Fast bounces, similar to spiccato but in the U.H. (upper half of the bow).

Rule of Down-Bow: Notion that the first beat of every measure should start down bow. Usually this feels right, but there are many exceptions, when up is more appropriate. Sometimes you have to work back from materials in upcoming measures to make sure the movements of the bow serve the phrase. Geminiani called this "the wretched Rule."

Slur: A curved line, below which or above which, all the notes are smoothly articulated together. Phrase breaks occur outside the slur. The primary distinction between a slur and a tie is that a tie unites one or more notes of the same pitch, requiring that the pitch not be replayed, but held the time required. Slurs slur notes of different pitches, as a rule.

Son filé: Fr., "filimented sound" or the sustained legato. See article *Strings* magazine: "Son Filé and the Bow Stretcher" (http://www.stringsmagazine.com/issues/Strings115/strings101.html), to study the production of this sound. Another method is as follows:

> Ex: Starting at the tip, keeping the bow parallel between the end of the fingerboard and the bridge, move the bow as slowly as possible to the frog (and back) making a nice sound and counting. See how long you can make this last. Very good for developing the small muscle control needed to play with sensitivity.

Staccato: Generally, short. Spaces between the notes. An important articulation developed by the control of the bow from the second joint of the bow hand on the stick. [For further study: martelé, jeté, slurred staccato, flying staccato.]

Sul tasto: Playing over the fingerboard (which produces a softer sound). Okay as an orchestral technique, not okay as a bad habit, due to lack of bow control or the affect of gravity if the violin is not held parallel (or above) to the floor. End of sul tasto passage may be indicated by "ordinario," often written as "ord."

Timbre: The quality of a sound, which distinguishes one sound from another; e.g. the violin versus the viola.

Tremolo: Orchestral technique of many small and measured or unmeasured up and down bows, accented or unaccented, at various dynamics, as indicated by the composer. Often used to fill the sound more full, or to create excitement or tension.

Vibrato: An oscillating of the sound, used to provide warmth to a note. Basically three kinds of vibrato: finger vibrato, hand vibato, arm vibrato, with string players tending to use one or more of these according to their own propensities. In the Baroque period vibrato was considered an ornament. In contemporary technique, continuous vibrato can be a problem and has to be controlled. Vibrato should not be used during the practice of scales, unless one is specifically using the scale to practice vibrato. Vibrato can also be a sign of nervousness and should be calmed, in that case. Judiciously used vibrato and portamento contribute to the emotional appeal of a performance.

John Cage and Merce Cunningham
1942 – 1992

The collaboration between John Cage, the composer, poet and artist, and Merce Cunningham, the dancer and choreographer, extended from 1942, when they met at Seattle's Cornish School, and continued until Cage's death in 1992. [Their personal relationship is well established from personal commentary but is not mentioned in the literature because the temper of the time was not "out" as it is today; I do not make anything of it in my report because I respect Cage's view, which is that he resented categories.]

This 50 year period began the last three years before the end of WWII (the same year that US forces landed on Guadalcanal) and three years before Truman dropped the bombs on Japan in Hiroshima and Nagasaki–and continued through and beyond the Korean (1950-1953) and Viet Nam (1954-1975) conflicts and the myriad changes of the 1960's. [There is some controversy regarding Cage's lack of participation in WWII; this has been explained by Cage having assisted his father, who was an inventor working at times for the US government, with some particular research which was significant to the war effort.]

The era of the 60's was characterized by a growing sense of planetary connection, concern for human rights (the women's movement, the civil rights movement), civil disobedience (protests, riots), technological quantum leaps, and numerous artistic, intellectual, political and economic upheavals. And this was the era when Cage came into prominence. In 1968 Cage and Buckminster Fuller were asked to participate in a dialog through the auspices of a newly formed interdisciplinary branch of the Department of Justice, headed by R.G.H. Siu, the purpose of which was to develop a framework of social justice values for President Johnson's "Great Society." Joan Retallack, the author of *Musicage: Cage Muses on Words Art Music* (Wesleyan University Press, 1996) was hired as a consultant, and brought in Cage and Fuller, who were thrilled to be given the potential to have an effect on society through their socialaesthetic notions.

In 1965-1967 Cage published his "Diary: How to Improve the World" and Fuller's geodesic dome had housed the US exhibition in Montreal. Cage's work expressed his awareness of world problems of hunger, lack of shelter, and the war in Viet Nam. Retallack interviewed both men extensively and then (without making copies) gave the tapes to a secretary in the Justice Department for transcription. Right after that, Humphrey lost to Nixon and when Nixon took over, the tapes became classified, Siu was fired, all of the materials from the interviews were classified and Retallack was not allowed to have them back. Joan Retallack was intensely embarrassed by these events, as she felt she had wasted the two men's time; she withdrew from working with them for a while but she and Cage reconnected later, the outcome of which were the interviews which resulted in her book, *Musicage*.

Cage's (and by extension, Cunningham's) political views are very much based on what he considered to be the obvious results of technological development, as exemplified in the work of Buckminster Fuller and others; that technology would eventually provide enough food and goods to care for everyone on the planet. To Cage, planetary ecology, responsible agribusiness (he was a vegetarian), and concern for all human life were key issues and he spoke about them often in his work. Cage "took his work...to be a contribution to the global conversation among those who care about the future of the planet." (*Musicage*, Joan Retallack, p. xxvii.) Cage's primary political stance was a support of anarchy, which he felt would be the most appropriate form of government in a world where everyone's basic needs (food, shelter) were satisfied and there was plenty of leisure to pursue artistic and personal goals. The world has again proven to be less interested in accomplishing these goals than Cage or Fuller would have liked, but the game is not over yet.

Economically, probably what is most significant about this era is the nature of the planetary interconnection with all people, occurring in response to technological developments; it is said that human technology changed more during these 50 years than in the last two millennia. The issues pertinent to this change were discussed in books by two important authors: (1) Alvin Toffler's *Future Shock* (Bantam Books, 1991), and (2) John Naisbitt's *Megatrends*, which, like Toffler's books, diagnosed current trends as they apply to contemporary social structures—work, the family, personal relations, business, and international concerns. In essence, what these books are saying is that this era, the one in which the Cage/Cunningham collaboration flourished, was an era of remarkable, technologicallyinspired, planetary wide change and rebirth. Primary to Toffler's thinking is the notion that human history may be subdivided into three developmental eras—the agricultural, the industrial revolution and now, what we're experiencing currently, the information age. Toffler offers a remarkably usable context for the current global confusion. John Naisbitt's *Megatrends* is currently out of print, but an additional book, *Megatrends 2000* covers trends into the 21st century. A useful analogy which I read somewhere (but have long since forgotten the source!) is with the space program: one might compare the venturing out of humans into space to the first venturing of sea-based life forms onto the surface of the planet. (This may be attributed to Carl Sagan, but I cannot be sure.)

In keeping with all of the important trends during this era is the sense of global interconnectiveness with all of the planet's myriad cultures and ethnicities, and specifically, in the United States, that of interest in and study of Asian cultures, particularly Zen Buddhism. Cage was immersed in the philosophy of Zen and spent two years attending weekly lectures at Columbia University, given by D.T. Suzuki. [See Zen and Japanese Culture by Daisetz T. Suzuki (Princeton University Press, 1993.) D.T. Suzuki is not to be confused with Shinichi Suzuki, founder of the Suzuki violin method.] The primary focus of Zen is to break through all the myriad forms of human superficiality and to get to what lies behind them all; Zen has no taste for complexities and feels that intellect is only one of many screens that interfere with taking hold of what is in fact, reality. Zen attempts to open the psyche up to a greater awareness of life, and this awareness is all inclusive with respect to other cultures; it moves one beyond the ordinary, just as the LSD-induced trances of the time were said to do. [Cage, by the way, was never interested in and probably never took drugs. He had friends who did, though, he says. Probably this was, among others, John and Yoko, who also introduced him to macrobiotic cooking.]

It should be noted that Zen is not a religion in any traditional sense, but a philosophy or way of life, one that accepted poverty (wabi, in Japanese, and the turning away from what is fashionable to what is simple and beautiful and honorable), and discouraged a dependence on worldly things such as power, wealth and reputation. This also was in keeping with current trends, the "hippie" movement and the then-current youth rebellion against parental values. With respect to Cage's voice, musically, Zen philosophy meshed with his sense of removing his own personality, history and taste from the compositions. The goals of both Cage and Cunningham were to let the sounds and images stand for themselves and let the auditors put into the works what they will.

From *Musicage*, p. xxix: "Cage worked in service of principles and values derived from what in lifelong study he took to be the best, the most practically and spiritually relevant, of Eastern and Western thought, hoping that someday global humanity might live with pleasure in anarchic harmony–in mutually consensual, non-hierarchical enterprise."

The year 1968 was a significant year in the United States; it was the "Summer of Love" in Berkeley, California, and the height of the hippie period in Haight Asbury. I was staying in Berkeley with a public school music teacher who was running for an administrative position on the school board and was involved in the free school movement. There were hippies everywhere (I was one, in my own Midwestern sort of way), marijuana was $10 for a shoe box, a lot of people experimented with LSD, and the University of California campus at Berkeley was full of long haired, beaded, students, most of whom seemed to carry musical instruments, had a dog with them, or both. Everyone shared, communal living was the order of the day, Elton John's "Tiny Dancer" was in vogue, and revolutionary ideas were in the air; Cage, Camus, Bertrand Russell, Henry Miller, R.D. Lang (*The Politics of Experience*), and Eric Hoffer (*The True Believer: Thoughts on the Nature of Mass Movements*, and *The Ordeal of Change*) were all popular books of the time.

The primary tenet was not to be "straight," which characteristic would be indicated by a support of Nixon politics and, specifically in California, Raeganism. What we supported were blacks, minorities, and women. Bobby Seale and the "Chicago Seven" had an effect on the Republican National Convention. There was outrage over the war in Viet Nam, our parents' racism, and over the notion that one should "act like a lady." Our mothers told some of us that, of course women could have jobs, but, of course, "they'd never compete with men." (Huh?? How could you have a job and not compete with men?) Households rang with screaming matches over religion (I was against it), race (we couldn't reconcile our parents' claims to be Christian while remaining bigots), and most of all, with ecological concerns and the War. Our parents were thinking with their own mindsets, conditioned by the Great Depression and the terms of WWII, which conflict was caused by the injustices of the Versailles Treaty and which war was probably, relative to Viet Nam, in retrospect, relatively justified.

The prevailing intellectual temper of this era was rather anti-intellectual and consisted primarily of struggle–the struggle between a younger generation of "over-fed, long-haired, leaping gnomes," as one rock and roll song put it, and those who, like my parents, clung to the past and the things that had served them then. This was the generation which had endured pre-war economic devastation and struggled intensively to provide their families with more security than they had, growing up. Thus when the GI's returned from the European conflict in 1945 (WWII ended in 1945, Viet Nam ended in 1975–30 years that convulsed with incredible social changes), what they wanted most were jobs, educations in some cases, and to buy a house and raise a family. Theirs was a society predicated on the status-quo; the division of the races, the subjugation of women in the home, the complete emotional commitment to the goals of the government, and obedience to authority. Business, government, law, education, the arts–all the sources of power and control–existed in what was a man's world based on two models; sports and the military. Women's place was in the home. Traditionally, men were the heads of households and there was no arguing with them on issues, particularly ones involved with the sacredness of their power.

The temper was anti-minority, anti-gay, anti-women, and sexually repressed. Any deviation from these social norms was met with shock, rejection and horror. The intellect as divorced from practical considerations, per se, was not looked upon with favor; the sort of intellectual experimentation favored by the avant-garde was viewed with suspicion, as being too frivolous, and was certainly not favored by a generation which had seen and survived poverty, global depression and war.

From Cage's *Empty Words*, (Middletown, Conn.: Wesleyan University Press, 1979. p. 5): "It may seem to some that through the use of chance operations I run counter to the spirit of Thoreau (and '76, and revolution for that matter). The fifth paragraph of Walden speaks against blind obedience to a blundering oracle. However, chance operations are not mysterious sources of "the right answers." They are a means of locating a single one among a multiplicity of answers, and, at the same time, of freeing the ego from its taste and memory, its concern for profit and power, of silencing the ego so that the rest of the world has a chance to enter into the ego's own experience...Rome, Britain, Hitler's Germany. Those were not chance operations. We would do well to give up the notion that we alone can keep the world in line, that only we can solve its problems. More than anything else we need communion with everyone. Struggles for power have nothing to do with communion. Communion extends beyond borders; it is with one's enemies also.

Thoreau said: "The best communion men [sic] have is in silence." Works by Cage/Cunningham affronted the bourgeois with avantgarde notions since the 1940's; by the early 60's, Cage was particularly active in New York though not always well received. He regretted but was not at all discouraged by unsupportive responses from New York audiences, and developed a stronger international following during a six month world tour. Throughout many of the collaborations, most of the audiences were those which had been insulated from both the abandonment of conventional tonality (as expressed in Schoenberg), the post WWII development of magnetic tape, and the beginnings of electronic music–characterized by Tompkins as the "great revolutions in twentieth-century music." [See Duchamp: A Biography, Calvin Tompkins. Owl Books, 1998].

A geographic outcome of the radicalism of the Cage/Cunningham era was the notion of the "global village," a phrase coined by Marshall McLuhan (*War and Peace in the Global Village*, out of print. ISBN #0671689967.) Interestingly, this phrase has passed into a sort of universal usage, along with another phrase from his book by the same title, "the medium is the message." Doing a search on Amazon.com revealed dozens of books with the phrase "global village" and Hillary Clinton's book *It Takes a Village* is also reminiscent of the phrase. What McLuhan meant by this phrase is the interconnectedness of all of mankind through the technological developments current at that time. McLuhan, Cage and Fuller had during the 1960's an Utopian sense of trying to save the world; Cage's work can be said to be a collaboration in that his aim was to work on the global problems of the world in a practical and constructive way. "Global Village" is also the title of an etching by Cage which he turned into a diptych in his home by placing it opposite a mirror which reflects a window giving a view to his back yard.

Cage's work consisted of a lifetime effort to dislodge "cultural authoritarianism (and gridlock)..." (*Musicage*, p. xxvii.) Thus the Cage/Cunningham collaboration, which began decades before the real flourishing of these various significant societal changes, had very strong intellectual underpinnings related to the broad changes in society; their ironic and sometimes bizarre works speak clearly to the issues of the time, the rebellion of youth, and the inevitable changes brought about by technology, which changes shocked and abused the sensibilities of the previous generation.

For further insights, see *Into the Light of Things: The Art of the*

Commonplace from Wordsworth to John Cage by George J. Leonard. University of Chicago Press, 1995.

Archives of Cage Listserv, Silence, Annotated Discography, and Autobiographic Statement:
http://www.newalbion.com/artists/cagej/

John Cage - Representative Works

Piano Works - 1935-1948. Collection for solo prepared piano. 40 pages. Published by C.F. Peters.

4' 33". For tacet (any instrument or combination of instruments). With performance notes. Composed 1952. 2 pages. Published by C.F. Peters.

Sonatas And Interludes For Prepared Piano. Collection for solo prepared piano. Composed 1946-8. 40 pages. Published by C.F. Peters.

Prepared Piano Music, Volume 1 - 1940-1947. Collection for solo prepared piano. 80 pages. Published by C.F. Peters.

Prepared Piano Music, Volume 2 - 1940-1947. Composed by John Cage (1912-1992). Collection for solo prepared piano. 78 pages. Published by C.F. Peters.

Ryoanji - Percussion Obbligato. Percussion part (spiral bound) for percussion obbligato (2 instruments of different material). With percussion notation. Photoprint edition - publisher prints this title after order is received. Composed 1983-85. 3 pages. Published by C.F. Peters.

Works for Piano, Prepared Piano and Toy Piano. Edited by Margaret Leng Tan. For piano, prepared piano and toy piano. Published by C.F. Peters.

Party Pieces (Sonorous and Exquisite Corpses). Edited by Hughes. For flute, clarinet, bassoon, horn, piano (5 scores needed for performance). 20 short pieces composed collaboratively by John Cage,Henry Cowell,Lou Harrison and Virgil Thomson(1949

Wonderful Widow of Eighteen Springs The (1942). For voice, piano. (Eng). Duration 2'. Published by C.F. Peters.

Radio Music (1956). For radio (s), 1 to 8 performer (s). To be performed as a solo or ensemble for 1 to 8 performers, each at one radio. Duration 6'. Published by C.F. Peters.

String Quartet in Four Parts (1950). For 2 violin, viola, violoncello. Duration 20'. Published by C.F. Peters.
Suite for Toy Piano. For toy piano (piano). Duration 8'. Published by C.F. Peters.

Third Construction (1941). For percussion (4). Duration 15'. Published by C.F. Peters.

Aria (1958)(Score in color). For Voice (any range). To be used alone or with FONTANA MIX,or any parts of CONCERT. Secular Choral Works. Published by C.F. Peters.

Living Room Music (1940). For percussion (4). Percussion and Speech Quartet. Duration 6'. Published by C.F. Peters.

Six Melodies for Violin and Keyboard (Piano)(1950). For violin, piano. Duration 15'. Published by C.F. Peters.

Two (1988. For flute, piano. Duration ca.15'. Published by C.F. Peters. Imaginary Landscape No.3 (1942). For percussion (6). Duration 3'. Published by C.F. Peters.

4' 33" (No. 2). (Solo to be performed in any way by anyone.) Composed by John Cage (1912-1992). for instrument (tacet). With performance notes. Composed 1962. Published by C.F. Peters.

Fourteen (1990). For piano solo, flute (piccolo), bass flute, clarinet, bass clarinet, horn, trumpet, percussion (2), 2 violin, viola, violoncello, contrabass. This edition: Photoprint Edition. Photoprint editions are made to order. Printed on high quality paper and cover stock, they are made on a Canon digital printer from clean digital masters. Most of the photoprint editions are saddle stitched, but larger books have wire spiral binding. Duration ca.15'. Published by C.F. Peters.

Music for?(1985)/Percussion1. For percussion. This edition: Photoprint Edition. Photoprint editions are made to order. Printed on high quality paper and cover stock, they are made on a Canon digital printer from clean digital masters. Most of the photoprint editions are saddle stitched, but larger books have wire spiral binding. Percussion 1 part. Duration ca.30'. Published by C.F. Peters.

Perpetual Tango (1984). For piano. This edition: Photoprint Edition. Photoprint editions are made to order. Printed on high quality paper and cover stock, they are made on a Canon digital printer from clean digital masters. Most of the photoprint editions are saddle stitched, but larger books have wire spiral binding. Published by C.F. Peters.

Composed Improvisation for Steinberger Bass Guitar (1989). For Bass Guitar. Duration 8'. Published by C.F. Peters.

Concert for Piano and Orchestra (1957-58). For piano solo. 63 pages,to be played,in whole or part,in any sequence; 84typesof composition are involved.To be performed,in whole or in part,in any duration,with any number of performers,as a solo,chamber ensemble,symphony,concert for piano and orchestra,aria,etc.(Se. Published by C.F. Peters.

One (1988). For piano. Duration 10'. Published by C.F. Peters.

Four 2 (1990). For SATB. This edition: Photoprint Edition. Photoprint editions are made to order. Printed on high quality paper and cover stock, they are made on a Canon digital printer from clean digital masters. Most of the photoprint editions are saddle stitched, but larger books have wire spiral binding. Secular Choral Works. Duration 7'. Published by C.F. Peters.

Music for?(1985)/Flute. For flute. This edition: Photoprint Edition. Photoprint editions are made to order. Printed on high quality paper and cover stock, they are made on a Canon digital printer from clean digital masters. Most of the photoprint editions are saddle stitched, but larger books have wire spiral binding. Flute part. Duration ca.30'. Published by C.F. Peters.

Forever and Sunsmell (1942). For voice, percussion (2). (Eng). Duration 5'.

A Flower (1950). For Voice and Closed Piano. Duration 4'. Published by C.F. Peters.

1007488. For piano. Duration ca.35'. Published by C.F. Peters.

Etudes Australes (1974-5) Books I and II. For piano. Book I:Etudes 1 to 8; Book II:Etudes 9 to 16. Published by C.F. Peters.

Etudes Australes (1974-5) Books III and IV. For piano. Book III:Etudes 17 to 24; Book IV:Etudes 25 to 32. Published by C.F. Peters.

First Construction (In Metal)(1939). For percussion (6) with assistant. Duration 9'. Published by C.F. Peters.

Four 6 (1992). For any way of producing sounds. (If performed as a solo,the 1st player's part is used and the title becomes One 7). Duration 30'. Published by C.F. Peters.

Freeman Etudes Books 1 and 2 (1977-80). Edited by Paul Zukofsky. For Violin. Published by C.F. Peters.

Freeman Etudes Books 3 and 4 (1991). Edited by Paul Zukofsky. For Violin. Published by C.F. Peters.

Imaginary Landscape No.4 (March No.2)(1951). For For 12 radios (24 players and Conductor). Duration 4'. Published by C.F. Peters.
Song Books Instructions (1970). For Solo Voice. Published by C.F. Peters.

Song Books Volume 1 (1970). For Solo Voice. Solos for Voice 3-58.Some songs may be used with Atlas Eclipticalis. Published by C.F. Peters.

Song Books Volume 2 (1970). For Solo Voice. Solos for Voice 59-92.Some songs may be used with Atlas Eclipticalis. Published by C.F. Peters.

ASLSP (1985). For piano. This edition: Photoprint Edition. Photoprint editions are made to order. Printed on high quality paper and cover stock, they are made on a Canon digital printer from clean digital masters. Most of the photoprint editions are saddle stitched, but larger books have

Concerto for Prepared Piano and Chamber Orchestra (1951). For piano solo, 1 (piccolo) 2 (english horn) 21 1121 percussion (4), piano/celesta, harp, strings (solo players only). Duration 22'. Published by C.F. Peters.

Credo in Us (1942). For percussion (4) (including piano and radio or phonograph). Duration 12'. Published by C.F. Peters.

Score (40 Drawings by Thoreau) and 23 Parts (1974). For Any instruments and/or voices, Tape. This edition: Photoprint Edition. Photoprint editions are made to order. Printed on high quality paper and cover stock, they are made on a Canon digital printer from clean digital masters. Most of the photoprint editions are saddle stitched, but larger books have wire spiral binding. Sacred Choral Works. Published by C.F. Peters.

Litany for the Whale (1980). For 2 Voices. Vocalise for 2 Voices. Duration ca.12'. Published by C.F. Peters.

Music of Changes: Vol. 1, Vol. 2, Vol. 3, Vol. 4. For piano. Duration 43'. Published by C.F. Peters.

Nocturne for Violin and Piano (1947). For violin, piano. Duration 4'. Published by C.F. Peters.

Speech (1955). For For 5 radios with news-reader. Duration 42'. Published by C.F. Peters.

Hymns and Variations (1979). For 12 Amplified Voices. This edition: Photoprint Edition. Photoprint editions are made to order. Printed on high quality paper and cover stock, they are made on a Canon digital printer from clean digital masters. Most of the photoprint editions are saddle stitched, but larger books have wire spiral binding. Secular Choral Works. Duration ca.20'. Published by C.F. Peters.

Winter Music (1957). For 1 to 20 piano. This edition: Photoprint Edition. Photoprint editions are made to order. Printed on high quality paper and cover stock, they are made on a Canon digital printer from clean digital masters. Most of the photoprint editions are saddle stitched, but larger books have wire spiral binding. Published by C.F. Peters.

Sixty-two Mesostics re Merce Cunningham (1971). For Solo Voice using Microphone. Published by C.F. Peters.

Dream (1948)(arranged for Viola Solo and Viola Ensemble). For solo viola, 4 viola. This edition: Photoprint Edition. Photoprint editions are made to order. Printed on high quality paper and cover stock, they are made on a Canon digital printer from clean digital masters. Most of the photoprint editions are saddle stitched, but larger books have wire spiral binding. Duration 5'. Published by C.F. Peters.

Eight Whiskus (Version for Violin)(1985). For Violin. This edition: Photoprint Edition. Photoprint editions are made to order. Printed on high quality paper and cover stock, they are made on a Canon digital printer from clean digital masters. Most of the photoprint editions are saddle stitched, but larger books have wire spiral binding. Duration 10'. Published by C.F. Peters.

Thirty Pieces for String Quartet (1984). For 2 violin, viola, violoncello. This edition: Photoprint Edition. Photoprint editions are made to order. Printed on high quality paper and cover stock, they are made on a Canon digital printer from clean digital masters. Most of the photoprint editions are saddle stitched, but larger books have wire spiral binding.

Published by C.F. Peters.

WGBH-TV (Correspondence and Notes)(1971). For For Composer and Technicians. This edition: Photoprint Edition. Photoprint editions are made to order. Printed on high quality paper and cover stock, they are made on a Canon digital printer from clean digital masters. Most of the photoprint editions are saddle stitched, but larger books have wire spiral binding. Published by C.F. Peters.

Thirteen Harmonies (from Apartment House 1776)(1986). Edited by Transcribed By R. Zahab. For Violin, Keyboard (2 copies needed for performance). This edition: Photoprint Edition. Photoprint editions are made to order. Printed on high quality paper and cover stock, they are made on a Canon digital printer from clean digital masters. Most of the photoprint editions are saddle stitched, but larger books have wire spiral binding. Duration 38'. Published by C.F. Peters.

Six Short Inventions (1934). For alto flute, clarinet, trumpet, violin, 2 viola, violoncello. This edition: Photoprint Edition. Photoprint editions are made to order. Printed on high quality paper and cover stock, they are made on a Canon digital printer from clean digital masters. Most of the photoprint editions are saddle stitched, but larger books have wire spiral binding. Duration 7'. Published by C.F. Peters.

Telephones and Birds (1977). For three performers. This edition: Photoprint Edition. Photoprint editions are made to order. Printed on high quality paper and cover stock, they are made on a Canon digital printer from clean digital masters. Most of the photoprint editions are saddle stitched, but larger books have wire spiral binding. Duration 30'. Published by C.F. Peters.

Concerto for Prepared Piano and Chamber Orchestra (1951). For piano solo. This edition: Photoprint Edition. Photoprint editions are made to order. Printed on high quality paper and cover stock, they are made on a Canon digital printer from clean digital masters. Most of the photoprint editions are saddle stitched, but larger books have wire spiral binding. Published by C.F. Peters.

Portraits of Anomaly: Nannerl Mozart, Fanny Mendelssohn, Clara Schumann

"The Education of women should always be relative to men. To please, to be useful to us, to make us love and esteem them, to educate us when young and to take care of us when grown up, to advise, to console us, to render our lives easy and agreeable–these are the duties of women at all time and what they should be taught in their infancy." Rousseau [1]

"Among a hundred praise-worthy female composers hardly one can be found who fulfills simultaneously all the duties of a reasonable and good wife, an attentive and efficient housekeeper, and a concerned mother." Johann Campe [2]

In examining our own culture, and in cross-cultural comparisons of gender identity, we have seen now, up until around ten years ago, male bias has "informed" the literature of most disciplines; other than certain superanomalous exceptions, women have been isolated in their nuclear families, and relegated to the "hot stove" and domestic sphere because of their reproductive functions. Men have been the masters of culture and a male world-view has prevailed. Women are seen as outside, and a threat to, the system that men represent. Power is in male hands and women have been trained to accept it. In this paper I will attempt to show how the three artists navigated the uneasy waters of social prejudice through the trajectory of their lives.

Although women had been composers since the Middle Ages [3], the advent of the 19th century brought a marked increase in the number of female musicians, along with journalistic recognition, and a wider audience. The greater participation of women in fields traditionally associated with men was brought about by European social and political currents, and especially by the invention of the piano. The climate of solo and chamber works (especially lieder, or song) fits comfortably into the domestic arena, a setting where women had long been accepted as performers. This contrasted with the public arena of large-scale works where opera, sacred and orchestral music were forbidden to respectable women. Female creative achievements of the 19th century–mainly lieder–include works which compare favorably with men, and some of which are equal to the best composers of the era.

As women were excluded from professional positions, (it is said there is no female Bach because no women had a position like his, as church organist with the duty of regularly composing music for religions services), modern musicological scholarship finds women absent from the conventional mainstream, not because of their non-existence, but due to the nature of musicology, which tends to focus on documents (fewer of which exist for women's music) and artists who were the most progressive and were leaders in style change, as women have not been (until this century).

Social prejudice was a central factor in the paucity of feminine musical genius in the period 1750-1900. In the eighteenth century it was believed that women did not possess the intellectual and emotional capacity to learn and that it was unnecessary and even dangerous for women to acquire knowledge, as it would detract from their true calling of wife and mother. Even Moses Mendelssohn, thought to be an illuminate of his age, cautioned his fiance: "Modest learning becomes a lady, but not scholarship. A girl who has read her eyes red deserves to be laughed at."[4]

As women were not allowed to go about without an escort, so concertizing was thought to endanger the morals and character of a young girl. This effectively cut off the meeting of helpful and influential individuals so necessary to catapult a name into prominence. Fanny Mendelssohn, though born into one of the most intellectually and culturally gifted families of the early 19th century, was not allowed to concertize in public until she was 32. Compositions, remaining unpublished, failed to draw the larger audience. Females belittled their own compositions, and required an inordinate amount of positive reinforcement to continue.

As women's horizons and accomplishments were confined to the home, there was a lack of professional training. When a women did receive training, there was a sharp discrepancy between the high level of training and the negative attitude of society. Women's work was thought to inspire pity in the eyes of experts. To be female implied being amateur, and the air of dilettantism marked any discussion of women's work. Women were required to sublimate their talents to the emotional support of others and to household responsibility. What might have been yielded to an individual women of genius or charm was not yielded to women collectively as a right. However, the growing need of women to support themselves transformed the question of women's right to work and hold professional positions into an issue of great economic importance.

During the 19th century, the problem became a matter of locating enough trained girls to take the feminine parts. The new interest in drama made them indispensable. Therefore, one of the new movements of the 17th and 18th centuries was the institution of girls' schools.[5] (Prior to this time, female music students were restricted to private tutoring in their homes, or to monastic schools, where they would become nuns.) Women had no access to study at cathedral schools or apprenticeship to a master player. Despite this, a few women, mostly singers, made their living in low-status jobs.

Nannerl Mozart

No history of Mozart fails to mention his able sister, Nannerl, who accompanied the young male genius and their parents on three European tours. And yet, as the catalog of their travels unfolds, there is always that point when the narrative continues without mention of the talented elder sister.

The girl Nannerl's talent is usually mentioned, however. On her third tour across western Europe with parents and brother, including London and Paris and lasting until 1766, the Baron Friedrich Meichoir Grimm judged that she played the piano brilliantly and performed the greatest and most difficult pieces with an astonishing precision. She was said by the historian Burney to have shown an early talent "scarcely inferior to her brother's."

The tragedy of the following sentence from Grove's will not be lost on people of feeling: "From 1769 on Nannerl was permitted to show her artistic gifts only at home." She was eighteen years old. While her brother triumphed as a composer and virtuoso abroad, she remained with her mother in Salzburg. When she was thirty-three she married a magistrate at St. Gilgan. After three children, and her husband's death, she returned to Salzburg and lived a simple, peaceful life as a piano teacher. People were anxious to study with the sister of the great Mozart. In 1839, the year of her death, she was found to be blind, languid, exhausted, feeble and nearly speechless–afflicted with poverty and loneliness.[6] She had tried her hand at composition, with results her brother approved, but none of her compositions survived.
The question remains, what might Nannerl have done if it were true that she was, indeed, as able as her famous brother–perhaps the supreme musical genius of all time? Though they were close until their respective marriages, and her diaries and letters are central documents

for the study of the Mozart family, one cannot help marvel at the unspeakable loss to the world.

Fanny Mendelssohn

Fanny Mendelssohn, a further development of the trajectory, showed early on a musical talent comparable to her brother's and was, like him, provided with instruction in piano and music theory from Berger and Zelter–at which she is reported to have equaled her brother. The Oxford Dictionary insults her twice, once by saying she was "almost as good a pianist as her brother," and again by calling her an "amateur pianist and composer."

Fanny Mendelssohn persevered in composing despite her father's stern admonition against her becoming a professional musician and his insistence that she focus on domestic concerns and not the world at large. Felix's good opinion of her as a composer, central to her self-esteem, and his pride at being the brother of such a talent, stopped short of total support:

> "I consider publishing something serious...and believe that one should do it only if one wants to appear as an author one's entire life and stick to it. Fanny...possesses neither the inclination nor calling for authorship. She is too much a woman for that, as is proper, and looks after her house and thinks neither about the public nor the musical world unless that primary occupation is accomplished. Publishing would only disturb her in these duties, and I cannot reconcile myself to it. If she decides on her own to publish, or to please Hensel, I am, as I said, ready to be helpful as much as possible, but to encourage her toward something I don't consider right is what I cannot do." [7]

Fanny was afforded a deep and penetrating introduction to the world via her comprehensive education and was then denied the opportunity to follow through on her training and participate fully in that world. Abraham Mendelssohn told her: "For you it (music) can and must only be an ornament. You must...prepare more earnestly and eagerly for your real calling, the only calling of a young woman–I mean the state of a housewife."[8] Though Felix's approval and support would have resulted in the publication of a much greater number of the 200 lieder she composed, her father and brother repeatedly discouraged her from considering composition as a career or publishing her works. Achievements of feminine lieder composers from 1775-1850 are magnificent and admirable, though mostly inaccessible to the public, awaiting serious scholarly investigation, publication, and performance.

When she married Hensel, a painter, at 24, Felix had already launched a brilliant career as composer and conductor. She followed her brother's triumphs closely, while devoting her own life to music "at home." Her isolation, centered as it was in the one outlet of Sunday musicals on the family estate in Berlin, allowed her to compose and conduct works of her own. Wilhelm Hensel encouraged her, though a very negative picture is painted of Felix's reaction to his sister's wish to publish and have her works known, and the notable effect of her limited public exposure on her productivity and self-esteem. She wrote:

> "If nobody offers an opinion, or takes the slightest interest in one's productions, one loses in time not only all pleasure in them, but all power of judging their value."[9]

Three of Fanny's early songs were published in Felix's Op. 8 and 9; a duet composed by her is said to be the best in the collection. ("An des lust-gen Brunnes Rand.") While similar to her brother's, these early efforts show certain individual traits and figurations. In addition, she composed one overture and five vocal works which include orchestra. The majority of her works, including large-scale cantatas and oratories, remain unpublished. The best composers and players of this era made constant efforts to avoid the extremes of sentimental salon music and pointless technique–two who happened to succeed were Fanny Mendelssohn and Clara Schumann.

Clara Schumann

Clara Wieck Schumann was accepted as one of the greatest talents of her century. What might have happened to her at an early time, I hope to have illustrated in the proceeding two synopses; what Clara Schumann has in common with them is the connection with some great artist or pedagogue. The Mozart children had Leopold, Fanny had the whole of the brilliant circle to which she was born, and Clara had her father, a man whose pedagogical instincts were said to be formidable.

Though more usually known as muse to her husband Robert (a Romantic figure party to a passionate friendship, a devoted wife and mother, a "consecrated loyal priestess"), Clara Schumann made a decisive mark on the musical life of the time, attaining a remarkable success in view of European society's general disapprobation of women in professional roles. As one of the genuinely great musicians and teachers of the century, she brought about many innovations in the musical as well as the personal sphere. To say that she ventured beyond the home is an astounding understatement; when her husband died, a sociological shift enabled fuller participation and she took up again the life of a concertizing artist she began at age nine, in order to support their seven children.

She was among the first to play recitals without the music in front of her and give recitals without supporting musicians. (In other words, as in modern practice.) Her programming and standards changed the character of the solo piano recital. She was a peer and had the respect of Paganini, Liszt, Thalberg, and Rubinstein–and was a tireless promoter of her husband's work as well as that of the young Brahms, who adored her. She popularized, through her exquisite playing, Beethoven's music, then considered baffling and obtruse. Her concerts were sold out, and she was everywhere greeted with wild applause, warm reviews, gifts and honors. Still she struggled to maintain her sense of priority as a composer:

> "I have already made a few attempts on the Ruchert poems that Robert noted down for me; however, it is not working–I have no talent whatsoever for composing."[10]

Despite her international success, she is often, in her husband's biographies, a subordinate figure–or a reproach. She has yet to be accorded the dignity of a full-fledged scholarly study. Many of the details of her life have been glossed over, omitted–and the correspondence abridged. And yet no other performer of her century, male or female, maintained a career over such a span of time, playing more than 1,300 publicized concerts in England and Europe. Though beginning their careers with flashy debuts and brilliant appearances, the bulk of her female contemporaries gave up careers when they married or found the pressure too straining. Clara took the whole job of concert-managing on herself; she rented pianos, had them moved and tuned, made all the arrangements for the halls, lights, heat, had tickets printed, advertisements placed in papers and on posters, and tended to her own costume.

Her father considered her an extension of himself, and brought to bear on her his extraordinary gift for pedagogy. In 1816 he married Marianne, whose grandfather was a well-known and accomplished flutist. No credit has been given to the contribution Clara's mother may have had on her daughter, though she was an uncommonly talented singer and pianist. When the Wicks divorced, Clara's mother was only allowed to see her children at Wicks' pleasure, since according to Saxon law they were the father's property.

Though her father successfully trained her as a child wonder (his program of moderate work, physical exercise, performance attendance and contact with distinguished musicians was also used on Clara's sister), he treated her with extreme harshness when she decided to marry. She and Robert Schumann had to take the matter to court; when they won and were allowed to marry, her father took all her savings from her earnings and gave her nothing with which to start married life. Though her husband loved and admired her, they both took it for granted that she would arrange her daily routine around him. In her diary: "My playing is getting all behindhand, as is always the case when Robert is composing. I cannot find one little hour in the day for myself."[11]

However, Clara Schumann did recognize her own importance as a pianist. Because of the seven children and a husband who ended his days in an asylum, she resumed her concert career at 35. (Robert: "We found the solution. You took a companion with you, and I came back to the child and to my work."[12]) She considered herself an artist first and a parent second. While on tour, the children were deposited with family friends, grandparents, or in boarding school. She wrote them constantly and the eldest children were put in charge of managing family reunions (often for an entire summer), and arranging concert tours and teaching engagements, as soon as they were old enough. Robert, survived by her by forty years, was amazingly enlightened for the time. During their fourteen-year marriage, and eight children (one died in infancy, and there was one miscarriage), very little is ever mentioned of resentment by either party.

Along with distinguished pupils and her fame for the integrity and breath of her playing, Clara Schumann's compositions include: a piano concerto (A minor), a piano trio, many piano pieces, several songs, and cadenzas for concertos by Mozart and Beethoven. Hensel and Schumann both composed large-scale orchestral works, and began to break away from the narrow circumscription regarding acceptable musical expression; both collections of their lieder merit recognition and inclusion in standard repertoire.

I hope these brief biographical notes have indicated the types of anomalous positions in which societal prejudice placed these three women of genius. There is something hopeful in their efforts; each person of this trilogy succeeded more than the last. Surely women of the future are continuing this trend, benefitting from a fairer distribution of educational and musical opportunities, as women become less anomalies and more acceptable as artists in society.

Notes

1. Women Making Music. The Western Artistic Tradition, 1150-1950. Jane Burrows and Judith Tice. University of Illinois Press. Chicago 1986.

2. *Ibid.* p. 226.

3. Hildegard of Bingen in the 12th century, Barbara Strozza in the 17th century, and Elizabeth Jacquet de la Guerre at the turn of the 18th century, to name a few.

4. *Ibid.*

5. During the reign of Louis XIV, the composer Lully began one of the first schools, which developed into L'Academie Francaise. Girls' tuition fees made such institutions profitable, and they soon existed in almost every major city. Ibid p. 236.

6. From the travel diaries of Vincent and Mary Novells, 1829. Grove Diction, p. 680.

7. Women in Music, p. 230.

8. Ibid, p. 245.

9. Ibid, p. 2430.

10. Ibid, p. 232. 11. Music and Women, Sophie Drucker. Zenger Publishing Company. Washington, D.C. 1977.

11. Ibid, p. 91.

BIBLIOGRAPHY

The Concise Oxford Dictionary of Music. Michael Kennedy, ed. Oxford University Press. New York. 1980.

A History of Western Music. Donald Jay Grout. W.W. Norton & Co. New York. 1980. Newest ed. of the Grout, 7th ed., Burkholder

The Musical Women, an International Perspective. Judith Lang Zaimont, ed. Greenwood Press. Westport, Conn. 1984.

Music and Women. Sophie Drucker. Zenger Publishing Co. Washington, D.C. 1977.

The New Grove Dictionary of Music and Musicians. Stanley Sadie, ed. MacMillan, London. 1980. Vol. 12.

Romantic Music. Leon Plantinga. W.W. Norton & Co. New York. 1984.

Women in Music, An Anthology of Source Readings from the Middle Ages to the Present. Carol Neuls-Bates, ed. Harper & Row. New York. 1982.

Women of Notes. 1,000 Women Composers Born Before 1900. Anya Laurence. Richards Rosen Press, Inc. New York. 1976.

Women Making Music. The Western Artistic Tradition 1150-1950. Jane Burrows and Judith Tice. University of Illinois Press. Chicago. 1986.

Women's Work in Music. Arthur Elson. Longwood Press. Portland, Maine. 1976 reprint of 1904 edition.

Unsung. A History of Women in American Music. Christine Ammer. Greenwood Press. Westport, Conn. 1980.

REPRESENTATIVE WORKS

Nannerl Mozart

Wolfgang Amadeus Mozart: Notenbuch fur Maria Anna (Nannerl) Mozart 1759. 1. Notenbuch fur Maria Anna (Nannerl) Mozart 1759 - 2. Londoner Skizzenbuch 1764 (Nr. 1-43), Anhang. Urtext der Neuen Mozart-Ausgabe. Edited by Wolfgang Plath. For Piano. Neue Mozart-Ausgabe. Serie IX, Werkgruppe 27/1. Collection; Playing Score; Urtext Edition; Complete Edition (cloth bound). Published by Baerenreiter-Ausgaben (German import).

Fanny Mendelssohn

Fanny Mendelssohn-Hensel(1805-1847): Sechs Melodien, Opp. 4, 5 (score). For piano solo. Original Works. New Issues. Reprinted from Schlesinger. Romantic, German. Score. Composed 1841. Published by Masters.

Fanny Mendelssohn-Hensel(1805-1847): Piano Music. For Piano. Piano Collection. 0. Masterwork. Book. Published by Dover Publications.

Fanny Mendelssohn-Hensel(1805-1847): Selected piano works (first edition). Edited by Fanny Kistner-Hensel. Piano (Harpsichord), 2-hands. Pages: X and 45. Urtext edition-paper bound. Published by G. Henle.

Fanny Mendelssohn-Hensel(1805-1847): Lieder. For One Voice and Piano. By Fanny Cecile Mendelssohn, Fanny Mendelssohn Hensel. (High Voice). Boosey and Hawkes Voice. Size 9x12 inches. 36 pages. Published by Bote & Bock.

Fanny Mendelssohn-Hensel(1805-1847): Faust II - Cantata. Edited by Suzanne Summerville. Goethe. For soprano, women's choir (SSAA) and piano. First Publication. Level: intermediate. Full score. Duration 12'. Published by Furore-Verlag (German import).

Fanny Mendelssohn-Hensel(1805-1847): Funf Terzette/Five Trios. Edited by Barbara Gabler. J.G.Droysen, H.Heine, A.H.von Platen, J.W. Von Goethe. For trio (soprano, alto, baritone). First Publication. Level: intermediate. Full score. Published by Furore-Verlag (German import).

Fanny Mendelssohn-Hensel(1805-1847): Piano Pieces 1828-1830.

Edited by Annette Nubbemeyer. For piano. Piano Pieces by Fanny Hensel Volume 8. Level: intermediate. Full score. Published by Furore-Verlag (German import).

Fanny Mendelssohn-Hensel(1805-1847): Prelude. Edited by Rosario Marciano. For piano. First Publication. Level: beginning. Full score. Published by Furore-Verlag (German import).

Fanny Mendelssohn-Hensel(1805-1847): Sonate c-Moll und Sonatensatz EDur. Edited by Liana Gavrila Serbescu, Barbara Heller. For piano. First Publication. Level: intermediate. Full score. Published by Furore-Verlag (German import).

Fanny Mendelssohn-Hensel(1805-1847): Sonate g-Moll. Edited by Liana Gavrila Serbescu, Barbara Heller. For piano. First Publication. Level: intermediate. Full score. Composed 1843. Published by Furore-Verlag (German import).

Fanny Mendelssohn-Hensel(1805-1847): Waldruhe. Edited by Barbara Gabler, Tilla Stohr. For trio (soprano 1 and 2, alto) and piano. First Publication. Level: intermediate. Full score. Duration 5'. Published by Furore-Verlag (German import).

Fanny Mendelssohn-Hensel(1805-1847): Wand'l ich in dem Wald des Abends. Edited by Barbara Gabler, Tilla Stohr. For trio (soprano 1 and 2, alto). First Publication. Level: intermediate. Full score. Duration 3'. Published by Furore-Verlag (German import).

Clara Schumann
Clara Schumann (1819-1896): Piano Music. Compiled by Nancy B. Reich. Collection for solo piano. Series: Keyboard. 64 pages. Published by Dover Publications.

Clara Schumann (1819-1896), Samtliche Lieder: Vol 1, Vol 2. Edition Breitkopf. Published by Breitkopf and Haertel (German import).

Clara Schumann (1819-1896): Marsch Es-dur. For piano. This edition: paperback. Edition Breitkopf. 16 pages. Published by Breitkopf and Haertel (German import).

Clara Schumann (1819-1896): Klavierkonzert a-moll op. 7. For Piano, Orchestra. Breitkopf Full Scores. Published by Breitkopf and Haertel (German import).

Clara Schumann (1819-1896): Sonate g-Moll. For Piano. This edition: paperback. Edition Breitkopf. 36 pages. Published by Breitkopf and

Haertel (German import).

Clara Schumann (1819-1896): Drei Romanzen op. 21. For piano. This edition: paperback. Edition Breitkopf. 20 pages. Published by Breitkopf and Haertel (German import).

Clara Schumann (1819-1896): Klavierkonzert a-moll op. 7. For Piano, Orchestra. This edition: paperback. Edition Breitkopf. 56 pages. Published by Breitkopf and Haertel (German import).

Clara Schumann (1819-1896): Quatre Pieces Fugitives op. 15. For piano. This edition: paperback. Edition Breitkopf. 16 pages. Published by Breitkopf and Haertel (German import).

Clara Schumann (1819-1896): Er ist gekommen (Ruckert) (Transposed to E minor). For medium/high voice. Language: German. Published by Classical Vocal Reprint.

Clara Schumann (1819-1896): Piano Music. Compiled by Nancy B. Reich. Collection for solo piano. Series: Keyboard. 64 pages. Published by Dover Publications.

Clara Schumann (1819-1896): Sechs Leider Op. 13. Arranged by Davidson. For SSA, piano. Choral. Published by Laurendale Associates.

Clara Schumann (1819-1896): Drei gemischte Chore. For mixed choir. Breitkopf Full Scores. Published by Breitkopf and Haertel (German import).

Clara Schumann (1819-1896): Konzertsatz f-moll. For Piano, Orchestra. Breitkopf Full Scores. Published by Breitkopf and Haertel (German import).

Clara Schumann (1819-1896): ... dass Gott mir ein Talent geschenkt. Arranged by Monica Steegmann. German. Special Import item. The price for this item includes a Special Import fee of $8.00. 280 pages. Published by Atlantis Musikbuch-Verlag.

Clara Schumann (1819-1896): Da Capo. German. Special Import item. The price for this item includes a Special Import fee of $8.00. 82 pages. Published by Matth. Hohner Verlag.

Clara Schumann (1819-1896): Praeludium und Fuge B-Dur op. 16.2. Edited by Joachim Dorfmuller. For organ. Level: beginning. Full score. Published by Furore-Verlag (German import).

Clara Schumann (1819-1896): Praeludium und Fuge d-Moll op. 16.3. Edited by Joachim Dorfmuller. For organ. Level: intermediate. Full score. Published by Furore-Verlag (German import).

Clara Schumann (1819-1896): Praeludium und Fuge g-Moll op. 16.1. Edited by Laurent Jospin, Vivienne Olive. For organ. Level: intermediate. Full score. Published by Furore-Verlag (German import).

Clara Schumann (1819-1896): Piano Music. Compiled by Nancy B. Reich. Collection for solo piano. Series: Keyboard. 64 pages. Published by Dover Publications.

FAQ - Learning & Techniques

(1) How to locate teachers and violin shops:

1. Check the Teacher Directories (see
http://beststudentviolins.com/Teachers.html)
2. Contact the music department string teachers of any local
universities: they may not take beginning students, or they may charge
more than you care to spend initially, but they are likely to know the
good local teachers, or recommend one of their abler graduate students.
3. Local Musician's union (AFM - American Federation of Musicians).
4. Local string repair and music shops; they often have lists of local
teachers
5. Contact the Suzuki Association or post to the listserv
String_Teacher_Support.
6. Post your request on a string-related listserv (see
http://beststudentviolins.com/listservs.html).

Personally, I would never send a child to a randomly chosen teacher, no
matter how highly recommended, without attending the lessons myself
in order to determine if:

• the teacher treats the child with respect;
• the environment is comfortable for the child; and
• the teacher has an instrument & adequately able to demonstrate on it.

(2) How to teach yourself the violin:

"Can I teach myself the violin?" is a question which comes up six or
seven times a day on YahooAnswers. This may be a function of the
economic times we live in, and also, frequently, there are no teachers
available in the Asker's area. The answer to that is, I don't think you
can, unless you are already a trained musician, and even then a good
teacher is necessary. It is not out of mere self-interest that teachers
insist that teaching oneself the violin is apt to be counterproductive and
frustrating. It is an instrument which requires individual, hands-on
guidance from an experienced teacher, and students frequently report
that their initial efforts to teach themselves were not very productive.
Nevertheless, I don't mean to be dismissive about this. There are people
who live in areas where there are no violin teachers locally, people who
would gladly go to a teacher if one were available. To them I would
recommend the following books and online services (see lists, below).
Note that Ivan Galamian, an Iranian teacher who taught at Juilliard for

many years, and trained a generation of eminent violinists, is the source of almost all technical issues currently in practice in modern classical violin. His assistant was Dorothy Delay, and her assistant was Simon Fischer.

FREE STRING VIDEOS:
Pinchas Zukerman Masterclass
http://www.artsalive.ca/en/mus/musicresources/webcasts.html

How to Play the Violin
http://www.expertvillage.com/video/137808_how-play-violin-doublestops-15.htm

How to Play the Violin
http://www.wikihow.com/Play-the-Violin

How to Start to Play the Violin
http://www.ehow.com/how_12397_start-play-violin.html

Michael Hegeman
http://www.youtube.com/profile?user=michaelhegeman&view=videos

London Symphony Orchestra master class
http://www.youtube.com/watch?v=VXG5j82FW1s

OnlineLessonVideos
http://www.youtube.com/user/OnlineLessonVideos

ProfessorV's Videos on YouTube
http://www.youtube.com/profile_videos?user=professorV&p=r

Roy Sonne
http://www.youtube.com/watch?v=rLGsG1uloc8

Todd Ehle
http://www.toddehle.com/id71.html

Violin Masterclass
http://www.violinmasterclass.com/index.php

The Violin Site
http://www.theviolinsite.com/lefthand.html

STRING PEDAGOGY BOOKS:
1. Auer, Leopold. *Violin Playing As I Teach it*
2. Fischer, Simon: *Basics*
3. Fischer, Simon: *Practice*
4. Flesch, Carl. *Art of Violin Playing*, Book One
5. Flesch, Carl. *Art of Violin Playing*, Book 2
6. Flesch, Carl. *Memoirs of Carl Flesch*
7. Galamian, Ivan. *Principles of Violin Playing and Teaching*
8. Gerle, Robert. *The Art of Bowing Practice*
9. Gerle, Robert. *Art of Practicing the Violin*
10. Roth, Henry. *Violin Virtuosos: From Paganini to the 21st Century*
11. Steinhardt, Arnold. *Violin Dreams*
12. Schwarz, Boris. *Great Masters of the Violin*

STRING METHOD BOOKS:
1. *Tune A Day,* Vols. 1-3 (available for violin, viola and other instruments): This is an excellent set of progressively more difficult books which includes good introductory explanations (I love book 1!) and pieces based on American themes and folk music (lots of Steven Foster pieces). I started on these as a child, and I still use them to supplement the Suzuki books, in order to go sort of sideways rather than forging ahead inappropriately, or forcing the student to play the same Suzuki pieces interminably. There is also a *Tune a Day* Scale Book, which may be used to proceed the Hrimaly.

2. *The Doflein Method*, Vols. 1-5: These are frequently the beginners' books used in Europe, used by traditional (or eclectic?) teachers who do not primarily rely on Suzuki for their beginning students.

3. Kerstin Wartberg, *Step by Step: An Introduction to Successful Practice for Violin*: There is some controversy about the use of this material by Suzuki teachers, but it comes highly recommended. Good stuff, by all reports.

4. New students are also likely to get the Suzuki books and CD's; these are very widely used internationally and are slowly coming out (circa 2008) in revised editions which have lots of explanatory text. Suzuki books are used by many teachers who have not taken Suzuki training; this training is expensive, and requires adherence to principles with which many teachers do not agree –that is, the initial teaching of the violin to very young children, by rote. Many of the ideas in the Method (or Philosophy) are quite good, however, especially the child-centered

Montessori-like notion that "Every Child Can" and respect for the student–versus the old "ruler over the knuckles" approach in traditional teaching. It is probably wise to keep an open mind.

Further study, see:
Violin Literature
http://beststudentviolins.com/sheetmusic.html#violinlit

Violin Scale Books
http://beststudentviolins.com/sheetmusic.html#violinscales

If you want to tread the usual path, after you've worked through one of the sets of traditional introductory books, you can then proceed with Wohlfahrt, Kayser, Mazas, Rode, Dont Op. 37, Kreutzer, Dont Op. 35, etc. You will absolutely need a private teacher to work through this material.

The least expensive way to get some of this material is buy the CDSheetmusic CD, which has the études. This collection also includes Hohman and Sitt, which are great, and Secvik, Dont Op. 35 and 37, Hrimaly, Kreutzer, Schradieck, Rode, Fiorillo. If you don't mind printing this stuff out yourself, it's worth getting. Bear in mind that after three downloads of the software, it locks. So you only want to download it with that in mind.

(3) Am I too old to learn the violin, which has always been my dream?

I would say, absolutely not. The benefits are enormous and you don't have to feel at all odd about it. There is one YahooGroups, "Beginning Adult Violin Study" (bavs) which has been online for eight years now and has over 3,000 members. This is a great place to get acquainted with other adults on the same path.

Initially, beginning students may come to realize that the violin is harder than they thought it was going to be; it takes at least five years to get into the violin. The beginning stages may be difficult for adults who are accomplished in other areas. In some sense, they have to become like children again, playing Twinkle and other simple pieces. It may also be difficult for busy adults to integrate consistent practice time into their busy schedules, but many adults manage to do this and have great success, enabling them to play in local orchestras, play gigs with friends, etc.

The advantages of the mental and physical effort needed to play an instrument far outweigh any drawbacks. If you have children, in particular, it is an advantage for them to see their parents give importance to this sort of effort.

Inspirational books for adult students:
• Adams, Noah: *Piano Lessons: Music, Love, and True Adventures*
• Cooke, Charles: *Playing the Piano for Pleasure*
• Green, Barry and W. Timothy Gallwey: *Inner Game of Music*
• Holt, John: *Never Too Late: My Musical Life Story* [See: John Holt page: http://beststudentviolins.com/Holt.html]
• Judy, Stephanie: *Making Music for the Joy of It: Enhancing Creativity Skills and Musical Confidence*
• Ristad, Eloise: *A Soprano on Her Head: Right-Side-Up Reflections on Life and Other Performances*
• Wilson, Frank: *Tone Deaf and All Thumbs?: An Invitation to Music-Making*

Discussion lists for adult students:
• Late Starter Musician: Magazine, Directory
http://www.latestartermusician.com/
• bavs, Beginning Adult Violin Study
http://launch.groups.yahoo.com/group/bavs/
• Musical Fossils, Freeing the Adult Piano Student
http://www.musicalfossils.com/index.html
• Musical Fossils YahooGroup
http://launch.groups.yahoo.com/group/musicalfossils/
• Adult Music Student Forum - http://www.amsfperform.org/
• String_Teacher_Support
http://launch.groups.yahoo.com/group/string_teacher_support/

(4) Since I am left-handed, can I learn to play and have a violin fitted for playing in the opposite way? (In other words, with the G string to the right, and holding the bow with the left hand?)

Much like the question about adult learners, this question is very controversial, and I would hesitate to answer positively one way or another. The literature is really not designed for this, and the problems of adjustment in reaching higher positions seem overwhelming when you consider what the configuration would have to be. It would require a re-fitting of the G bar inside the instrument, and a reshaping of the bridge, at the very least.

I think a lot depends on what sort of music you want to play; there are very many areas of music where a left handed player would be at no disadvantage. I'm thinking of popular players in rock, C&W, Jazz and other musics. I don't see it as a problem in those venues, though my knowledge in this area is limited. I do think that in so-called "art music," left-handed players are very rare, since the ensemble playing in orchestra or chamber music requires consistent bowings, and even consistency with respect to fingerings for uniformity of phrasing. I know of only one such player whom I encountered in a university orchestra, and do not know of any others.

While, oddly enough, the question of refitting the violin comes up rather often, this is, naturally, a separate issue from someone who is merely lefthanded and wants to study the violin with a traditional hold. One player suggested that being left-handed is an advantage because of the requirements of the left-hand technique, and certainly there is nothing to prevent a left-handed person from taking up the instrument. My guess would be that the percentage of left-handed string players is the same as the percentage of left-handed people in the general population, though I have no hard data on this. If anyone has research on this and would like to contribute it, that would be great. See:

Playing the Violin and Fiddle Left-Handed.
http://www.captainfiddle.com/playvioleftbook.html

(5) Can you give me some advice about how to play the "wiggly thing," i.e., vibrato?

This is a large and important subject which is best managed under the supervision of a teacher, or at least with videotapes. Having said that, it is common that students will see teacher and other players vibrato and, usually around the second, third or even forth Suzuki books, will want to acquire this technique themselves. My introductory remarks on the subject usually are something like:

There are primarily three sorts of vibrato: finger vibrato, hand vibrato, arm vibrato. Vibrato is very personal, and also dependent on the style of the work in question. Zukerman suggests a "continuous vibrato," but performance practice requires that one recognize that in early music, vibrato was considered to be an ornament and used sparingly. Students normally exhibit a desire to learn this technique, struggle for some time to acquire it, and then wake up one day with a vibrato. Vibrato should be used knowingly and deliberatly, rather than continuously and nervously.

Resources on Vibrato

• Violin Masterclass - http://violinmasterclass.com/vibrato.php
• "Vibrato to your Heart's Content", John Krakenberger
http://www.viola.com/articles/vibrato.html
• The Violin case
http://www.theviolincase.com/Newsletter/Aug05.htm
• The Violin Site - http://www.theviolinsite.com/vibrato.html
• Folk of the Wood - http://www.folkofthewood.com/page2687.htm
• Violin Tips - http://www.violintips.com/info/vibrato.html
• Experts About.com
http://en.allexperts.com/q/Violin-2164/vibrato.htm

(6) What is the distinction between "weight" and "pressure" with respect to playing double (and triple) stops?

Galamian students (Davidovici, Luby, Bedelian–the three I studied with) relay to their students the notion, taken from Galamian (and from his teachers, one supposes, though I have not followed this through), the distinction between "weight" and "pressure" in bowing. In Galamian's *Principles of Violin Playing and Teaching*, (Prentice-Hall, 1962), I located the exact passage (page 57):

> What counts in tone production is not the amount of pressure used but, if one may so term it, the quality of the pressure. This is determined by the manner in which the pressure is transmitted. The main point is that it must not, under any circumstances, take effect as a dead weight, inelastic and inarticulate, that would crush the vibrations of the string or, at best, produce a tone of inferior quality. Instead the weight of the arm and hand and the pressure from the muscles should be transmitted through the flexible and well-coordinated system of springs, natural and artificial, which was outlined...

(7) What is best approach to producing smooth bow strokes?

Bring bow stroke up from the bottom wrist slightly bent up. Make sure the hair has a constant firm contact on the string. As you approach the upper part of the stroke and are turning around, kind of throw your fingers up to make the turn, lowering your wrist at the same time. At the top of the turn, squeeze the bow as you lower the top of your hand. Bring your hand down squeezing and gradually release as you reach the bottom. Then lead with the top of your wrist. Leaving the fingers behind, gradually bringing your fingers through the stroke to end up top again to make the next turn. It's like driving your car around a corner, you don't stop, but bring it around smoothly. Watch the hand and wrist of good players.

(8) What technical routine do you use to stay in shape?

Violin and viola: scales, études, pieces. Piano in the morning, early. If you have a lot of performance responsibilities, "routine" is not quite the right word. Professionals practice all the time, and the more you practice (with supervision if you're new to this), the better you'll get– assuming you're practicing correctly and not practicing mistakes. This is what a good coach or teacher is for. Practice should be "mindful"–in other words, it should be pleasurable and interesting, not dull or "routine." That's why no one who plays really well can answer this question, because it's so personal. You play what you're interested in, or required to play, and you LISTEN to yourself. Awareness is everything. Otherwise, you're wasting your time.

(9) What is the usual progression of violin études?

Etudes: I use an eclectic combination of materials; at the Minuets in the first Suzuki book, I add *A Tune a Day* Book 1 (for the younger students) and the *Tune A Day* Scale Book (an excellent book!) for the older ones. I find the *Tune A Day* Book 1 and Book 2 helpful for ensemble practice and to review topics in musicianship. I introduce Wohlfahrt Book 1 at the beginning of Suzuki Book 4 (Seitz concerti - see Suzuki Repertoire List), beginning of Suzuki Book 4, Mazas-Kreutzer, followed by Rode, Gavinies and Dont Op. 35.

Along with the first Wohlfahrt, I add Trott *Melodious Doublstops* Bk. 1 and then Bk. 2, and the Whistler, *Introducing the Positions*, Bk. 1 and then Bk. 2. At Book 2 in those series, we can begin to add Schradieck (Book 1, Book 2, Book 3). Along with the Schradieck, I introduce Carl Flesch *Scale Studies*. [See Indiana University String Academy Sequence of Etudes, which coordinates the études with the Suzuki books: http://www.music.indiana.edu/special_programs/sa/repertoire.shtml]

It should be noted that there are violin teachers (Dr. Schmeider at Rice and later, at USC, is I believe an example) who don't use any études at all, in their teaching, and they have great results with students. On the other end of the spectrum are teachers who load you up with Sevcik, endless hours of purely mechanical study, and some people swear by this method.

Scale Books: After the *Tune a Day* Scale book, I use Hrimaly. Between the Hrimaly and the Carl Flesh, I've started using the Barbara Barber *Scales for Advanced Violinists* or *Scales for Advanced Violists*. I use the first two pages, with all the different bowings, applied to all keys in three octaves. I have a small box with small cards with all the major and minor keys written on them, and the student picks a card, which is their scale for the week. In order to develop a consistency in the fingering, I have the students shift up into third position on the A (or D on viola) string, and then shift down on the top string. Every three octave scale starting with a 2nd finger has the same fingering. Thus the students are easily able to memorize all the scales in every key. See:

Handout: Violin/Viola, Piano: 3 octave fingerings
http://beststudentviolins.com/3octave_fingerings.html (key signatures, and a system of memorizing fingerings for three octaves scales)

Handout: Analysis of Carl Flesch Scale System
http://beststudentviolins.com/scales.html

Free one- to three-octave Printable Violin and Viola Scales
http://www.theviolincase.com/music/freeviolinsheetmusic.htm

Sevcik: The use of Sevcik exercises is somewhat controversial, I think. I recently purchased a complete set of violin and viola works, and in examining these, I think they are incredibly useful. See:

Sevcik for Violin:
Op.1, Bk. 1, Op.1, Bk. 2, Op.1, Bk. 3, Op.1, Bk. 4 Sevcik for Violin (Scales and Arpeggios)
School of Bowing Technics: Bk. 1, Bk. 2
Preparatory Trill Studies, Op. 7: Bk. 1, Bk. 2
Shifting the Position and Preparatory Scale Studies, Op. 8 Preparatory Exercises in Double-Stopping, Op. 9

Sevcik for Viola:
Selected Studies in First Position
School of Bowing Technics: Part 1, Part 2, Part 3. School of Technique: Part 1, Part 2, Parts 3 & 4. Preparatory Trill Studies, Op. 7 - Part 1
Changes Of Position And Preparatory Scale Studies Preparatory

Exercises in Double-Stopping, Op. 9

Also see: John Krakenberger: Violin-Viola Pedagogy: Sevcik yes or Sevcik no http://personales.ya.com/j-krakenberger/english/arteng6.pdf

Etude List with Composers' Dates
Tartini (1692-1770): Devil's Trill and Art of Bowing

Locatelli (1693-1764): L'Arte del Violino in 1733

Gavinies (1728-1800): 24 caprices in 1800(?)

Kreutzer (1766-1831): 42 studies in 1800

Rode (1774-1830): 24 caprices in 1814-1819

Paganini (1782-1840): 24 Caprices in 1820

De Beriot (1802-1870): L'Ecole transcendentale

Ernst (1814-1865): 6 Polyphonic Etudes

Dont (1815-1888): Op. 37, Op. 35
Vieuxtemps (1820-1881): 6 concert studies Wieniawski (1835-1880): L'Ecole Moderne

Etude List from Leopold Auer: In the last chapter of Leopold Auer's *Violin Playing as I Teach It* he lists the following works in the following order:

PRACTICAL REPERTORY HINTS-What I Give My Pupils to Play

Kreutzer 40 Etudes
Rode 24 Caprices
Viotti Concertos A minor, E minor
Rode Concertos A minor, E minor
Kreutzer Concertos D minor, D major
Spohr Second Concerto D minor
Vieuxtemps Reverie, Morceau de Salon in D minor,
Ballade et Polonaise, Tarantelle in A minor, Fantasie Appassionata
Rode Etudes
Rovelli Etudes
Dont 24 Caprices
Spohr Concertos Nos. 7, 8, 9, 11, Vocal Scene
Wieniawski Légend, some of the mazurkas, Polonaises in A
Sarasate Spanish Dances Vol. 1, Vol. 2, Vol. 3, Vol. 4, Nocturnes

After mastering the Rode 24 Caprices:

Concertos of Mendelssohn, Beethoven, Brahms, Tchaikovsky
Movements from Bach's six sonatas for violin solo [See footnote regarding the Bach violin concerti.]
Beethoven, two Romances
Kreisler transcriptions of "older masters" (he does not indicate which)
Kreisler Collection: Vol. 1, Vol. 2, Vol. 3
Auer's own transcriptions of pieces by Beethoven, Schumann, Tchaikovsky
Ries Troisième Suite
Elman transcriptions of pieces by Grieg, Rubinstein, Fauré "and others"
Favorite Encores, Concert Favorites
Zimbalist Danses Orientales, Suite dans le style ancien
Achron Hebrew Melody and Hebrew Lullaby
Tartini Sonata in G Major Op. 11 No. 12, The Devil's Trill Sonata G Minor
Various "other sonatas by the older Italian masters"
Vieuxtemps Concertos Nos. 2, 4, 1, 5.
Wieniawski Concerto No. 1, F sharp minor, Concerto No. 2, D Minor
Ernst Fantasie brillante on themes from "Otello", Aires hongrois Ernst F sharp minor Concerto
Paganini Concerto in D major
Last group of compositions which represent the maximum of technical difficulty:
Bach-Wilhelmj Air on the G String
Handel Larghetto
Handle Sonatas E, A, D
Bruch Concerto
Saint-Saens Concerto (No. 3, B Minor?)
Lalo Symphony Espagnole
Paganini 24th Caprice in A minor, Perpetual motion

FOOTNOTE (Dover ed., p. 97):
"With respect to J.S. Bach's two Concertos for violin, I have never given them to my pupils to study because, from my point of view, only the two slow movements in them are musically valuable and really worthy of their composer; while the first and last movements of each Concerto are not very interesting, either musically or technically. This, of course, is my own humble opinion."

(10) What is the best way to achieve good intonation in string playing?

As an intellectual concept, this is a difficult area, particularly if you're primarily right-brained and not given to mathematical and scientific thinking, though this sort of thinking can in some degree be learned, with effort. There is an excellent discussion of these issues in Dr. Michael Kimber's "Scales, Arpeggios, and Double Stops for the Violist." This book, available online on Dr. Kimber's page, has several pages of really interesting text at the beginning, referring to methods of practicing the material and intonation issues in string pedagogy. Extremely valuable resource. See his diagram explaining intonation differences.

As a practical matter, there are a few concepts that teachers use, including the "ringing tones" in Suzuki. These are the fourth finger/lower open string and third finger/upper open string pitches which should match, and also the notion of "frame" formed, initially, by the first and third fingers (with a "high" or a "low" 2), and somewhat later, the frame formed by the octave reach of first and fourth finger (around the 3rd Suzuki book, I suppose, along with the Wohlfahrt studies).

A refinement of this idea may be found in John Krakenberger's article on "Laterality," published in the April 2007 ed. of *Strad* magazine:

> What has left-wrist suppleness to do with good intonation? Firstly, I make a distinction between correct intonation and sensitive intonation. The former hits the note accurately but may just miss the place on the string that produces vibrations in sympathy with the instrument itself or with surrounding sounds. If you can tune in to these, the sound improves, becoming richer and rounder: this is what I call sensitive intonation. To produce this requires the left hand to be supple enough that the fingertips are extremely sensitive subliminally to the vibrations coming back from the string. Incidentally, this feedback also produces endorphins in the player, and once you get a student to feel this you are on the right track. The human has an insatiable appetite for endorphins and will look for more sensations of the kind; thus, gradually, sensitive intonation becomes automatic.

An additional concept may also be introduced, having to do with the roles that pitch steps (of the scale) play within the context of any given key. Stringed instruments are not equally tempered the way the piano is, and thus, key context is everything when it comes to intonation on a stringed instrument. The leading tone, for example, is higher, and half-steps can be smaller, within the context of the key (than they are on piano). Playing with piano, one may attempt to adjust to the equally tempered notes, but this is not accurate for the violinist.

Scale Steps and their Corresponding Triads

I	Tonic
ii	supertonic
iii	mediant
IV	Subdominant
V	Dominant
vi	submediant or superdominant
vii°	leading tone

Regarding naming scale steps in minor: The names of the scale degrees are the same in major and minor, with one exception: when the seventh degree isn't raised with an accidental to make a half-step with the tonic, it's better to call it "subtonic" instead of "leading tone". ("Flat seventh" or "lowered seventh degree" will also work).

• Other perspectives include: Within the key context: 3 and 7 are high, the perfect 5th is wide
• Tendency tones: 2 goes to 1, 4 goes to 3, and 6 goes to 5. The exception is that 7 goes up to 8, whereas the others tend to fall down to the tonic triad tones

Four different kinds of intonation:
1. Pythagorean Intonation
2. Just Intonation
3. Equal Temperament
4. Expressive Intonation

See:
• *How Equal Temperament Ruined Harmony* (and Why You Should Care), Ross Duffin
• *Tuning and Temperament: A Historical Survey*, J. Murray Barbour
• *Temperament: How Music Became a Battleground for the Great Minds of Western Civilization*, Stuart Isacoff

This discussion takes an entirely different turn if we were to address

baroque performance practice:
• *The Development of Musical Tuning Systems*, Peter A. Frazer
• *Pythagorean Tuning and Medieval Polyphony*, Margo Schulter
• *The Just Intonation System of Nicola Vicentino*. This article originally appeared in 1/1: Journal of the Just Intonation Network, 5, No. 2 (Spring 1989), 8-13.

(11) At what stage in students' development do they begin vibrato and shifting?

Interesting to pair shifting and vibrato, since they really are in so many ways, related concepts. I have some ancient Paul Rolland tapes, where beginning students are doing tapping and other exercises to develop the flexibility necessary for both of these practices.

By the time the student gets to Suzuki Bk. 4, shifting is necessary for Seitz concerti, and vibrato should be online by then, also. Towards the end of Bk. 3 I introduce the Wohlfahrt studies and numerous exercises for developing a freer left hand, even in the Hrimaly. [I don't think it's wise to get into the habit of practicing scales with vibrato, all the time, but according to Dr. Michael Kimber you can practice scales with or without vibrato, but it should be either with or without, but not both, and deliberately, not habitually. If you're not careful, vibrato can be a hindrance to developing pure intonation, "frame," and "ringing tones."]

Depending on the age of the student–with adults there is *much* more verbalization–ideas about both vibrato and shifting are mentioned early on, but not addressed directly until maybe mid- Bk. 3. But indirectly addressed by seeing that the left hand is flexible, free, and able to operate independently of holding the instrument, which should be more a function of the collarbone and shoulder.

(12) Should a teacher who is primarily a violinist teach viola?

I played the violin for many decades, teaching and performing, and then started studying viola seriously several years ago. I am enamoured of the sound and what the study of this instrument does for my overall musicianship.

The question is, should a violinist, however familiar with the violin etude and chamber music repertoire, be teaching viola? Even beginning viola? (I mean privately, private studio). I wonder about the ethics of doing this, particularly if there are good viola teachers available. Same with cello. In a rural area, with no other options, perhaps it's excusable.

But in a larger city, with numerous other teachers, I wonder.

While many of the standard studies for violin are available for viola (Mazas, Rode, Dont, Kreutzer, etc.), one ought not to neglect the original études for viola: Hoffmeister, Campagnoli, Fuchs, and others. Violin études of course have to be selected and/or edited judiciously for study on viola: ones that feature useless extreme-high positions (that are VERY stressful on the left hand on viola) and nearly or literally impossible reaches (tenths–ouch!) are not going to do an advancing viola player much good, and indeed can easily lead to counterproductive frustration. Even such a thing as over-use of the fourth-finger extension in first position is going to be an issue for most players on a adult-sized viola.

Fuchs has a note in the introduction to one of her collections mentioning that a lot of violin études fairly well neglect the middle range of the instrument. You could play violin études all week without learning that the instrument has a third string (slight exaggeration only!), thus without playing much in the register that is the bread-and-butter, most highly characteristic part of the viola's range.

In general, a teacher in this situation would need to be aware of the needs of advanced students, or students with exceptional potential, whereas teaching beginning students would probably be okay, at least initially or until the student was ready for more advanced studies. Care should be taken, however, that the teacher who is primarily a violinist continues to study the viola and continues to understand the pedagogical aspects of viola playing. These differences include but are not limited to: broader vibrato, differences of tone production with the bow, more use of second position, and different fingerings.

(13) How can I get my child to practice?

This is often, for parents, a very serious and sometimes troubling issue in music study. They should be told that it is normal for students to not want to practice, and home practice should be supervised by the parents until the child is older and has developed more independence. There is an excellent book about this, Cynthia V. Richards' *How to get your child to practice without resorting to violence*. In general, the recommendations in the book include:

1. Remain calm but firm; don't nag, threaten, get angry, or give up. Brushing teeth is not optional, and neither is practicing. 10 minutes a day is fine at the beginning.

2. Create a musical environment: this will include listening to the Suzuki CD's, other CD's of classical music or other musics, going to concerts, and listening to NPR (National Public Radio) programs with classical music. Have music on all the time, or at least during meals and before bedtime.

3. Make it fun and enjoyable. Let the child be happy and loved at all times. Never make being loved contingent on whether they practice, or whether they do well.

4. Use lots of praise, even for the smallest thing, and even if it sounds awful. There is always something positive to say: "You really worked hard" "That sounded pretty good" "That was much better than last time." No negative or derogatory remarks!!

Also recommended:
• Cutietta, Robert: *Raising Musical Kids: A Guide for Parents*
• Fink, Lorraine: *A Parent's guide to String Instrument Study*
• Morris, Carroll: *Suzuki Parent's Diary: Or How I Survived My First 10,000 Twinkles*
• William & Constance Star: *To Learn With Love: A Companion for Suzuki Parents*
• Nathan, Amy: *Young Musician's Survival Guide* (for older children, middle school and up)
• Books by and about Dr. Suzuki
http://beststudentviolins.com/PedagogyBookstore.html#suzuki

(14) Why we play.
1. The feeling of being a part of an ancient tradition
2. Sharing, if only briefly, with the greatest minds of the past
3. The sense that you are pursuing the thing for which you are most suited
4. The pleasure of accomplishing something difficult and highly competitive
5. The pleasure of the audience
6. The sensual pleasure of the music, particularly when it goes well
7. The pleasure of working with your colleagues
8. The identification of the self with the profession
9. The joy of forgetting the Self
10. Dressing up, making money, the pleasure of having good equipment
11. The sense that you are contributing in some small way to the peace and intelligence of the world

12. The sense that you may be inspiring people with hope and beauty – and perhaps inspiring some children to have a better life.

(15) I have been playing for some time but my technique is not very good. What is your recommendation?

What I do with my students and myself is to divide the time spent with the instrument into three sections: Scales/arpeggios, études, and pieces. To develop a firm foundation, I would start with Wohlfahrt and Hrimaly, and then progress forward in the order mentioned above. [Wohlfahrt-KayserDont Op. 37-Mazas-Kreutzer, followed by Rode, Gavinies and Dont Op. 35. Scale books: Hrimaly-Schradieck-Flesch-Galamian (in that order).] You could also add the Whistler, Introducing the Positions and the Trott Melodious Doublestops. It goes without saying that you will need a teacher to guide you; someone who is closely acquainted with this literature and has a history of developing students to a high level of proficiency.

(16) If there is an harmonic alteration, that alteration is good for the whole measure: is the alteration also good in all octaves, or just for the note that's altered?

Dr. Brad Lehman: Depends on the composer, country, and century. In music before the late 18th century (maybe the early 19th) there was no international convention that all composers had to agree with, in any of their notation, as to the normal duration of accidentals.

There are also some spots in CPE Bach, where the sharp or flat is supposed to be carried forward across the barline, if we happen to be within a port-de-voix, and preparing a note that becomes an appoggiatura. No chromatic slithering within a complex ornament: if a note is being sharpened or flattened, it stays sharpened or flattened all the way through that same ornament, even if it extends across a barline that would normally cancel it.

Example: To the right is a short example from one of CPE Bach's sonata movements. In the first note in the right hand, bars 3 and

5, the C-flat has to be carried across from the anticipation in the previous bar, even though it doesn't say so. (Anticipation + appoggiatura + resolution = port de voix.) This happens similarly in other pieces of his, as well: a bunch of notes together comprising an ornamental unit, and a sharp/flat needing to be carried all the way through, even if it crosses a barline.

Joel Jacklich: Back in the days of "musica ficta," (later Medieval, Renaissance, and earliest Baroque), rules governing proper intervals meant that certain notes above the bass (or, in the earliest days the tenor, which used to be the lowest voice before the advent of the contratenor bassus or "bass") had to be altered to avoid the tritone (the augmented 4th or diminished 5th, the "so-called "devil's interval," which was considered so unstable as to be avoided at all costs). Every good musician knew these rules, so there was no need to notate them in the music. Also, in general, until Petrucci in 1501 and his first published music book for polyphonic music printed from moveable type, there wasn't much argument about what the notes were. The composer himself generally passed out the manuscript parts, rehearsed the musicians, and he would be the arbiter of correctness.

After music began to be published, the music could be purchased by someone hundreds or thousands of miles from the composer. The composer was no longer there to "put things right." It became the responsibility of the publisher to make things clear to the performer (many times an amateur performer who didn't always know "the rules"). Each publisher set up his own essential "house rules" for where to include accidentals. There was no common agreement.

Remember that in the days of Bach, key signatures would often be one accidental off from our current system. A piece in D major might have only one sharp (F#) with the C# (the "leading tone," most often the most prominent old *musica ficta* note in the old days) getting a written accidental. Key signatures, as we know them, weren't standardized until starting about 1750.

The idea of whether to put an accidental in all octaves of a chord, or just in one (and assume that the others were also thus affected), again, comes from individual publishers. One will find some 18th century and even 19th century publications that include only one accidental. However, as we get to the late 19th c. and into the 20th c., the Garner Reed quote (given in earlier posts) becomes the generally accepted norm for the music publishing industry. The accidental must appear in any (all) octave(s) in which the note must be altered. Once written, an accidental remains in effect (but only for the single line or space upon which it is written) for the rest of the measure until cancelled by the bar line. If such an altered note (whether it has an accidental attached to a note, or whether it is a later note in the measure on the same line or space as an altered note) is tied across the bar line, then the accidental is also tied across. In that case, the accidental will continue until the tie (or continuous unbrokenn series of ties) ends, even if that is many measures later. And in such a case, no accidental is needed on any of those later continuously-tied notes.

The above rules generally cover tonal music. With the advent of atonal (particularly dodecaphonic [12-tone, serial]) music, Some composers, an accidental covers only the note to which it is attached. If it is followed by another note on the same line or space, then it, too, needs an accidental, if it is to be altered. Otherwise, without the accidental, an unmodified note (even if it follows a modified note on the same line or space within the same measure) reverts back to its plain, whitenote state.

In the case of atonal music, it seems to make sense to notate each individual note requiring an accidental with an accidental even if it is in the same measure as a previous accidental on the same line or space. It does make the music easier to read for the performer. Again, not all 20th c. composers do this, only some. Many still follow the standard rules (i.e., Gardner Reed).

See also:
• Notation texts - http://beststudentviolins.com/guide.html#notation
• Theory and Ear Training texts
http://beststudentviolins.com/guide.html#etss
• Score Reading/Conducting texts
http://beststudentviolins.com/guide.html#conducting

(17) How can I produce a blues scale on the violin/viola?

Doesn't matter what instrument you use, or what key you're in, a blues scale consists of:
* the root (first note of the scale)
* lowered (minor) 3rd (no 2nd scale step)
* the 4th
* lowered 5th
* natural 5th
* lowered 7th (no 6th step)

* root (octave higher)

So, for example, a blues scale in C would be:
C - E flat - F - G flat - G natural - B flat - C

A blues scale has seven notes and includes a flatted 3rd, 5th and 7th. These three flatted notes are often referred to as "blue notes." See: *Essentials of Music Theory: Complete Self-Study Course*, p. 111.

(18) What is the best method to produce a straight bow?

Getting students to play on the so-called "Kreisler Highway"** is a difficult task for the teacher. Some of the ideas that I use to get a straight bow include:

1. We discuss the math notion of "parallel." The bow needs to be parallel between the bridge and the fingerboard;
2. We discuss the terms (and sounds of) "Ponticello" and "Sul tasto." Ponticello is the sound, used primarily in contemporary music, produced by playing on or very near the bridge; alternatively, sul tasto is the sound produced by playing on the fingerboard, a softer sound requested in the score by some composers, for affect. Neither are appropriate for most playing;
3. We discuss how the arms of humans beings, specifically the right arm, naturally move in a circular motion. So in order to maintain the parallel placement of the bow, it is necessary to push outwards, toward the front of the player (sorry – difficult to express verbally);
4. We discuss the notion of "cutting the string." Not a nice image, I realize, but useful in sound production on the violin: the bow "cuts" the string at the "sounding point" (Galamian's "point of contact"); sound is produced by the "spinning out" of the vibrations, created by a perfectly parallel "cutting" of the string, controlled by the second joint of the index finger of the bow hand.

Simon Fischer's *Basics*: Simon Fisher was a protégé of Dorothy DeLay, who was of course, Galamian's assistant. His articles regularly appear in *Strad*. The book has some wonderful exercises, and is the best book for self-teaching on the violin that I know of. The book has very explicit, detailed directions and explanatory photographs. I use these exercises in my teaching. The first chapter of the book is about the bow hand, and well worth examining.

One of my favorite exercises is #36, page 20 (Peters ed., 2004):

Fig. 23 Moving the hand along the bow

In this exercise the hand moves along the bow while it rests on the string without moving. Because the bow is parallel with the bridge the arm has no choice but to make exactly the correct movement. This is one of the best exercises because it gives you the feeling of drawing a straight bow.

The exercise requires an assistant [2] who rests the bow on the string at the point holding it exactly parallel to the bridge (Fig. 23). Use only the screw of the bow to hold it, to leave as much room as possible for the player's hand.

Chapter Outline (with numerous subheadings, not listed here):

A. Right Arm and Hand
B. Tone Production
C. Key Strokes
D. Left Hand
E. Shifting
F. Intonation
G. Vibrato

RE: Private Teaching Studios

(19) How can I develop a private teaching studio?
Important question, especially for those of us whose income is primarily from teaching and performing.

Ideally, you want to have such a good reputation as a private instructor, that all your referrals come in by word of mouth. But you may, initially, need to hang flyers in the local shops. I like designing a flyer with my phone number listed numerous times at the bottom, so that prospective students can take a strip of paper with the phone number.

Some of the places where you could place ads (bring your own box of pins) might include:

1. grocery stores
2. laundromats

3. any school (higher education; often need to get permission)
4. some coffee houses
5. some libraries
6. churches (get permission)
7. some copy places have bulletin boards
8. all the local music stores (I mail two flyers and a small stack of business cards every six months or so)
9. Montessori schools, religious schools (sometimes they have newsletters, also)
10. some privately owned, "hippy" type restaurants will let you tape a flyer to their door glass
11. some other private businesses will sometimes allow you to tape a flyer to their glass door
12. some bookstores may allow you to post your flyer (ask first) 13. some teachers who teach instruments other than the one you teach will not mind having a few of your business cards; I send these periodically in a nice card

Books on developing a private studio:

1. Bonnie Blanchard: *Making Music and Enriching Lives: A Guide for All Music Teachers*
2. Philip Johnston: *The PracticeSpot Guide to Promoting Your Teaching Studio*
3. Milana Leshinsky: *77 Ways to Build Your Private Music Practice*
4. Martha Beth Lewis: *Business Practices in the Private Music Studio*
5. Mimi Butler: *The Complete Guide to Making More Money in the Private Music Studio; The Complete Guide to Running a Private Music Studio, Second Edition; The Complete Guide to Raising Parents In The Private Music Studio*
6. David R. Newsam: *Making Money Teaching Music*
7. Steve Stockmal: *How to Make Money Teaching Music: The Music Teacher's Manual*

My recommendations also include:
1. Develop a contract (set boundaries); see mine at Studio Page

2. Design a webpage: Free sites:
• Angelfire
• FreeWebs

Pre-designed sites:
• Music Teacher's Helper

3. Advertise regularly the local newspapers.
4. Get business cards and include email address, URL, and phone.
5. Play as much locally as you can.
6. Contact music schools, music stores, luthier shops; any and everyone associated with string music in your area
7. Develop a quartet for weddings and social functions 8. Contact the newspapers to see if they will do an article on you
9. Announce your studio in university publications
10. Design a flyer and post at schools, and any public bulletin boards. Montessori Schools are good.
11. Contact local public music teachers and see if you can give demonstrations, guest conduct, and get referrals
12. Join the local Music Teachers National Association (MTNA) and the local; musicians' union (AFM); American String Teachers Association (ASTA); and the Suzuki Association if you're a Suzuki teacher. Attend all functions. Follow up all calls.

(20) What areas might be covered in a private teacher's studio policy?

My policy has the following:

§1. Cancellations: Request 24 hour notice.

§2. Dismissals: The student's feelings are key.

§3. Illness: Children who are ill should stay home.

§4. Instruments: 100% trade in policy for student instruments.

§5. Fees: About middle ground for this area.

§6. Lesson Time: Not early, not late.

§7. Makeups: Only with two week advance notice.

§8. Parents: Observations.

§9. Parking: On the street but not in anyone's driveway.

§10. Recitals: Two per year, adult students not required.

§11. Retainers: Monthly fee remains stable.

§12. Time-out: Vacation policy.

(21) What are some of the techniques teachers use to approach beginning students?

I will be happy to attempt to explain these things, though they would be better demonstrated in person. I am sure there are thousands of such techniques used by teachers:

* I draw the violin and bow and we study parts of instrument and bow

* finger numbers; if student is also studying piano with me, the distinction is made between piano finger numbers and violin finger numbers

* ask parents and student permission to place tapes on violin and bow: three finger tapes (for "frame") on fingerboard, and two tapes in centre of bow, to begin "Pepperoni Pizza"

* "left hand technique" (violin hand) and "right hand technique" (bow hand)

* how to hold violin (1-2-3): (1) violin is held at arm's length, scroll up, parallel to student's body; (2) position of violin is reversed, with scroll down; (3) violin is placed in correct position to left, on collorbone, with violin parallel or above to floor, and elbow under violin. Next step is to practice holding violin without hands, and then shaking hands under violin

* how to hold the bow (1-2-3): (1) thumb is placed, under frog for little ones, crooked near grip for adults and older children (thumb and 2nd finger make "doggie" circle); (2) first three fingers are dropped across stick, tilted slightly toward the tip, with space between 1st and 2nd finger (importance of 2nd joint of 1st finger for the purposes of controlling articulations is later examined—often); (3) pinky finger is curved on inside of bow (add Pinky Pad)

* "rocket ships": bow is held in correct position, and "launched" (with rocket noise) from floor towards ceiling

* "tick-tock": bow is held in correct position, slowly making windshield washer movement

* "the spider": bow is held from the back, careful not to touch the hair, and hand crawls up bow—up is easy, going down is much harder

* "the stretch": (for adult or older students), bow is held in correct position, then fingers are extended flat, and then bow is drawn into the palm

* "squeelies": start with bow at tip and draw slowly to frog, while running finger up and down strings (great for Halloween)–is preparation for shifting and vibrato exercises

* "ticks": hold bow in correct position, and make tiny notes at frog and at tip–this is to develop strength in hands and focus on straight bow

* son filé: start at one end of bow and slowly draw bow to opposite end, counting, with bow parallel to the bridge

* "choo-choo train": very small bows in the middle, spaced notes, getting faster and faster–is prelude to "Wish I Had a Watermelon" variation, i.e., two sets of 16th notes, each starting down bow

* "hovering" fingers: develop notion of hovering, e.g. the bow is hovering over the pencil

* "Moon Man Silent Landing": bow is brought down between the two center tapes on the bow, on the sounding point ("point of contact"); "Pepperoni Pizza" is developed from there, starting on the E string.

* "pump handle": the seven levels of the right arm, four string levels and three combination levels

(22) I'm a music teacher with an online Studio Policy (as you recommended) but I receive a lot of odd emails that I suspect are phoney. What should I do?

REPORTING FRAUD

Like a lot of people, I am very tired of receiving emails, attempting to defraud me via some obvious scam. However, please note that one should never answer those emails: many of those people are hardened criminals, and there have been some reports of people being killed from meeting such individuals, in person. Do not, in other words, attempt to take the law into your own hands, or catch these people on your own.

How to respond to scam emails:

1. Get the Full Header. In Yahoo mail Classic, this link is at the bottom right of the email, under the row of buttons;

2. Copy the header by dragging your mouse over it, and hitting Control/C;

3. Hit Forward, and paste (Control/V) the header into the top of the email and then forward it to any of the following emails, as appropriate:

> spam@uce.gov – for all scams: This is a service associated
>
> with http://www.ftc.gov/spam/
>
> spoof@paypal.com – PayPal scams
>
> spam@craigslist.org – CraigsList scams

* You should also CC ("carbon copy") the email service they use, e.g.: abuse@yahoo.com or abuse@gmail.com or abuse@hotmail.com In other words, abuse @ __whatever the email service is, will be followed up by that service. They very frequently close the account, and may even check the IP number.

* If you have a statcounter (I use the excellent one at http://www.statcounter.com/ which is free), you can get the IP number of the offending visitor to your studio policy or resume, and you can block that IP at your file manager.

PayPal is very good about following up on these, and they do close them down; after doing this about 1,000 times, I stopped receiving most of the PayPal scams. PayPal will send you a notice back, too, that they received your forward. The gov email doesn't, but I'm sure they're working on this.

(23) What are some of the advantages of studying music?

I believe that music study is productive for anyone, at any age. The benefits may be said to include (a) Sense of accomplishment, self-esteem; (b) informs one's knowledge of human history and aesthetics; (c) teaches self-discipline and awareness; (d) is enjoyable and pleasurable; (e) gives meaning and purpose to life; (f) inspires self-knowledge and psychological insight; (g) teaches patience and persistence; (h) promotes physical coordination; (i) develops attention to fine detail; (j) teaches humility; (k) provides a release of emotions; (l) allows one to share concepts with some of the best minds in human history; and in chamber music performance (m) teaches one to work with and respect others.

For children, in particular, it is thought that music study supports high academic performance and positive socialization. Individuals responsible for decision making on college entrance applications look at private music study and orchestral experience, as very positive factors. For adults, it is an aide to memory and physiological coordination and wellbeing. [See also: Why We Play, page 90.]

It has been amusingly pointed out by a denizen of the Early Music forum (rec.music.early) that the same advantages may be had by baking bread. I think that is accurate; anything done well will produce similar results.

(24) How much music history and music theory do you cover, or attempt to cover, in the private lessons?

I have found that I follow pretty much the "Unit Objectives" from the Lesson Plans in my Math/Music Curriculum unit: [See: http://beststudentviolins.com/curriculum.html#objectives]

1. Drawings of how a piece of music makes the student feel.

2. 2. Drawings of staves, notes & rests, dynamic markings, clefs; creating a collage of music symbols.

3. Numbers as they relate to music (pitch, rhythm, conducting).

4. Acoustic properties of sound. Meaning and importance of A=440.

5. Use of electronic instruments (metronome, pitch devices).

6. Simple 2/4, 3/4 and 4/4 conducting patterns (down-beat & up-beat).

7. Recognition of instruments, sight and sound.

8. Recognition of major and minor chords.

9. Recognition of major and minor scales.

10. Recognition of V-I and IV-I cadences.

11. Recognition of steps and half-steps.

12. Vocabulary of dynamics: Italian, French, German, English (say aloud in class).

13. Vocabulary of keys, scales and intervals.

14. Vocabulary: pitch, timbre, dynamics, duration, rhythm.

15. Learning of parts of the scale via solfeggio, numbers and letters.

16. Improvisation using all black keys (pentatonic scale) and percussive instruments.

17. Passing around of musical artifacts: things from the violin case.

18. Introduction of personalities: Mozart, Beethoven, Bach, Cage.

19. Student conducting.

20. Student repetition of rhythmic patterns.

21. Student repetition of pitches.

22. Student singing of one-measure pitch-rhythm patterns.

23. Concert decorum; coaching of how students should behave during demonstration visits by guest musicians.

A timeline for determining when these subjects are understood depends upon whether the student has begun lessons: (a) early, as in the Suzuki method, or;(b) more traditionally, at seven, eight or even nine years of age, or; (c) begins as an adult, which is also very common nowadays. As a general rule, it takes several years to integrate all of these concepts within the framework of learning an instrument. I would expect students who have had three or four years of private and group lessons to have grasped this material.

With a new student with prior training–either in public or private school, and with or without private lessons from a prior teacher–☐ evaluations have to be made in order to determine where the student's training needs to begin. One way is a brief written or oral test. (See: Music Pre/Post Test)

It should be stressed that this is not a test anyone can "fail" but merely evaluative. If given orally, which is probably best during a private lesson venue, it will quickly become apparent if the student knows or does not know this material. Thus running through the entire test is not always necessary. Most students are not going to know this information initially.

(25) What is the purpose of practicing scales?

I found this interesting observation on the rec.music.makers.piano. It was written by a jazz pianist/teacher, but I think it's very worthwhile and applies to strings:

> Why Practice Scales:
> There are many possible answers, depending on your background and your goals. For a complete beginner, they help build finger dexterity by giving you something to play that you can work on without being slowed down by reading. They also teach you what notes are found in each key, which makes reading music go more smoothly as you'll cease having to read each note one at a time and start to see patterns within the key. If you're planning on playing jazz or any other style with improvisation, it teaches you what notes are available for use in improvisation, and teaches your hand good fingering habits that will hopefully come into play while improvising.

Handout: Violin/Viola, Piano: 3 octave fingerings
http://beststudentviolins.com/3octave_fingerings.html (key signatures, and a system of memorizing fingerings for three octaves scales)

Handout: Analysis of Carl Flesch Scale System
http://beststudentviolins.com/scales.html

Free one- to three-octave Printable Violin and Viola Scales
http://www.theviolincase.com/music/freeviolinsheetmusic.htm

Galamian has a scale study method covering much the same material, but includes more contemporary harmonies, more diverse choice of fingerings, and a separate book with bowing options. Notes are only note heads, which is different than the Carl Flesch.

An even more contemporary scale and arpeggio study book with a jazz/rock influence is Mark Wood's *Electrify Your Strings*. This may be studied with an acoustic instrument and is well worth examining.

For fiddlers, I recommend the Mel Bay *Fiddling Chord Book*.

Violin Scale Books

A Tune A Day Beginning Scales for Violin
Barbara Barber: *Scales for Advanced Violinists*
Susan Brown: *Two Octave Scales And Bowings For The Violin*
Paul Rolland, James Starr: *Three Octave Scale Fingering Alternatives*
Hrimaly: Scale Book - violin
Schradieck: *School Of Violin Technics*: Bk. 1, Bk. 2, Bk. 3
Sitt: *Scales Studies For Violin*, Op. 41
Carl Flesch: *Scale Studies* - violin
Galamian *Contemporary Violin Technique*: Vol. 1, Vol. 2.

Viola Scale Books

Barbara Barber: *Scales for Advanced Violists*
Susan Brown: *Two Octave Scales And Bowings For The Viola*
Castleman/Koob: *Tonal Applications of Finger Patterns*
The Galamian Scale System For Viola (Volume 1)
Mogill *Scale Studies* - viola
Schradieck: *School Of Viola Technics*: Bk. 1, Bk. 2, Bk. 3
Carl Flesch: *Scale Studies* - viola
Dr. Michael Kimber: *Scales, Arpeggios, and Double Stops for the Violist*

(26) What is a cost effective and reliable way of recording students? In order to audio record students, I use the following combination of things, which are reasonably priced, and easy to use:

1. Laptop or PC
2. Audacity software, (free)
3. lame_enc.dll, (free)
4. Microphone
5. Boom

Placement of microphone(s) is very important. For ideas about microphone placement see: James Boyk's *To Hear Ourselves As Others Hear Us: Tape Recording As a Tool in Music Practicing and Teaching.* You may be able to get a better price on his book by visiting Professor Boyk's homepage.

(27) What are some of the questions perspective students ask?
These are the questions that I get asked the most frequently:

Music Lesson FAQ (Frequently Asked Questions)

1. How much do you charge?
2. How old do you have to be?
3. I have x-number of children: Do you have group rates for my children, or may I bring the younger ones to the lessons?
4. Can we use a keyboard to start piano lessons?
5. I (or my child or children) want to study fiddle, or jazz, exclusively: can you do that?
6. Can you come to our home to teach us?
7. Do you teach guitar, mandolin or 'cello?
8. Do you teach group piano?
9. May I take lessons twice a month, or every once in a while?
10. Do you take autistic, learning disabled or other differently abled students?
11. What methods do you use?
12. Where can I purchase a violin or viola?
13. What is your background and how long have you been teaching?
14. How do I contact you for further questions?

(28) What are some of the legal issues associated with a private teaching studio?

Issues in the home studio:
(a.) If you teach in your home you can have liability issues if anyone gets hurt there. It's recommended that you have home owner's insurance, or renter's insurance;

(b.) You should have your instruments and other equipment insured if they are costly; the AFM (American Federation of Musicians) has good instrument insurance. Regular carriers will often not be able or willing to cover this;

(c.) Private teachers need to have a very clear and specific lesson policy, written out, perhaps available online, and in hard copy for new students to sign, so that misunderstandings don't occur. I have one online at: http://beststudentviolins.com/Studio.html which covers the contingencies I have encountered over the years. If there is a question, we can always refer to the policy, such as the following:

§1. CANCELLATIONS: Please think and plan ahead, and remember your lesson time. If you need to cancel a lesson, make every effort to give teacher as much notice as possible, at least 24 hours. Makeup lessons are not given without 24 hour notice.

§11. RETAINERS: The flat monthly fee covers four lessons, and occasionally five, per month–except for November and December, when it covers three lessons. Regardless of the number of lessons you receive in a month, the fee remains the same. No monthly refund will be given, once lessons are started.

(d.) Unfortunately, in this era, one needs to be sensitive and take care with respect to touching students. The Suzuki process of having the parent in the room is a wise one. I would never touch a student if a parent is not there, and especially so if the parent seems confrontational or otherwise emotionally unstable.

(e.) In my opinion, a teacher must be willing to dismiss or let go of students, or parents, who are emotionally volatile, or inappropriate in behavior.

Regarding dealing with difficult situations:
In terms of telling students that it's not working out, the central issues, for me, are dishonesty, primarily: not paying on time, no shows/no calls (I give them three and then ask them to find someone else to work with), and behaviors which are otherwise counterproductive.

Legal issues online:
(a.) If you have a studio policy or other information online about your teaching, associated with your email address, you are apt to receive a lot of fraudulent messages, attempting to get you to accept a stolen or bad check, and then return an overage amount to the thief. I have a Teacher Directory and an online Studio Policy, and regularly receive messages of this type, based on my online presence.

See: Fraud Against Music Teachers
http://beststudentviolins.com/FRAUDagainstMT.html

(b.) If you do business online, you must educate yourself about online security issues, including concerns about wireless security, hacking, phishing, spam and identity theft. If you put your name, phone number, address and resume online, you are bound to encounter difficulties. To start, I recommend the following:

The End of Privacy, Charles J. Sykes
Desktop Witness, Michael A. Caloyannides
Emotional Vampires: Dealing With People Who Drain You Dry,
     Albert Bernstein Kindle ed.
Net Crimes and Misdemeanors, J. A. Hitchcock
The Gift of Fear, Gavin De Becker
The Sociopath Next Door, Martha Stout
Snakes in Suits: When Psychopaths Go to Work, Paul Babiak
*Without Conscience: The Disturbing World of the Psychopaths
     Among Us*, Robert D. Hare

(29) How long will it take me to get really good at the violin?

That question is probably one of the top four or five most "frequently asked" on YahooAnswers and various violin forums. The answer is that it takes about five years to really get into the violin. According to the following research, it takes 10,000 hours to master it.

Two recently published books reference a study about violin students; Malcolm Gladwell, *Outliers: The Story of Success* and Geoff Colvin, *Talent is Overrated: What Really Separates World-Class Performers from Everybody Else.* The study indicates that success in violin performance is directly related to the amount of practice.

The material below, from Peter Norvig's *Teach Yourself Programming in Ten Years* support this thesis as well:

Researchers Bloom (1985), Bryan & Harter (1899)*, Hayes (1989), Simmon & Chase (1973)** have shown it takes about ten years to develop expertise in any of a wide variety of areas, including chess playing, music composition, telegraph operation, painting, piano playing, swimming, tennis, and research in neuropsychology and topology. There appear to be no real shortcuts: even Mozart, who was a musical prodigy at age four, took 13 more years before he began to produce world-class music.

In another genre, the Beatles seemed to burst onto the scene with a string of number one hits and an appearance on the Ed Sullivan show in 1964. But they had been playing small clubs in Liverpool and Hamburg since 1957, and while they had mass appeal early on, their first great critical success, Sgt. Peppers, was released in 1967.

Samuel Johnson (1709-1784) thought it took longer than ten years: "Excellence in any department can be attained only by the labor of a lifetime; it is not to be purchased at a lesser price." And Chaucer (1340-1400) complained "the lyf so short, the craft so long to lerne." Hippocrates (c. 400BC) is known for the excerpt "ars longa, vita brevis", which is part of the longer quotation "Ars longa, vita brevis, occasio praeceps, experimentum periculosum, iudicium difficile", which in English renders as "Life is short, [the] craft long, opportunity fleeting, experiment treacherous, judgment difficult." Although in Latin, ars can mean either art or craft, in the original Greek the word "techne" can only mean "skill", not "art".

* Bryan, W.L. & Harter, N. "Studies on the telegraphic language: The acquisition of a hierarchy of habits. Psychology Review, 1899, 8, 345-375 ** Chase, William G. & Simon, Herbert A. "Perception in Chess", Cognitive Psychology, 1973, 4, 55-81.

(30) How can I develop good sight reading skills?

Sight reading is learned by doing; it takes a quick wit, direction from an experienced teacher, and practice. I require sight reading in every lesson. Being a good sight reader requires a combination of two elements:

1. Learning as much music theory, music history, and related subjects, as one can manage. Having, in other words, a deep interest in music, in general; and

2. Practical experience in sight reading. This is acquired by joining as many formal or informal groups as one can locate, and also regularly attending to new music in the home practice.

A few things to keep in mind:

1. At the head of every piece of music, there are three areas to examine initially: the clef signs, the key signature and the time signature;

2. One should also have some general idea about the style period;

3. Glance through the piece if you have time and look at the form and chord structures. Determine, at minimum, whether it's in a major or minor key, and note any development or recapitulation materials.

Knowing how to sight read well is the prized skill of many studio musicians. These are great, great players who can "sightread the bugs off a wall," and are highly trained, highly experienced, reliable, professionals. Some of them also teach, some privately, some in university. Studio musicians are typically used for recordings and film music. They are frequently AFM (or the Canadian counterpart) members. See: American Federation of Musicians

(31) Do you use fingerboard tapes with your students, and if so, what kind of tape?

I use the following products to set up new students' violins:

* Fingerboard tapes: Normally tapes will start to "migrate" (move out of the correct position), at which time you can determine if a second or third set of tapes is productive. The "ringing strings" caused by sympathetic vibrations of fingers being put in just the right place should be the goal; fingerboard tapes are used initially, as introduction only.

See also:
Violin/Viola Fingerboard Charts
http://beststudentviolins.com/fingerboard.html

* Pinky pads: Used for the tip of the pinky finger on the bow hand. There are other products you can buy, but I feel that they are too restricting and possibly could cause damage. A pinky pad should be placed slightly on the inside (toward student) of the bow stick, rather than the very top of the stick. These pads will need replacing several times before they're abandoned. You can use Fiddlebrite to clean off any messiness caused by the pinky pads (or by fingerboard tapes). Make sure not to get Fiddlebrite on the bow hair.

* Masking tape: I still use small strips of masking tape to "fence" the initial middle area of the bow for the Twinkle. I find that masking tape stays in place better on the tiny bows, than the fingerboard tape does. (Masking tape is the brown packaging tape that comes in 1" strips.)

(32) What is the best way to develop effective practice habits?

QUESTION: My goal for right now is making sure I set aside time to practice every day. Any ideas other than will-power?!

TEACHER RESPONSE: I have lots of ideas about this. There is this wonderful book called How to get your child to practice without resorting to violence. The ideas also apply to adults, in a self-monitoring way. But mainly I suggest the following:

1. Don't think of it as "practicing." Think of it as "spending time with the instrument."

2. There are sort of two ways of "practicing": the wrong way and the right way. The wrong way is sort of watching the clock and sawing away for a certain number of minutes. The right way is to forget the clock and actually PLAY the instrument with intense focus.

3. You should never "practice" for more than 20 minutes at a stretch. If you can do two, three, or more such "practice" sessions a day, you will get good at playing the instrument.

4. But never underestimate the value of "practicing" even just for 10 minutes. If you're really listening, your muscles and musicianship will benefit.

5. Having even a general idea of both short-term and long-term goals is helpful. Keep track of what you're doing, and certainly what is required from the teacher every week (if you have a teacher). One of the best books you can get on this is Barry Green's The Inner Game of Music. I think every working musician alive has read this book.
6. I require that all students have a three-ring notebook with filler paper,

and I do lots of handouts and put their current work on a page in the front of the book every week. It's helpful to keep records of what you're doing and where you're going. If you have a good notebook, you can always refer to it if you forget something. I give students who have been with me a year an Elson's Pocket Dictionary.

Fiddle and Alternative Styles

(33) Teaching Fiddle
I frequently have students contact me who are studying law or working on a Ph.D. in a science subject, who are clearly not planning on becoming professional musicians (though some approach that level), but who "want to know everything" while mainly their focus is fiddle. In these cases, I use the *Tune a Day*, still, and also Suzuki book 1, but add the *American Fiddle Method*, but using more an aural tradition. By

observing the posts on Fiddle-L, a forum based at Brown University, I have come to understand the real distinction between classical music orientation and folk/fiddle orientation. Learning fiddle is not done by the book, but by listening and teaching improvisation techniques. To faciliate my own learning in this area, I collect recordings, including mp3 files of fiddle songs from Amazon.com, and popular country CD's (I like Garth Brooks' fiddler). I am learning these by listening, with no reference to written notes. And then, teaching the fiddle parts, also without reference to written notes. This is the way folk and popular music is frequently learned, and I highly recommend it.

Like studying the viola, studying fiddle takes the classically trained violinist out of their comfort zone, and is wonderful for the development of their musicianship. There are also sociological and cultural issues, and it's incredibly interesting.

(34) How many different fiddle styles are there?

The distinction is between so-called "art music" and popular or folk music is no longer very meaningful, as the social classes that participate in these art forms are pretty much completely across-the-board. In other words, highly educated individuals enjoy playing "fiddle," and discovering what that art form is about, and students from all social classes (not just the privileged), study classical music.

Sometimes people are taken aback by the term "art music," assuming that this phrase suggests that other musics are not art (understandable, actually). But nothing could be further from the truth. The phrase "art music" is found in every musicology textbook, and simply means a distinction between academically oriented music versus popular or folk musics. It is not pejorative.

If you trace the history of music from the Renaissance to the present, it is evident how events in music mirror the socioeconomic events in human history. In the early development of Western "art music," this music was mostly created for the European wealthy class. There was no middle class until the Industrial Revolution.

At that time, entrepreneurs began designing larger concert halls to accommodate the middle class, who could afford concert tickets, and the modern stringed, keyboard, brass and woodwind instruments came into being, in response to the acoustic needs of these big halls.

This is an important fact that students should understand. The "pianoforte" (our modern piano) was so called because it could play both loudly and softly; an ability unknown in the previous keyboard instruments (like the harpsichord), which were designed for the small "chamber" ensembles, which were an entertainment of the wealthy.

In Arnold Steinhardt's *Violin Dreams* he wrote about his visit to Mark O'Connor's summer fiddle camp:

> where violinists of all types – jazz, bluegrass, country and western, blues, rock, Texas style, old-time, classical, and Cape Breton -gathered to teach and play. (p. 240, 2006 ed.)

He mentions eight styles other than classical. (a) Should there be other styles on this list?; and (b) What are the definitions of each?

Responses on Fiddle-L:
In addition to those already mentioned, I'm aware of the following fiddle styles: Irish, Scottish, French, Swedish, New England, Midwestern, Quebecois, Southwestern, Alaskan, and Northwestern. These are just the ones I can pull out of my head at the moment, and I'm sure there are many more. . .they vary widely in the type of music played, the bowing styles, and ornamentation. Within Irish fiddle music alone there are as many different styles as there are counties in Ireland.

The list is definitely incomplete. There are other musical cultures in which the violin or fiddle is used extensively, and the style or styles in which the instrument is played would not fit any of the categories already listed. For instance, the violin is a very important instrument in Indian classical music. It is also played quite a bit in Greek traditional music. The category "Gypsy" would not be adequate to represent Hungarian traditional playing as well as Romanian fiddling. We also have all the Native American traditions of fiddle playing, Metis (ND and Canada), Tarahumara and other Northern Mexico tribes, Bolivia, etc...

I can think of five very different fiddle styles in Michoacan. Around Lake Patzcuaro (Morelia, Uruapan); Tierra Caliente part of Michoacan; the southern coast; Tarascan (native fiddle); and modern Mariachi, which is found everywhere but seems strongest to its roots in the western part of the state.

Let me suggest a few styles that have thus far not been mentioned: Son Huasteca, from Veracruz on the Gulf Coast side of Mexico and the son and gusto styles from La Tierra Caliente, over on the Pacific side. Is it proper to call that Son Calientano. And the fiddle is used in Michoacan, in a configuration that differs from its neighbors (Son Michoacano?), Also there's some wonderful fiddle music from the Andes that is unlike any other I've heard. Have you tried to list the various Indian styles in North America? Waila, Athabascan, Metis from the Red River Country, North Woods styles (Anishanabe, Menominee, etc.) And don't forget the Poles (several varieties right here in Chicago), and the Danes, and the Finns, and the South Slavs.

I'm not sure if you can even list all the styles, even in one specific geographic region. West Virginia probably has a half dozen different styles, to the discerning ear, as does North Carolina. Eastern Kentucky is different from Western Kentucky, East Texas/ West Texas, Southern Missouri/Northern Missouri. Thus far, we have:

    * American fiddling (e.g., New England, Northwestern, Midwestern, Southwestern, Appalachian, Missouri, Tennessee)

* Balkan
* bluegrass
* blues
* Cajun
* Canadian (e.g., Ottawa Valley, Western/Midwest, North Dakota Norwegian, Ottawa Valley, East Coast, West Coast (Métis), Red River, Prince Edward Island)
* Cape Breton
* country and western
* English
* French
* Greek
* Gypsy (e.g., Serbian, Armenian)
* Hungarian
* Indian raga (e.g., Hindustani, Carnatic)
* Irish (e.g., Donegal, Kerry, Clare, Galway)
* jazz
* Kletzmer
* Mariachi
* Maritime
* metal
* Mexican
* Northumbrian
* Norwegian
* old-time (e.g., ragtime) * Quebecois

* rock
* Romanian
* Scottish
* Shetland
* Southwestern
* Square Dance
* Swedish
* Swing
* Tarahumara
* Texas style
* Western Swing

Bibliography

* *Beau Solo*: 12 Cajun Fiddle Tunes Transcribed from Michael Doucet's CD, Drew Beisswenger
* *Canadian Fiddle Music*, Edward A. Whitcomb
* *Celtic Music: A Complete Guide*, June Skinner Sawyers
* *Danse ce soir: Fiddle and Accordion Music of Quebec*, Laurie Hart
* *The Fiddle Music of Prince Edward Island: Celtic and Acadian Tunes in Living Tradition*, Ken Perlman
* *The Fiddler's Fakebook*, David Brody
* *Fiddle Traditions Musical Sampler from the pages of String Magazine*, Hal Leonard Corp.
* *Hill Country Tunes*, Sam Bayard
* *Howe's 1,000 Jigs and Reels*: Clog Dances, Contra Dances, Patrick Sky. Better known as 1000 Fiddle Tunes, this influential book first appeared in Boston (1884). (Coles, Chicago, 1940). Always influential, this new 1996 Mel Bay edition contains 1050 tunes plus history.
* *Irish Fiddle Solos*: 64 Pieces for Violin, Pete Cooper
* T*he Jewish Music Companion* (Book with CD): Historical Overview, Personalities, Annotated Folksongs, Velvel Pasternak
* *Old Time Fiddling Across America*, David Reiner. 66 carefully transcribed tunes from excellent fiddlers across various regional and ethnic traditions, as well as history, bowing and cross-tuning discussions, and stylistic analyses.
* *Old-Time Kentucky Fiddle Tunes*, Jeff Todd Titon
* *O'Neill's Music of Ireland*, James O'Neill
* *Traditional Scottish Fiddling*, Christine Martin
* *Under the Moon*, Martin Hayes

FAQ - Violin/Viola Care & Specs

(1) Issues regarding purchase of starter instruments.

Ten years ago, when this FAQ was originally conceived, my recommendation was to rent a violin at first, in order to determine if the child would remain interested. However, based on experiences with my own private students and given the favorable economic climate between the US and China regarding Chinese instruments, many of which are fine instruments and quite good quality at exceedingly reasonable prices, my views have changed. Currently, one can purchase a beautifully setup starter for $180.00 (viola, cello and bass are consecutively higher, since they're larger instruments), it is more economically sound to just purchase such an instrument. If you work with a teacher the instrument can be sold when the child outgrows it, or traded in for a better and larger instrument. I think, now, that this is the way to go. It's simply that if you can purchase an instrument outright for the price of a few months rental, it's more sensible to purchase it.

The contributing factor in the change of my views is the quality of these instruments. Certainly there are still shoddy instruments, but there seem to be a lot of very nice instruments coming from China nowadays, which are beautiful to look at, play well, have no problems, come with a very attractive case and bow (also with no problems) and at reasonable prices. The bows come furnished with real horsehair; this once-dear stuff has now become so reasonably priced that one can hardly find synthetic hair any more.

NOTE: The advanced player, who is no doubt under the tutelage of an experienced teacher, doesn't need my help–aside from perhaps the admonition to play a lot of instruments in combination with bows, and find what pleases you the best, paying less attention to the price and more to the sound. Fine instruments are a major investment and many professional players spend decades paying off the instrument, acquiring it through a loan from a local musicians union or bank. Sometimes players, because of their exceptional abilities, enjoy instruments given to them as gifts, but most players buy them or borrow them. As orchestras are ranked, in the top tiers the string professionals require instruments starting in the $30-$60K range.

(2) Requests to appraise an instrument

This must be done by a reputable shop. I get frequent requests about specific instruments, but that is not my area of expertise, and it cannot be done over the internet without a direct examination from a reputable expert, which most violinists are not. Labels are often faked!

People often write me about instruments with Stradivarius labels, violins which have turned up in an attic, closet, cupboard, or garage sale. The "Stradivarius" label often has a tiny *copie de* above the word Stradivarius, which means a copy of a Stradivarius, or an instrument built on that model. If repaired, these instruments may be good student instruments, but unfortunately they're seldom or never valuable. What must be done in every case is to locate a professional repair person who can do an adequate appraisal.

(3) Are the violin and the fiddle the same instrument?

Well, yes and no, it depends. What it depends on is who's playing it, and in what cultural context you're speaking. Growing up in the midwest, I felt uncomfortable using the term fiddle, because what that meant, then, was country and western fiddle. However, you hear violinists of the highest calibre, like Stern and Perlman, for example, referring to the violin as a fiddle...but their cultural context is Eastern European, which included gypsy-like so-called "fiddle" music, which is not the same at all as the American genre. The instrument itself may be the same, though folk players of violin (and other players who are playing something besides art music) may take more liberties with respect to the way the instrument is held, its fittings, and so on. Aside from some small details, however, the instrument is pretty much the same; there is no separate genre, fiddle, which is not also a violin.

(4) What's the difference between the violin and the viola?

Violins come in "fractional sizes" (4/4, 3/4, 1/2, 1/4, 1/8, 1/16, even a tiny 1/32). The 4/4 is full size, suitable for nearly all adults. The 7/8 size is frequently used by adults who are very petite.

Violas: While violins come in fractional sizes, violas are measured in inches (17", 16 1/2", 16", 15", 14", 13", 12"). For students changing from violin to viola, or adding viola after studying violin, the 14" viola is approximately the same size as a full size violin. Many violists start on violin. It may be difficult to find a 12" viola with a good sound on the C string.

The 16" is the usual adult size. Any size above the 16" may be difficult for young people to handle and is not recommended. Viola length is measured in centimeters in Europe (41cm, 41.5cm and 42cm), and there is no exact standard with respect to size. Many professional violists play a 17" viola; Michael Tree (of the Guarneri Quartet), Bruno Giuranna, Gerard Coussè.

The viola is a fifth lower in pitch than the violin; the lowest string on the viola is the C string. The viola's second string, the G, is the violin's lowest string. Violas have no E string, the top string on violin. The A=440 (the violin's second string), is the top string on viola. The viola is primarily written in the alto clef (though high registers may be written in treble, like the violin). Violists have to be conversant with both clefs.

The violin and viola étude repertoire is much the same, with additional works in viola by Fuchs, Campagnoli and others. Some of the literature for violin has been transcribed for viola (and visa versa), but viola literature is quite different. (See: Advanced Viola Literature http://beststudentviolins.com/lit.html#adv_vla_lit)

Note that the viola is "not just a big violin." Violists will have you assassinated if you even think that. Playing the viola requires a very different touch, different fingerings, different position work, different vibrato, and an entirely different mindset with respect to its role in the orchestral and chamber music repertoire. Violists are very sensitive about this.

Viola Resources

Suzuki Viola books and CDs
http://beststudentviolins.com/sheetmusic.html#viola

Viola Fingerboard Chart
http://beststudentviolins.com/fingerboard.html#viola_fingerboard_chart

Viola Resources
http://beststudentviolins.com/violas.html#violaresources

Barbara Barber Books and CDs
http://beststudentviolins.com/sheetmusic.html#barber

Viola Literature (études)
http://beststudentviolins.com/sheetmusic.html#violalit

Advanced Chamber Literature
http://beststudentviolins.com/lit.html#adv_chamb_lit

Viola Concertos
http://beststudentviolins.com/lit.html#viola_concertos

Viola Scale Books
http://beststudentviolins.com/sheetmusic.html#violascales

Free Viola Music
http://beststudentviolins.com/freemusic.html#freeviolamusic

Advanced Viola Literature
http://beststudentviolins.com/lit.html#adv_vla_lit

Viola da Gamba
http://beststudentviolins.com/lit.html#gamba

Viola List
http://launch.groups.yahoo.com/group/viola/

American Viola Society
http://www.americanviolasociety.org/

International Viola Society
http://www.viola.ca/ivs/ivs_home.html

Duets
Violin/Viola, Viola/Viola, Viola/Cello

Trios with Viola
http://beststudentviolins.com/lit.html#trios

Viola Outfits
http://beststudentviolins.com/violas.html#studentviolas

Step-Up Violas
http://beststudentviolins.com/violas.html#violastep-up

Master Level Violas
http://beststudentviolins.com/Professional.html#proviolas

Master Level Viola Bows
http://beststudentviolins.com/Professional.html#probows

Viola Cases
http://beststudentviolins.com/bobelock.html#viola

* Barrett, Henry: The Viola: Complete Guide for Teachers & Students *
Dalton, David: Playing the Viola
* Giorgetti, Ferdinando, Franco Sciannameo An Historical Introduction
* Hoffheimer, Michael: Fiddling for Viola
* Madden, Maxine: Sounds on Strings: Getting to Know Your Viola *
Maurice, Donald: Bartók's Viola Concerto: The Remarkable Story of
His Swansong
* Menuhin, Yehudi and William Primrose: Violin & Viola
* Stowell, Robin: The Early Violin and Viola : A Practical Guide
* Tertis, Lionel: My viola and I: A complete autobiography
* Williams, Amedee Daryl: Lillian Fuchs: First Lady of the Viola
* Zeyringer, Franz: Literatur Für Viola

(5) How can I determine if this violin or viola is the right size?

Student Violin Size Chart
* Age: 12-Adult/ 4/4 size
* Age: 10-11/ 3/4 size
* Age: 8-9/ 1/2 size
* Age: 6-7/ 1/4 size
* Age: 5-6/ 1/8 size
* Age: 4-5/ 1/10 size
* Age: 3-4/ 1/16 size

Student Viola Size Chart
* Age: Large Adult/ 16" and larger
* Age: Average Adult/ 15.5"
* Age: 10-12, Small Adult/ 15"
•   Age: 9-12/ 14"
   * Age: 7-9/ 13"
   * Age: 6-7/ 12"
•

There are a number of ways of determining the correct size of violin or viola for the player:

* Stretch the left arm under the instrument, and have the player wrap their fingers around the scroll. If the elbow is slightly bent but not too bent or too straight, it fits.

* Stretch the left arm straight out under the instrument, and under the scroll, and if the instrument's scroll ends flush with the pulse, it is just right.

(6) What is the best way to protect the violin from extremes of temperature and humidity?

There is a lot of disagreement about whether the two items used to manage this problem are necessary: hygrometers measure humidity levels; humidifiers correct dryness. Hygrometers in cases are either digital or analog (dial), and are not always accurate; in some cases the hygrometer has to be recalibrated regularly.

Sometimes there is a plastic vial (a humistat) which contains water and supplies humidity for the case. It clips in place somewhere down around the pegbox/scroll portion of the case and can be adjusted to allow more or less water vapor to escape. If there is not one of these vials accompanying the hygrometer itself, you can purchase a humidifier to put in the f holes of the violin. Both Strettos and Dampits seem to work well, although Dampits are more of a hassle since you have to resoak them frequently. Many musicians keep a humidifier in the music studio (aim for a steady 50-60% humidity), which protects stringed instruments and pianos.

Certainly there are players who question the usefulness of these products and wonder whether any kind of humidification is a good idea for string instruments, in terms of avoiding cracks. Humidifying an instrument in its case may be unnecessary except in extremely dry environments. It's conceivable that too much humidity could cause problems with insects and otherwise damage the wood. The constant changing of the moisture content of the wood can't be good for the instrument; if the maker has selected well seasoned wood, the best thing to do is let the instrument adjust to the prevailing humidity or lack thereof.

For example: like Italy, Los Angeles is classed as a Mediterranean

clime by geologists. Violins sound better in L.A. then they do in the
humidity of NYC, but players often don't have any problems- or use
humidifiers. Dryness may be good for fiddles - avoiding extremes, of
course.

(7) How do I replace a string?
Please see:

• How to Change a Violin String, (free video)
http://www.ehow.com/video_2375311_tune-violin-newstrings.html
• How to change violin/viola strings, (written instructions)
http://www.ehow.com/video_2375311_tune-violin-newstrings.html
• How to String a Violin, Music Education Online
http://www.childrensmusicworkshop.com/instruments/violin/howt
ostring.html

(8) Rosin
Most new student violin outfits are provided with a cake of rosin. Take
this out of the case and scratch the top of the rosin in a cross-hatch
pattern. Just for the first time, not after. Hold the rosin steady in one
hand and draw the bow hair over the rosin; a good deal on either end,
and then back and forth. Shake off the excess and then take a clean, dry
rag and dust off the bow stick and frog. Keep a clean, dry rag in your
case and dust off the violin after playing every time.
Rosin is needed to "catch" the strings; a new violin will not play
without rosin on the bow. Normally, a bow should be rehaired once a
year, or every six months if you play a lot, depending on the quality of
the original hair. I've seen the costs of rehairing a bow anywhere from
$25 to $45, or more, depending on what part of the country you live in.

Sometimes new players confuse "hair" with "strings." Strings are the E-
A-D-G on the violin, which one tunes (or A-D-G-C on the viola - the
viola is a fifth lower than the violin); "hair" is bow hair.

Note that in order to prevent the bow stick from being warped, it is
very important to remember to loosen the hair (with the end adjuster)
before you put the instrument away, and then tighten the bow hair again
when you play. Hair should be about a fingertip width between the stick
and the hair.

(9) Strings

Many students start their study of the violin with a so-called "student" outfit. To improve the sound of this instrumnent, a better set of strings (Dominants, for example, versus the metal strings usually shipped on the cheaper instruments), and some better rosin (such as Hill), is recommended.

Strings are usually available in Weich, Medium and Stark: Yielding, Medium, and Strong (respectively, lower, medium, and high tension). I always order the "Medium."

How often you change your strings depends on how much you play. Students should probably try to change their strings every year; professionals who play a great deal, every six months, or sooner. Always change a string if it begins to sound dull or begins to unravel.

Regarding ball-end and loop-end strings:

Ball-end strings can work either with a tailpiece slot or with a tuner. Which is appropriate depends on the material of the string. Synthetic core strings are meant to be used without a fine-tuner, most metal-core strings meant to be used with one.

Loop-end E-strings work only with a tuner designed for loop-end E strings. Ball-end E-strings work either with a tuner designed for ball-end strings or (usually? always?) with a loop-end tuner if you take the ball out.

Gut core strings generally end in a knot and loop of gut, but this is not designed to be used with a fine tuner.

I think it may be accurate to say that the Dominants are the most purchased strings, followed perhaps by the Evah Pirazzi; players frequently choose a different E-string from the one that comes in a set with the other strings they use. In the viola world, for the past several years, it seems to be Dominants, followed by Obligatos. I use the Pirazzi's on both my violins and violas; they sound rich and warm to me. I don't use a different E string on the violins.

The steel strings are frequently fitted on the so-called "student" instruments, and also by "fiddle" players. However, most Celtic fiddlers prefer synthetic core strings. Steel core is an "old-time" fiddle thing – they like the brightness. It may even be more an Appalachian old-time than a New England old-time (contra) thing.

Some kinds of steel-core strings (with a steel rope or similar core rather than a plain steel wire as core) are intended for classical playing and do not have the extremely bright "steel" sound (e.g., Helicore). They are more popular on viola and (especially) on cello than on violin. They are also suitable for electric instruments with magnetic pickups (as are the plainsteel core strings, depending on what sound is required).

The better sounding strings are wound aluminum over perlon, which is a synthetic, which replace the old gut strings used in baroque instruments. Gut strings are still available for baroque instruments and sold as the Corelli brand or (better) hand made by Damian Dlugolecki.

(10) Set-up
Some inexpensive student instruments come with the bridge tucked into a little packet of tissue paper, under the tailpiece. This is a security measure to protect the instrument, in transit from Asia. The SV-175 Cremona Violin Outfits (for example) are adjusted in the shops, but will need to have the bridge set up by the purchaser or their teacher. [For a diagram of the parts of the violin, please see *Violin acoustics: an introduction*: http://www.phys.unsw.edu.au/jw/violintro.html#Strings]

Set up Instructions:
Violin bridges have a flat side and a rounded ("belly") side. The "belly" side needs to face the scroll. Loosen the strings and set the feet of the bridge between the nicks in the F holes, with, as mentioned, the rounded side of the bridge facing the scroll and fingerboard. Make sure the bridge is straight up and down, at right angles to the top of the instrument, and not tilted in either direction.

Sometimes, (though rarely), a bridge will break, so I keep an adjustable bridge in my case. Though one can purchase bridges, pegs and soundpost setters online, these tasks should really be left to a luthier who has the equipment, training and experience to do the job correctly.

(11) Tuning Instructions:
Tuning an instrument takes some skill and usually the teacher will help with this. On a violin, the strings are E, A, D and G, as indicated on the treble staff, below; the viola strings are a fifth lower: C, G, D and A, and the viola clef is the alto clef. Click on the link, below, for a free online tuner.

For further help with where the notes are on the violin and viola, see:

Violin/Viola Fingerboard Charts:
http://beststudentviolins.com/fingerboard.html

Open strings on the violin:

Violin Range: From G below middle C to four octaves above middle C (the highest note on the piano).

Viola Range:

See:
Online Tuner (Interactive!)
http://www.seventhstring.com/tuner/tuner.html

Online Metronome (click on outside ring to change setting)
http://www.metronomeonline.com/

Violin Diagram (parts of the violin)
http://www.phys.unsw.edu.au/jw/violintro.html#Strings

The A is 440, which is the international pitch standard. This is the A above middle C on a keyboard (assuming the keyboard is in tune). One can also purchase a pitch pipe or chromatic tuner. The chromatic tuner is a recommended choice, as the tuner will indicate whether the pitch is too high or too low.

Fittings:
A matched set of string fittings includes the pegs, chinrest, tailpiece and end button. The only items you might replace yourself are the chinrest and tailpiece; replacing of the end button and pegs requires the services of a luthier to fit them properly.

(12) My pegs are not working right; how do I fix them?

If your pegs are not sticking, you can gently try to press them inward toward the peg box. But don't force them. Sometimes players put pencil lead or chalk on the peg to make it stick, but the best way is to use peg drops or peg dope.

(13) My chinrest came off; how can I fix it?
The chinrest can be tightened, using a little tool called a chinrest wrench. You can also use a bobby pin (hair pin) if you don't have anything else. Make sure that the cork between the metal of the chinrest and the wood of the violin, is in place, so you don't damage the instrument. As always, it's best to have a luthier do this, if you can.

(14) My tailpiece came off; how can I fix it?
You can, if you need to, replace the tailpiece yourself if the leather bit at the end is broken. There is a great deal of pressure at that spot, so you will need to replace the tailpiece or take it to a luthier and have them do it. Below are some examples of tailpieces you can purchase online.

(15) Cleaning/Polishing and Removing Dust Bunnies
1. Never use any household products on an instrument; only use those products especially designed for violins. Rubbing alcohol and four-in-one oil are the only two exceptions I can think of; rubbing alcohol for the strings, and a tiny dab of oil on the bow screw if it's fussy. No Elmer's Glue, furniture polish, chemicals of any kind, varnish remover, etc.
2. Use a small amount of polish/cleaner and gently buff with a dry cloth until dry.
3. Let the instrument sit out for a while (out of its case), so it can air dry.
 4. If you are going to use polish, don't polish over twice a year; in between times, just dust the instrument off with a clean, dry cloth after playing. Too much polish can lead to build-up and attracts dirt.
5. If you're not clear whether your violin has a French polish, test a tiny spot before using any product. Discontinue immediately if the area becomes
sticky.
6. Don't let rosin, skin oils or dirt build up on the strings or the wood; the best way to keep the instrument clean is to wipe it off with a dry cloth after every playing session.
7. In the process of cleaning/polishing the instrument, if you see any cracks, take it to a luthier and have them repaired. Don't polish the instrument until this is done; polish in the cracks will interfer with the repair.
8. In the process of cleaning/polishing, make sure not to move the bridge or damage the f holes; take care that you don't snag your cleaning cloth on the intricate carving of the bridge.

9. If the instrument has a really thick build-up of rosin and dirt, you should take it to a luthier and have it cleaned.

10. Carefully shake the polish before using, and use a small amount, about the size of a small coin. Fiddlebrite

11. Fiddlebrite: This is a great product offered by Elderly Instruments. A luthier told me that it's really not a polish, but a cleaner. And it may be used to clean the stick of the bow (don't get it on the hair), the violin wood, and the strings. It is appropriate for all so-called "student instruments," but you should not use it on expensive instruments with French varnish (which young beginners should not have anyway, in my opinion.) For very expensive instruments, you should use regular cleaner and polish, or better still, just dust the instrument and have it professionally cleaned periodically.

12. Cautionary note: Don't confuse Fiddlebrite with the regular cleaner and polish products. Fiddlebrite may be used to clean not only the wood, but the strings. Other products are designed only for the wood of the instrument (not the fingerboard, either, but the wood of the body of the instrument) and must not be used on violin strings.

13. An alternative way to clean violin strings, is to take a couple of clean, dry cloths, folded several thicknesses; place one, several thicknesses, on the violin wood directly under the "playing area" (the area between the end of the fingerboard and the bridge), and place another cloth, at least double thickness, on the fingerboard, between the fingerboard and the strings. Then take another clean, dry cloth and put just a tiny dab of rubbing alcohol on the tip of a corner of the cloth, and clean your strings with that. You must not get any of the alcohol on the wood of the violin, or on the fingerboard. Make sure that the cloths you use don't have soap or chemical residue on them. Using alcohol to clean the strings must be done very carefully, as any drop of alcohol on the wood may damage the wood permanently. I prefer using the Fiddlebrite. An additional alternative way to clean the strings is to use the cork from a wine bottle. I've never done this, but it's often mentioned.

14. The common way of removing dust bunnies from inside the violin is to put 1/2 cup of DRY uncooked rice in the f holes, and then turn the instrument upsidedown, and shake out the rice.

15. Other issues: when you take the violin out, check the strings to make sure they're not unravelling, make sure the bridge is sitting up straight, make sure the chinrest is not loose, make sure the fine tuners are not rattling. Don't forget to loosen the bow and remove the shoulder rest when you put the instrument away.

(16) What on earth is a "Violin Hickey"?

A violin/viola hickey is a dark, usually roundish abrasion on the neck, caused by extensive playing or practicing, perhaps from skin sensitivity to metals in the screws (chrome, nickel) and the chin rest itself (chemical dyes). Metal parts made of titanium alloy are more expensive (but lighter); some producers have started making the screws out of surgical stainless steel. A violin/viola hickey can be serious if it becomes infected.

To address this concern, some players use the Wittner hypoallergenic chinrest and a Strad pad. It is recommended that the neck and chin rest be kept very clean, perhaps with witch hazel. And experiment with different chin rests and shoulder pads, to find the most comfortable setup.

(17) Why is my Viola making a buzzing sound?

A buzzing sound could be caused by any or some of the following:

1. loose fine tuner (loose metal doughnut)
2. lowest point of fine tuner pivot, barely touching top plate
3. string slot on the nut too deep, causing open string(s) to buzz against the fingerboard
4. seam that has come unglued
5. crack in the instrument somewhere
6. chin rest rubbing against the tailpiece or saddle
7. loose chin rest hardware
8. a high spot on the fingerboard
9. unglued fingerboard
10. loose purfling
11. loose lining
12. top and/or bottom block poorly glued
13. dirt in the f holes
14. loose sound post
15. loose collar or pin on decorated pegs
16. misplaced tailpiece
17. gap between bassbar and plate (one has opened up due improper or "sprung" fitting)
18. the bridge protectors are floating on the strings in the afterlength area
19. problem with endpin cork, ring, tip or screw
20. a label on the inside of the instrument can come loose, and buzz at a certain frequency
21. dead string falling apart; loose winding

22. loose string end in the pegbox
23. shoulder rest buzzing back of fiddle
24. loose sliding mute
25. loose wolf eliminator
26. buzz caused by an object in the room buzzing in sympathy with a certain note; sometimes can be mistaken for a buzz in the instrument
27. buzz caused by player's personal effects, jewelry or a button, etc.
28. check the bow; a screw loose on the threaded post can buzz.

Aside from making sure it's not a problem with a fine tuner (*1-2), or some problem extraneous to the instrument, (*21-28), you should take it to a luthier and have them examine the instrument, as only a luthier can do the repairs.

FAQ - Auditions & Gigs

(1) What is the best way to avoid being nervous at a jury or an audition?

* Prepare the music carefully, leaving nothing to chance. Everything should be so well prepared, you can play it cold, no matter what. This requires you to divide your practice up into "preparing time" and "performing time," a concept Galamian talks about in *Principles of Violin Playing and Teaching.*

* You should make an effort to tend to your health–that is, have had enough sleep, eat potassium rich foods like bananas, don't eat meat, fried foods or dairy (vegan is best, but at least avoid heavy foods), and exercise. But don't hurt your hands! I recommend walking, lifting light weights (I have a pair of 4 lb. Chinese barbells which I use regularly, lots of reps) and do yoga and stretching. Swimming is also good. Bicycling is good, but you can hurt your hands if you don't do it right, so be careful. Lots of fresh air and sunshine and positive thoughts.

* Be philosophical. Why do we study music? To make a big deal out of ourselves? No. If anyone does art to aggrandize themselves, they're doomed from the beginning. We do art to be in contact with the best human minds, to make beauty, and to express the best in humanity. We do it out of love. We do it because we can't do anything else. Given all that, so what if you aren't perfect? Only god is perfect. Do your best, give it everything you've got, and then make music and enjoy yourself. That's what counts. Forget yourself.

* Remember the little things which the listeners are going to be looking for (particularly if one of your listeners is a conductor), and which will indicate if your training is solid. These include stylistic accuracy, rhythmic integrity, attention to phrasing and dynamics, good intonation, and musical sensibility. Bach is different than Brahms. Dynamics don't just happen, you have to make them happen. Everything in the score is there for a reason. Plan the bowings and phrasing ahead of time (though some leeway is allowed for interpretive inspiration of the moment). This is all very hard work and time consuming, but don't blow any of it off and expect it to happen automatically when you go in to play. It won't.

Also see the following:

Books on Practicing

1. Madeline Bruser, *The Art of Practicing: A Guide to Making Music from the Heart*
2. Burton Kaplan, *Musician's Practice Log*
3. Burton Kaplan, *A Rhythm Sight-Reader*: Bk 1, Bk 2
4. Burton Kaplan, *Practicing for Artistic Success: The Musician's Guide to Self-Empowerment*
5. Stuart Edward Dunkel, *The Audition Process: Anxiety Management and Coping Strategies* (Juilliard Performance Guides, No 3)
6. Margret Elson, *Passionate Practice: The Musician's Guide to Learning, Memorizing, and Performing*
7. Jack Grassel, *Power Practicing*
8. Don Greene, *Audition Success* (A Theatre Arts Book)
9. Don Greene, *Performance Success: Performing Your Best Under Pressure* (Theatre Arts)

(2) How do I break into the music business (i.e., get gigs?)

Any or some combination of the following recommendations will probably work for you:

1. Take private lessons (or lessons through your university) from the top person in your area; often the concertmaster or principle of the local symphony, or someone who plays professionally and teaches. There are often local "artist teachers" who are very good;

2. Be willing to play for free a little bit, especially initially to meet people, or if you're very young or new to the business. That is, play in church, play in community orchestras, play as much as possible. However, at some point, this business of "bring your instrument and we'll feed you" becomes profoundly offensive. Please don't say this around me unless you want a lecture; normally, you don't consult a doctor or lawyer for free when you're at a social function, and you shouldn't ask a professional musician to play for free, either;

3. Pay your AFM dues, Musicians' Union dues, which are initially perhaps around $120, and then a bit every year, like $30. This is how you get your "name in the book" and is really important. Make sure your phone is in working order with the same number as that "in the book";

4. Be reliable: be on time, be pleasant, don't gossip, be nice to everyone ("the music world is a very small world" is not an adage for nothing), and keep your word so people know they can rely on you;

5. Practice a lot. Every day. Know your stuff. Be ready when the opportunities come;

6. Get as good equipment as you can afford and keep getting better. Experiment with new products, talk to people, visit local shops frequently. Try to be charming and people will be more apt to help you;

7. Don't get into interpersonal conflicts with people, no matter how annoying people are. Everyone is concerned about their own lives. Once a conflict starts (and it will) take a deep breath, stop the interaction, and back off (even if, and especially if, you know you're right and the other person is a jerk). Don't be a push-over, either, but just rise above it all and most of all, be forgiving and let things go;

8. Keep learning, whether you're in school or not;

9. Even if you're not playing in them, attend as many concerts as you can. If you're deeply interested in music, you will do this;

10. Don't do weird things. Don't just not show up. If you say you're going to do something, either DO IT or call and apologize for not being able to. Reputation is everything in this business.

Aside from the first, initial things, there are other, more controversial issues to talk about. These might include:

1. This is not a moral judgment, but drugs and alcohol ruin more musicians than anything I can think of. If you need something to relax, take up a sport. Weight lifting, Pilates, bike riding, swimming, tennis. Anything but drugs. In my experience, musicians tend to examine spiritual practices, read a lot of self-help books, and participate in retreats and yoga and that sort of thing;

2. If you really want to devote your life to music, you're going to have to think about getting the best instrument you can. This is expensive and scary, particularly since all shops are not totally free of self-interest. Play a lot of instruments until you can recognize the sound you want. Sometimes you can get an instrument for $300, say, which sounds as good as one for much more, but you've got to keep looking.

131

A good bow costs $1,000 and up. Other expensive issues to examine are insurance and tax issues (the AFM will help with this);

3. You have to have the right clothes. I know–Thoreau: "Distrust any enterprise that requires new clothes". . .but if you're going to be playing a lot of concerts you really do need comfortable, elegant clothes;

4. At some point, you may want to investigate things like brochures, head shots, business cards, management, etc. Most of us don't, but many do, and it's something to think about, particularly if you're developing a quartet;

5. You might find profession periodicals useful, including the AFM publication "International Musician," Strings, ASTA, SSA, etc.;

6. You will at some point, if you have not already, have to think about what direction you want your work to go: how professional, what level, does it include teaching or master classes, how much travel. And if you teach, what level do you want to teach? Public school, private studio, university? All of these arenas have different requirements with respect to qualifications. It's not true that most players have doctorates in performance, but many have Masters (M.M.) and that seems to be the norm. Try to go to the best school you can; you'll have more exposure to the best players, teachers, and opportunities;

7. Auditioning–whether for jobs or scholarships–is a learnable skill. You can get good at it if you work at it. Do as many auditions as you can until it becomes commonplace and non-scary.

The musical life is a good life. You don't have to get dirty and you meet a lot of nice people. You're in the business of creating beauty, which is a noble way to spend your time. There is no end to what you can learn. And teaching, if you like it, is a joy - something you can do when you're old and you truly having something to share. Good luck!

(3) How can I recover if I lose an audition?
You have my sympathies. Losing an audition is tough, and there are not too many musicians who don't go through this at one time or another. Remember the adage that the only person who never fails is the person who never tries anything. My recommendations, in no particular order:

1. Try to analyze your playing objectively; gather together all the resources you can–excerpt books and recordings, books about auditioning, books on string pedagogy–and read and study them, as well practicing as many hours as you can get in;

2. Find out who the most eminent teachers are in your town (won't be difficult to determine) and study with them; they were probably on the committee (did you say that you auditioned behind a screen? Even if you did, teachers can recognize the playing of their own students);

3. Try to get with someone, perhaps at a summer institute or workshop (check AFM publications, and other string-related magazines), who specializes in preparing players for auditions. Borok, for example, who used to teach at SMU but is now at U of H, is known for doing this. And there are others;

4. Know that many times, one may lose an audition based on the unfortunate chance that just so many positons were open, and some exceptionally good players, or well-connected players, showed up at the same time you did;

5. You can feel badly for a while–you're entitled–but then take it as a challenge, I'd say.

(4) ICSOM Statistics (International Conference of Symphony & Opera Musicians):

It should probably be added that positions in major orchestras are not only highly competitive, but shrinking in number due to economic conditions. One very successful professional player noted on the newsgroup that repeated failures to win auditions may be simply that the person, however intelligent, may lack critical physical abilities, and that, regardless of how hard the person wishes to win a major job, or how hard they may work, it is cruel, they say, to not try to gently guide them into some other field where they might have greater success– given that doing auditions is an extremely expensive and time consuming activity.

In terms of winning a major orchestra job, the newsgroup violinist is absolutely correct. I think it is accurate to say that the majority of musicians on the planet do not have high paying jobs, and that seeking a position in an orchestra with a smaller budget is often a good compromise, as is freelancing and teaching (only if you enjoy teaching, please–not as a fallback position!!), and also combining some other field with music. If you lose an audition, you can also ask to be put on the sub list, and then decide where to go next with your playing. [And I would mention to young people that, if you find yourself in an emotionally painful situation, please know that painful feelings go away eventually. These feelings won't last forever.]

There are many fine musicians who are also Phd's in some field, or physicians, or computer professionals, or lawyers, or police officers. Many really fine musicians have second jobs, or are doing music as their second job. There are many more ways to go than just getting a high powered orchestra job, in other words. It also doesn't follow that if you get a graduate degree or degrees in instrumental performance, even from a first rate music school, you will automatically earn a good income. There are a lot of unemployed people with doctorates.

ICSOM is comprised of 52 American orchestras. These orchestras comprise virtually all of the American orchestras that pay a full-time living wage. Interesting statistics:

• There are 52 ICSOM orchestras employing a total of about 4,200 musicians.
• During the academic year 2002-2003, American colleges, universities and conservatories graduated 14,601 students with degrees in music.
• During the 2003 calendar year there were 159 openings for musicians in ICSOM orchestras.

So in this, as in everything, there are no guarantees. One has to make choices and sometimes they are difficult. If a good player likes teaching, that is certainly an option, and freelancing, as well, provides opportunities to perform for a living, and freelancing does not require long-term commitments or painful auditions; often the jobs are given on the basis of past performance. If you can "sightread the bugs off the walls" and are an otherwise reliable player who does not mind travel, freelancing may be the answer. Even with freelancing, it takes years to develop contacts and the skills necessary to play in pick-up or back-up gigs. Everyone has to find their own combination of things to do, but there are certainly a lot of options, and one lost audition is only an audition.

(5) What is involved in developing a press kit?

A press kit should include:
• An 8x10 photo (print one on your computer; take it to a local copy shop; have them make color copies on card stock)**
• a business card

• a 3-4 song demo CD (most people won't go to websites to listen to you) Don't include full tunes on the demo CD, or use a voice-over. Some people like the CD so much, they decide to use that in lieu of hiring real musicians.
• Free websites can be had at MySpace, Angelfire, and often through one's service provider.
• an introductory cover letter
• a bio
• a fact sheet that is easy to read so that whoever has it can look up some quick facts
• sticker, button or other promo material like that (people love stickers!)
• a folder to put it all in.

Example: use three-prong folders, and put the cover letter, fact sheet, bio, etc. in the prongs so that it is easy to page through, and put the other stuff in the left pocket. Those folders also have a place for business cards. I then made postcard size pics w/ the band name on it and glued it to the front of the folder. Eye catching colors are good.

You could also include...
• a DVD of a live performance
• newspaper reviews
• a list of upcoming gigs

Keep a record of who you sent or gave these to, so that you can make a follow up phone call.

See:
• *This Business of Music Marketing and Promotion*, Tad Lathrop.
• *This Business of Music: The Definitive Guide to the Music Industry*, M. William Krasilovsky.
• *Legal Aspects of the Music Industry: An Insider's View*, Richard Schulenberg.
• *What They'll Never Tell You About the Music Business: The Myths, Secrets, Lies (& a Few Truths)*, Peter M. Thall.

Newspaper reviews are extremely important. And don't skimp on the folder. The standard issue is a very high quality glossy card stock folder. If you want to be really classy, make a really professional looking label (photo, logo etc) on the outside. The important thing is that everything you put in the press kit is extremely professional looking. Do nothing halfway and nothing that looks cheap.

Card stock color copies of a publicity photograph are not very useful.

The quality of even the best photocopy is too poor for digital scanning purposes. Publicity offices want to have easy access to digital images, so that these can be placed in programs, concert calendars, newspapers, etc.

If you have a publicity photo made, don't skimp on the quality:
• Have photographs made (on photographic paper) by a professional. In many places one can have dozens of copies of a publicity photograph for around $80.
• Ask the photographer to provide digital images of the publicity shots (on a CD)
• Have color and black-and-white images made
• Have some interesting shots. When one is filling-up a concert calendar with images of musicians, nothing is worse than a spate of dull, uninspired photographs of performers clutching their instruments and looking serious. The publicity office where I worked was always glad for shots of musicians laughing, or posed in interesting backgrounds, or both!
• On the other hand, don't be so artistic that your face is lost in shadows or you're too small to see for all the periphery. In other words, work with a professional photographer that has experience with publicity shots for musicians.

Issues in Choice of Undergraduate Programs

(6) As a general rule, what are the audition requirements for undergraduate programs in violin and viola?

The answer to this question really depends on what university music school or music conservatory the student is auditioning for. Standards vary, and performance levels are not consistent throughout the many options a music student may have. With respect to exceptionally able students in smaller, perhaps local programs, the phrase "big fish in a small pond" is often heard. However, there are other combinations possible, since the quality of the pond (and the performance opportunities) is the real issue.

More importantly, the career goals of the student must be kept in mind from the onset. If, for example, the student really wants to be a professional instrumental player, they need to go to one of the dozen or so top professional schools; the majority of performers come from those schools. To get in, students should study with those teachers in summer programs before auditioning. Alternatively, if the student's focus is teaching, considerations are different; if they want to do public school, there's licensing to deal with. For private teaching, some schools have String Projects and other great pedagogical programs. As a general rule, studies indicate that the best players make the best teachers.

Choice of an undergraduate program should probably be based on a few primary considerations:

1. The emotional maturity of the student;
2. The available financial package (including scholarships, grants and loans);
3. The performance level of the student;
4. The student's work ethic, commitment and future goals.

1. With respect to the emotional maturity of the student; whether or not they're ready to move far from home, or would benefit from being in a nearby state or other good undergraduate program, is a key issue. If the student lives near a great state school (Indiana, for example), that is often the choice. Students vary widely in their emotional development; some really would benefit from doing an undergraduate program near home, and then, after four years, going on to a more demanding graduate program further out of state. Human adolescence has stretched beyond the teenage years, by some reports. This is not meant as a pejorative comment against young people. On the contrary, it is more like a recognition that human evolution has progressed to the point that maturity requires a broader educational base, and probably an additional 10 years or so, compared to past eras.

2. Schools vary widely with respect to the scholarship funds available. Many solid state school programs offer the so-called "orchestra scholarship," which is not dissimilar to a football scholarship: students commit to three weekly, two and a half hour rehearsals and the concerts each term, and are given tuition waivers for this. Just like a sports team, orchestras must have certain numbers of players to exist. This is a huge benefit, and parents should be made aware of this, particularly in light of the rising costs of education.

3. and 4. Students vary widely in their abilities, commitments, and goals. Finding the right teacher is key, in this sense, a teacher who will support the student's goals and inspire a higher level of performance. Incidentally, my recommendation has always been that the student contact the teacher with whom they wish to work, rather than taking an audition, cold. That teacher will either be a direct, deciding factor on

the admissions committee, or will be consulted regarding the student's admission. So the smart thing to do is for the student to contact the teacher directly, stating that the student wishes to study with them.

(7) Sample Undergraduate Audition - Violin/Viola

Prospective students should consult the program catalogs online or hardcopy, to determine the specific requirements of any particular program. As a general rule, the minimum requirements for an acceptable undergraduate audition are probably something like:

1. First movement of a concerto, the more advanced the better. From memory, is also a good idea, and the whole work, from memory, better still.

Violin: Mozart may do for some schools; Barber or Mendelssohn first movement would be a step up from that. Both would be better. See: Student Violin Concertos

Viola: Hoffmeister Concerto is a good first work. See: Viola Concertos

Of course, Mozart (D Major, A Major or G Major in violin) and Telemann (viola) are the standards, but probably one should try to avoid the Suzuki materials and demonstrate that the student has moved beyond the Suzuki books.

2. Some schools may require two contrasting movements from Bach [violin, viola];

3. All three octave major and minor scales and arpeggios; thirds, sixths, octaves and fingered octaves are also recommended; [Carl Flesh (violin, viola); Trott Melodious Doublestops, (violin, viola)];

4. A list of worked on études is recommended, and these should include the following:

Wohlfahrt: Books 1 & 2, violin; viola
Kayser: violin; viola;
Mazas: violin; viola;
Dont Op. 37: violin; viola;
Kreutzer: violin; viola;

Dont Op. 35 [violin; viola], Gavinies and Paganini are not unexpected, though not required for many undergraduate entrance levels;
Sevcik [violin, viola] and other études may be included, if the student has been exposed to them;

On viola, Hoffmeister études, Campagnoli, Fuchs.

5. Orchestra experience, chamber music experience and sightreading ability. Private lessons for at least four or five years is recommended.

6. Keyboard proficiency is an advantage, as well, along with at least some general knowledge in music theory and history, the conducting patterns, and perhaps some specialized interest, such as baroque performance practice, jazz, or contemporary composition and literature.

(8) M.M. and DMA Audition Requirements - Violin/Viola

Requirements will vary according to the difficulty of the program, but in general, perhaps something like this:

VIOLIN:
* All major and minor scales and arpeggios (if required): Flesch, Galamian Vol. I, Vol. II
* Bach: Sonatas and Partitas, Cello Suites (trans.) or Six Violin Sonatas
* Etudes (if required): Kreutzer, Rode
* Concertos: Possibilities might include Barber, Mendelssohn. See: Advanced Violin Literature and Student Concertos.
* Sonatas (if required): Brahms Sonatas or Beethoven Sonatas Vol. I, Vol. II. See: Violin Sonatas

VIOLA:
* All major and minor scales and arpeggios (if required): Flesch, Galamian
* Viola transcriptions of Bach: Sonatas and Partitas, Cello Suites or Six Violin Sonatas: Vol. I, Vol. II
* Etudes (if required): Kreutzer, Rode, Campagnoli
* Concertos: One to three movements of Hindemith Der Schwanendreher, Walton, or Bartók.
* Sonatas (if required): Brahms Op.120 Sonatas or Schubert "Arpeggione"

The DMA auditions are more of the same but as a rule, memorization of an entire concerto, Bach Sonata or Partita and Paganini; sometimes just the content of an hour long recital..

Survival Guide for String Students & Parents

How can I determine if this violin or viola is the right size?

Student Violin Size Chart
* Age: 12-Adult/ 4/4 size
* Age: 10-11/ 3/4 size
* Age: 8-9/ 1/2 size
* Age: 6-7/ 1/4 size
* Age: 5-6/ 1/8 size
* Age: 4-5/ 1/10 size
* Age: 3-4/ 1/16 size

Student Viola Size Chart
* Age: Large Adult/ 16" and larger
* Age: Average Adult/ 15.5"
* Age: 10-12, Small Adult/ 15"
* Age: 9-12/ 14"
* Age: 7-9/ 13"
* Age: 6-7/ 12"

There are a number of ways of determining the correct size of violin or viola for the player:

* Stretch the left arm under the instrument, and have the player wrap their fingers around the scroll. If the elbow is slightly bent but not too bent or too straight, it fits.

* Stretch the left arm straight out under the instrument, and under the scroll, and if the instrument's scroll ends flush with the pulse, it is just right.

Most shops which sell instruments, and many violin teachers, have a Viometer, a plastic mechanism which measures the instrument size. You can go into the shop and have them measure the player.

Tips on Purchasing Instruments

1. Talk to your private teacher before you buy an instrument. If your teacher has experience teaching in your city, they will very likely know the quality of the instruments available through music stores and luthier shops, and the best places to rent or purchase.

2. Someone will need to help you determine what size is appropriate for your student. Violins, for example, come in 1/16, 1/10, 1/8, 1/4, 1/2, 3/4, 5/8 and then the full size, 4/4. Music stores do not always do a

good job of this. Some teachers enjoy polishing instruments, rosining the bows, and noticing when the next size is appropriate, but others are less effective.

3. In order to study a stringed instrument effectively, you need to have a good, long-term relationship with a teacher, a luthier, and a music store. Children will outgrow a series of instruments and if you have no ongoing relationship with a reliable person or shop, you will entail more expense in the long run, than you should.

4. Don't let family members, however well meaning, make purchases of instruments without some input from a professional person. You don't want to be stuck paying $400 for a used, torn-up rental that is not only not worth $400 as is, but is actually worth far less, and will not bring in much as a trade-in (if you "rent to buy"), as well as being unpleasant and difficult to play.

5. Some instruments on EBay or for $75 at Target, may appear to be bargains, but it is often the case that they need so much additional setup work, that they are not the bargains they appear, and will not be pleasant to play. One of my students had the one from Target: the bow was unusable, and the case and the instrument were cheap and did not and could not be made to sound well. A lot of times children ask for those colored violins, but I have never seen one which sounds decent, and they don't fit in with orchestra, if the child is playing in orchestra. Colored bows are fine, though.

Buying versus Renting

Ten years ago, when the FAQ was originally conceived, my recommendation was to rent a violin at first, in order to determine if the child would remain interested. However, based on experiences with my own private students and given the favorable economic climate between the US and China regarding Chinese instruments, many of which are fine instruments and quite good quality at exceedingly reasonable prices, my views have changed. Currently, one can purchase a beautifully setup starter for $180.00 (viola, cello and bass are consecutively higher, since they're larger instruments), it is more economically sound to just purchase such an instrument. If you work with a teacher the instrument can be sold when the child outgrows it, or traded in for a better and larger instrument. I think, now, that this is the way to go. It's simply that if you can purchase an instrument outright for the price of a few months rental, it's more sensible to purchase it.

The contributing factor in the change of my views is the quality of these instruments. Certainly there are still shoddy instruments, but there seem to be a lot of very nice instruments coming from China nowadays, which are beautiful to look at, play well, have no problems, come with a very attractive case and bow (also with no problems) and at reasonable prices. The bows come furnished with real horsehair; this once-dear stuff has now become so reasonably priced that one can hardly find synthetic hair any more.

NOTE: The advanced player, who is no doubt under the tutelage of an experienced teacher, doesn't need my help—aside from perhaps the admonition to play a lot of instruments in combination with bows, and find what pleases you the best, paying less attention to the price and more to the sound. Fine instruments are a major investment and many professional players spend decades paying off the instrument, acquiring it through a loan from a local musicians union or bank. Many players, because of their exceptional abilities, enjoy instruments given to them as gifts, but most players buy them or borrow them. As orchestras are ranked, in the top tiers the string professionals require instruments starting in the $30-$60K range.

People often write me about instruments with Stradivarius labels, violins which have turned up in an attic, closet, cupboard, or garage sale. The "Stradivarius" label often has a tiny *copie de* above the word Stradivarius, which means a copy of a Stradivarius, or an instrument built on that model. If repaired, these instruments may be good student instruments, but unfortunately, they're seldom or never valuable. What must be done in every case is to locate a professional repair person who can do an adequate appraisal.

Care of Orchestral Instruments – DO's
1. Always wipe off any dust or dirt with a clean, dry cloth and put your instrument back into the case or rack when you are finished.
2. Clean your instrument every six months with a SMALL amount of special VIOLIN polish.
3. A set of strings costs anywhere from $20-$50 or more; there are three basic kinds: gut, synthetic, and steel. Strings should be changed at least once a year. Players who play a great deal, every six months.
4. Rehair your bow every 6-18 months (the more you play, the more often you change).
5. Always use BOTH hands to put the bow into the case and secure it before you close the cover. Damage to bows most often occurs due to

closing the case on the bow. CRUNCH.
6. Get a better brand of rosin.
7. If you live in a dry climate, look at using one of the following: Humistat, Humidifier, Dampit, Hygrometer.
8. Get a good shoulder rest.

DONT'S - NEVER do any of the following

1. NEVER use anything on an instrument which was not specifically designed for the violin; no Elmer's glue, furniture polish, or anything of that sort. (NEVER do repairs yourself, anyway.)
2. NEVER put any cleaner or lubricant on the neck or fingerboard or the hair of the bow. Use special cleaners or polish VERY carefully; a little goes a long way.
3. NEVER force a peg that won't turn.
4. NEVER let someone else pick up your instrument, play it, care for it.
5. NEVER leave your instrument in a car; hot or cold temperatures will damage it.
6. NEVER leave your instrument on the floor. Number one cause of instrument damage; it gets stepped on or run over. No kidding; picture your violin with your foot through it.
7. Andrew Wu from SHAR wished to add: "Please do not leave your violin while in an open case, especially with the shoulder pad still attached. It is very easy for the case to close and crush the top of the instrument. With winter here it is very important to keep instruments in an environment of 45-50% relative humidity. This will hopefully avoid the need for repairs which could cost in the hundreds. I recommend an evaporative humidifier. Remember not to leave the instrument in the car for any reason; the cold can do just as much damage as the heat."

Orchestra Etiquette

1. NEVER comment on another player's ability, good or bad. If you can develop a reputation of never being heard saying anything bad about anyone, it will serve you well. The music world is a very small world.
2. NEVER criticize another player to a conductor; it's none of your business.
3. Show respect to players in the front positions, e.g., the concertmaster.
4. NEVER touch another player's instrument – don't touch the percussion instruments when you pass by them.
5. NEVER take yourself too seriously; always leave room for laughter.

Music History/Theory Guide to Studying for Placement Tests

Good luck in preparation for your auditions and placement tests. These tests are required (with rising levels of difficulty) in order that it may be determined whether the student needs remedial work.

Graduate school can be difficult, and one wonders, sometimes, if the time taken to complete the degree(s) is worth the sacrifice in practice time. Doctoral work, in particular, is very stressful; lots of the best players stop at the M.M. in performance. However, if you want to teach in a university, a doctorate is increasingly more of a requirement, I think it's safe to say. Being called "Dr." the rest of your life is not a small thing, either. It was once mentioned to me that most university courses are only "introductory" in nature, which is sobering thought, but accurate, I believe. I would also recommend *Getting What You Came For: The Smart Student's Guide to Earning an M.A. or a Ph.D.* by Robert Peters. It's not musical, but it's a very useful book.

See:
The Music History Placement Exam
http://www.sfcmhistory.com/Placement/Placement_web_instructions.htm

Norton site: Flashcards
http://www.wwnorton.com/college/music/grout7/flashcards/index.htm

Score ID Practice Page
http://www.sfcmhistory.com/Placement/ScoreID_2008.pdf

Audition requirements for undergraduate programs in violin and viola?
http://beststudentviolins.com/AuditionsGigs.html#6

Sample Undergraduate Audition –œ Violin/Viola
http://beststudentviolins.com/AuditionsGigs.html#7

MM and DMA Audition Requirements - Violin/Viola
http://beststudentviolins.com/AuditionsGigs.html#8

RESEARCH TOOLS
Good beginning books for self-study:
Essentials of Music Theory: Complete Self-Study Course
Alfred's Essentials of Jazz Theory

Standard texts:

Burkhart, Charles: *Anthology for Musical Analysis*

Dallin, Leon: *Techniques Of Twentieth-Century Composition*

Grout, Donald: *A History of Western Music*

Berlioz, Hector and Richard Strauss. *Treatise on Instrumentation*

Berry, Wallace. *Form in Music*, Second Edition

Burkhart, Charles. *Anthology for Musical Analysis*

Burney, Charles: The following works are out of print though accessible via established music libraries or interlibrary loan (with fees attached, in some cases). But to get titles and ISPN numbers, Amazon.com offers the following:

Music, men, and manners in France and Italy, 1770 : being the journal written by Charles Burney during a tour through those countries undertaken to collect material for a general history of music.

Memoirs of Dr Charles Burney, 1726-1769

The Letters of Dr. Charles Burney: 1751-1784

Dr. Charles Burney's Continental Travels, 1770-1772

An eighteenth-century musical tour in Central Europe and the Netherlands: being Dr. Charles Burney's account of his musical experiences

An eighteenth-century musical tour in Central Europe and the Netherlands : being Dr. Charles Burney's account of his musical experiences

Memoirs of the Life and Writings of the Abate Metastasio, Including Translations of His Principal Letters.: Including Translations of His Principal Letters (Da Capo Press Music Reprint Series)

A General History of Music, from the Earliest Ages to the Present Period (1789)

The great Dr. Burney; his life, his travels, his works, his family, and his friends by Percy Alfred Scholes

Dr. Burney As Critic and Historian of Music by Kerry S. Grant

The only book I could locate about Burney which is not out of print:

Dr. Charles Burney: A Literary Biography by Roger H. Lonsdale

Donington, Robert. *Baroque Music, Style and Performance: A Handbook*

Fux, Joseph. *Study of Counterpoint*

Grout, Donald and Claude V. Palisca. *A History of Western Music*, Sixth Edition. Newest ed. of the Grout, 7th ed., Burkholder

Jeppesen, Knud. *Counterpoint: The Polyphonic Vocal Style of the Sixteenth Century*

Kennedy, Michael. *The Oxford Dictionary of Music*

Machlis, Joseph. *Introduction to Contemporary Music*

Neumann, Frederick. *Ornamentation in Baroque and Post-Baroque Music: With Special Emphasis on J. S. Bach*

Perle, George. *Serial Composition and Atonality: An Introduction to the Music of Schoenberg, Berg, and Webern*

Pincherle, Marc. *Vivaldi: Genius of the Baroque*

Piston, Walter. *Harmony*

Plantinga, Leon. *Romantic Music: A History of Musical Style in NineteenthCentury Europe* (Norton Introduction to Music History)

Rameau, Jean Philippe. *Treatise on Harmony*

Randel, Don Michael. *The New Harvard Dictionary of Music*

Rosen, Charles. *Sonata Forms*

Rosen, Charles. *The Classical Style: Haydn, Mozart, Beethoven*

Slonimsky, Nicolas. *Baker's Biographical Dictionary of Musicians*

Turek, Ralph. *The Elements of Music*

Ear Training Texts:

Stefan Kostka:

Tonal Harmony, With an Introduction to Twentieth-Century Music Student Workbook and CD for use with Tonal Harmony Audio CDs for use with Tonal Harmony

Ralph Turek:

The Elements of Music, Vol. 1

Workbook for the Elements of Music, Vol. 1

The Elements of Music, Vol. 2

Workbook for the Elements of Music, Vol. 2, not listed: email vendor to make sure you're getting the correct book.

Elements of Music Vol 1&2 2e Cd

Notation Texts:

Adler, Samuel. *Study of Orchestration*, Third Edition

Fux, John. *Study of Counterpoint*

Gerou, Tom and Lusk, Linda. *Essential Dictionary of Music Notation: The Most Practical and Concise Source for Music Notation*

Kennan, Kent and Grantham, Donald. *The Technique of Orchestration and CD Recording Package*
Read, Gardner. *Music Notation*
Persichetti,Vincent. *Twentieth-Century Harmony: Creative Aspects and Practice*
Piston, Walter. *Orchestration*
Piston, Walter. *Counterpoint*
Piston, Walter. *Harmony*: 5th ed.
Rimsky-Korsakov, Nikolay. *Principles of Orchestration*
Stone, Kurt. *Music Notation in the Twentieth Century: A Practical Guidebook*
Strange, Allen. *The Contemporary Violin: Extended Performance Techniques* (The New Instrumentation)

Performance Practice:
MUST HAVE: Judy Tarling's *Baroque String Playing for Ingenious Learners*, available in the US through Boulder Early Music Shop

Apel, Willi. *Italian Violin Music of the Seventeenth Century*
Boyden, David. *The History of Violin Playing from Its Origins to 1761 and Its Relationship to the Violin and Violin Music*
Carter, Stewart. *A Performer's Guide to Seventeenth-Century Music*
Donington, Robert. *Baroque Music: Style and Performance*
Donington, Robert. *The Interpretation of Early Music*
Donington, Robert. *String Playing in Baroque Music*
Neumann, Frederick. *Ornamentation in Baroque and Post-Baroque Music: With Special Emphasis on J. S. Bach*
Stowell, Robin. *Performing Beethoven*
Stowell, Robin. *Violin Technique and Performance Practice in the Late Eighteenth and Early Nineteenth Centuries*

Score Reading/Conducting:
Samuel Adler. *Study of Orchestratio*n, Third Edition
Hector Berlioz. *Treatise on Instrumentation*
Dave Black. *Essential Dictionary of Orchestration*
George Burt. *The Art of Film Music*
Deryck Cooke. *The Language of Music*
David Daniels. *Orchestral Music*
Robert W. Demaree. *The Complete Conductor*
Harold Farberman, Thom Proctor. *The Art of Conducting Technique: A New Perspective*

Cecil Forsyth. *Orchestration*

Norman Del Mar:
Anatomy of the Orchestra
Conducting Beethoven: Overtures, Concertos, Missas Solemnis
Conducting Beethoven: The Symphonies
Conducting Berlioz
Conducting Brahms
Conducting Elgar

Michael Dickreiter, Reinhard G. Pauly. *Score Reading: A Key to the Music Experience*
Knud Jeppesen. *Counterpoint: The Polyphonic Vocal Styles of the Sixteenth Century*
Norman Lebrecht. *The Maestro Myth: Great Conductors in Pursuit of Power*
Alfred Mann. *The Study of Fugue*
Brock McElheran. *Conducting Technique for Beginners and Professionals*
Reginald O. Morris, Howard Ferguson. *Preparatory Exercises in Score Reading*
Walter Piston. *Orchestration*
Jean Rameau. *Treatise on Harmony*
Nikolay Rimsky-Korsakov. *Principles of Orchestration*
Jeff Rona. *The Reel World: Scoring for Pictures*
Max Rudolf. *The Grammar of Conducting: A Comprehensive Guide to Baton Technique and Interpretation*
Felix Salzer. *Structural Hearing Tonal Coherence in Music* (Two Volumes Bound As One) [Schenkerian analysis: read Piston and Fux first.]
Hermann Scherchen. *Handbook of Conducting*
Arnold Schoenberg. *Structural Functions of Harmony*
Gunther Schuller. *The Compleat Conductor*
Ernst Toch. *The Shaping Forces in Music: An Inquiry into the Nature of Harmony, Melody, Counterpoint, Form* (The Dover Series of Study Editions, Chamber Music, Orchestral Works, Operas in Full Score)

Musicology

Note that human life does not lend itself well to restricted categories
and both the dates and the styles are subject to change and debate among scholars.

Historical Era	Approximate dates	Representative Composers (Small sample)
Medieval	ca. 500-1450	Hildegard von Bingen, Machaut, Landini, Léonin, Pérotin.
Renaissance	1450-1600	Josquin, Dufay, Palestrina.
Baroque Also see: 1725-1770 Roccoco (and/or Galant)	1600-1750	Bach, Vivaldi, Tartini, Geminiani, Handel.
Classical	1750-1820	Haydn, Mozart, Beethoven.**
Romantic Also see: Nationalism - Grieg, Sibelius	1820-1910	Schubert, Schumann, Chopin, Paganini, Brahms.
Contemporary, also referred to as 20th Century or Modern. Includes subcategories such as: Impressionism: Debussy, Ravel Expressionism: Schoenberg, Berg, Webern Americana: Copland Neo Classicism: Stravinsky, Copland Neo Romanticism: Piston, Barber, Hanson Experimentalism: Brown, Cage Minimalism: Glass, Reich	1910-present	Bartók, Bernstein, Cage, Babbit, Gershwin, Varese, Messiean, Stockhausen, Takemitsu.

** From A History of Western Music: "Through external circumstances and the force of his own genius he transformed this heritage and became the source of much that was characteristic of the Romantic period. But he himself is neither Classic nor Romantic; he is Beethoven, and his figure towers like a colossus astride the two centuries." [Donald Jay Grout. (3rd Edition with Claude V. Palisca.) W. W. Norton & Co., Inc. New York. 1973. p. 521.

Two Essays on the Development of Student Orchestras

Orchestra Etiquette and Protocol

For my students and any other interested parties, I have listed below, in no particular order, a few things string students and parents should know. All of the following concerns will not be relevant for younger groups, but are important in the Youth Symphony and then later, in High School orchestra and professional or semi-professional orchestras:

1. Never be late to a rehearsal. Early is better. Students should be in their seats and warmed up at least 10 minutes prior to the rehearsal. It goes without saying, never be late to a performance!

2. Do not talk during a rehearsal (certainly not during a performance). Sometimes if you're marking parts (bowing, etc.), you may whisper in the sections, but not loudly and better not at all.

3. Always position your stand so that you can see both the music and the conductor. You are learning how to play in orchestra, so you will need to develop the ability to watch the conductor, if only out of the corner of your eye, at the same time you are reading the music.

4. A note on posture: The best way to sit is centered, with legs slightly apart and feet flat. Women fought for years to be able to wear dress slacks to perform, for this very reason: centered with legs apart promotes breathing and comfort. It's not unusual in professional life to play 10 or 12 hours a day-performances, rehearsals and practice included. Please do not cross your legs, or wrap them around a chair leg. Sit slightly forward and don't slouch as it might in time injure your back.

5. Both you and your stand partner can mark the music, but often the inside person on the stand (the person on the other side of the audience), should mark the parts. If you do not have time to mark the parts during the rehearsal, during the break take your part to the first stand and see if you can get the rest of the bowings. Bowings must be consistent within the section; it is up to the first chairs and conductor, however, to coordinate the bowings between sections.

6. Always bring several sharpened pencils to the rehearsal. Pay close attention to what the conductor says, and lightly mark the music in easily erasable, black pencil (not red or blue!), and NEVER in pen!! Don't overmark the parts with unnecessary markings.

7. Pay careful attention to the conductor and section leaders regarding protocols for entering and exiting the stage, and for acknowledging applause after the concert. The rule is to sit or stand when your section leaders do, unless the concertmaster is individually greeting a soloist or shaking hands with the conductor. Do what everyone else does–and don't forget to SMILE at the end of the concert!

8. Follow the leadership of the first stand players, even if you disagree. Be kind, courteous, unassuming, pleasant, etc. Don't gossip. Be encouraging to others. Listen to others in your section and blend in.

9. Always practice the parts and be able to play everything well. During rehearsals you may place an * in the margins next to the hard bits, and look at them during your practice sessions at home. More often than not, the musicians who become professional players are those who go home and practice their parts after the rehearsals. (In other words, they care about their playing and performance.)

10. If they're available, try to listen to recordings of the pieces you're playing in orchestra, and more than one interpretation. If you can't find the exact piece, listen to pieces by that composer. Best yet if you can find an orchestra score and examine all the parts, so you know where your section fits in. This would be an activity that future composers and conductors would follow; anyone college bound would benefit enormously as well.

11. If you're playing standard repertoire, it would be helpful to have a copy of the first violin part (or viola, or cello part) for study purposes, to be placed in your library. Copies correctly marked with good bowings are helpful when you have auditions or unexpected performance opportunities. However, there are copyright issues involved: some works are in public domain, and may be copied, but to be safe, it is advisable to buy a CD ROM with the repertoire, and then print out and mark copies in that way. [*See endnote.] This is an important legal issue that musicians should be aware of; apparently some schools have gotten heavy fines for unauthorized copying of materials. No original copyrighted materials may be copied and used in large quantities for ensembles, without express permission.

12. Try to always have your instrument in top condition; carry an extra set of strings, have a mute on the instrument or near you if the part unexpectedly says "con sordino," and be sure your bow hair is in good condition. You may want to have an extra bow if you have passages in "col legno" or if you are performing outside, or in a large venue with very hot lights, like a circus or rock concert. Carbon fiber bows are good for this purpose and will save wear and tear on your good bow.

13. Keep your focus up by sleeping well the night before a performance, and eating right: bananas are good for nerves if you get nervous before a concert, though if you don't have a solo there's not much reason to feel nervous, in my opinion. Your colleagues are all there and you have nothing to fear. Enjoy your youth and freedom; when you become professionals, you'll have even less time (and less time for sleep.)

14. Enjoy yourself but pay close attention. If you make a mistake, don't let it show by your face or demeanor.

15. Regarding auditioning, see "How to avoid being nervous at an audition" (from the Violin/Viola FAQ). I think with young people, especially, you shouldn't stress about it. Just show that you're working hard and you care about your playing, do your best, be yourself, and you'll do fine.

I'm sure there are other things I could mention, but these are the ones that come to mind. I hope you enjoy playing in orchestras as much as I do. When you're immersed in that sound, there's really nothing as wonderful!

[*] See:

90 Orchestral Masterworks CD-ROM
http://beststudentviolins.com/Orch_CD.html
Complete Parts Violin I and II and Viola: I, II, III, IV, V, VI, VII, VIII, IX, X.

Orchestra Discipline

1. Balance: There is always a concern in orchestras about balance, so that each section can be heard in the way the composer intended. Depending on the training and sophistication of the group, as well as the size of the string sections and the quality of all the instruments, one of the concerns is that the brass sections don't overshadow the rest of the orchestra, particularly if you have brass players who have formerly only played in bands. It must be emphasized that orchestral playing is sometimes more subtle and more soloistic than some other kinds of musical experience, and thus careful attention needs to be paid for ensemble playing between the smaller choirs of instruments.

2. Intonation: Players need to be periodically reminded about intonation, as this is affected by the hall, the temperature, the quality of the instruments, and numerous other more subtle factors. Thus retuning is called for, particularly at the beginning of the orchestral musician's training. Casals likened developing good intonation to having a conscience. What typically happens is that young musicians who have not had their attention drawn to this important factor will, at the beginning of their more professional training, find that it seems as if they are playing more and more out of tune, when in fact what is happening is that they are only just realizing that they are playing out of tune.

3. Rhythmic accuracy: Rhythm is the "soul of music," and generally students will not maintain a very high accuracy unless they have been trained to do so. For example, it is likely that the distinction between dotted rhythms and triplets is not going to be very great, unless this is carefully demonstrated and the teacher insists on correctness.

4. Bowing/breathing articulations: Articulations are created differently by the different instruments, but the similarities are striking. The stringed instruments are "singing" instruments, and thus should be played with vocal articulations in mind. For the most part, articulations in the strings are created through bowing technique. It is important to get the string sections to understand that their bowings must be consistent, both within their section and with respect to the other string sections, as well as consistently phrasing in a coordinated way with the non-string sections. This is primarily the work of the conductor, but also of and with the concert master and the section leaders. Decisions about bowings should be made prior to rehearsal, as much as possible, and parts should be marked. See "Sectional Rehearsals."

Responses to conducting gestures must be consistent and reliable in order to produce the required sounds. These gestures include attacks, various articulations (e.g., staccato, legato, passages or notes), cut-offs, dynamic changes, changes in meter, reception of cues, and so on. The success in most of this is dependent on the skills and training of the conductor, particularly the communication of the tactus, and the general musicianship, imagination, and self-discipline. It is really bad form for a conductor to get angry with a group when they are not producing what the conductor is imagining; mind reading is not one of the required skills in orchestral playing, though sometimes it helps.

5. Orchestral discipline: There must be some strong, overriding conception of each piece, which is agreed upon by the time of performance. The better trained and more professional the group, the less rehearsal time is required. Just like a University is not a democracy but a benevolent dictatorship, so an orchestra is more like an army than anything else. There may be, and often is, grumbling in the ranks, but the leader of the orchestra must lead or nothing can be accomplished. I've seen orchestras fall apart because of lack of respect for conductors; conducting is a very demanding job.

Thus, the respect factor is worth a second look. And not to belabor a point, and at least to some extent with women especially, it is good to let the students know from the beginning that the director has extensive experience in the professional world (if this is the case), a high level of training, and a low tolerance for unprofessional behavior.

6. Seating: Seating is a more important issue than many conductors think it is. I think policy decisions have to be made in teaching situations; are you going to rotate, so more students can get different kinds of experiences-OR are you going to seat students primarily on the basis of your evaluation of ability, in order to get the maximum potential, musically–OR are you going to consider other factors, such as seniority, good behavior, etc.? And what do I mean by "good" behavior? Are the most musical students the most polite, the least resistant, the more pliable? No, unfortunately not. I think often the best musicians may be the most difficult, but lessons have to be learned about reliability, and sometimes this is going to be the ideal time for these lessons to be learned.

With older groups, it might be helpful to point out what professional life is like for musicians; being on time, being prepared, attitude, etc., can mean the difference between being hired again, or taken off a list–

since there are so many good players to choose from, anyway, as a rule, and professional people do not want to be bothered with prima donna behaviors. These are the cold facts of professional life, whether in the musical sphere or elsewhere, and students would do well to be prepared for this.

7. Sectional Rehearsals: These rehearsals are sometimes dismissed as unimportant, but really they are a great time to teach technique, ensemble playing, and to continue the focus on professional behaviors and responsibilities. Graduate students or section leaders can be good resources for leadership during these rehearsals, though that can engender resentment if it's not handled properly. Throughout professional life, there is always some underlying negativity which is based on competition or other negative feelings. Rehearsal time is a great time to demonstrate professional attitudes. Personal issues can and should be set aside for the greater good of producing beautiful music, which is really the point of everything. It is important not to lose this sense of purpose.

8. Motivation: In a teaching situation, the agenda is to impart knowledge, demonstrate or encourage the development of skills, and harness youthful enthusiasm. While I maintain that too many long lectures during orchestra are counterproductive, students as they are developing need to have the experience of knowing the commonly shared cultural information that so many have shared before them; that Beethoven wouldn't take any nonsense from anybody, that Mozart was brilliant and funny, that the world is both larger and smaller than they think it is, and the 18th, or any other century, is not as far away in time as they think it is. Music is a way of rising above the petty concerns of life, a way of connecting with the best minds in history, and of connecting with the world at large. Hopefully, students will develop the sense that playing music is a privilege, and find that working toward a better performance is a positive and enriching experience.

Administration of Postsecondary Music Departments

Originally an embellishment on traditional curricula, schools of music have become multidimensional disciplines requiring managerial skills similar to those needed in bureaucracies like businesses and government. Universities are now big businesses, intertwined with more or less six levels of authority: federal, state and local government, the multi-campus academic administration, the university or college itself, different colleges within the university, and the lowest operating unit, the department (Clark, 1983). [2] As of 1994, there were around 80,000 department chairs, of which 1,745 were in postsecondary music departments (Lucas, 1994).

The development of school administration parallels "scientific management," which was developed during the early 20th century by Frederick Taylor, Henri Favor, and others. Early undergraduate degrees in music were sometimes entitled "Instrumental Music Supervisors' Program." A successful teaching career and a masters was the usual prelude to administrative responsibility. An administrative job in music often has a bewildering range of responsibilities beyond the usual administrator's duty because of public performances, unusual assortments of (often very costly) equipment, and the unique needs associated with music programs, divisible into areas of curriculum, personnel, and space, equipment, and fiscal operations.

The role of the music department chair is far broader–more ambiguous–than it previously was. This role requires that the chair be both a champion of his or her discipline and a liaison between the administration and the faculty. This role conflict is ambiguous and contributes to stress levels in departmental leadership (Brown, 2001), complicated by the uncertainty or deceivingly informal nature of faculty committees, issues on academic freedom, and budgetary pressures. Ambiguity also characterizes the hierarchical placement of the academic chair in collective bargaining–an issue which has been resolved inconsistently.

A music executive is expected to be a competent musician and teacher, as well as administrator. Competencies of a successful music administrator include a certain amount of unselfishness (they must defer their own interests in order to guide colleagues), the ability to delegate responsibilities, vision and flexibility, efficiency, inner drive, mental and emotional maturity, verbal/written/spoken facility, broad interests, aboveaverage intelligence, and the ability to work with diverse personalities. One of the concerns in this position is managing faculty who may find it difficult to submit themselves to the discipline of a collegiate setting, since they have spent most of their adult lives in the professional music world (Brown, 2001). Stability is particularly important, and the lack of serious personal flaws such as laziness, undependability, conceit, pessimism, temper, obsessive behavior, lack of objectivity, oversensitivity to criticism, timidity, dishonesty, lack of objectivity, and moral or mental instability.

Preparation for this job really means polishing the abilities of those individuals who have already attained high levels of maturity, which are not accessible merely by diplomas. Normally the choice is made from current faculty members who are known entities. The power in the position is not power "over" but power to influence, a chance to shape dialog by setting tone and content. Since influence is more intangible, a great measure of the chair's effectiveness depends on personal qualities rather than any inherent power in the position itself. Since six to eight years is the longest usual tenure in these positions, they are usually "tours of duty" rather than career jobs.

From being minor figures, department chairs are now part of institutionwide leadership structures, and deal with a broader range of issues, such as assessments, computers, diversity, distance learning, union contracts, employment regulations, and maintaining good relationships with support staff. The music department chair is a first line supervisor, and may be compared to a foreman in an hierarchical business venture. Like the foreman, the chair comes up from the labor pool (the faculty) and is a liaison between upper management and workers (the faculty).

In the past, a department chair was often primarily chosen on the basis of having a distinguished scholarly reputation and a high level of teaching and/ or research excellence; the job was often more of a figurehead or symbolic in nature, and required little in the way of administrative skills. Currently, two-thirds of department chairs are hired from faculty, and have no management skills. Lack of institutional vision can become a detriment to the greater community. Even today in the Chronicle of Higher Education ads for department chairs, the job listings most often mention requirements of a national reputation in a discipline and the likelihood of developing innate loyalty to the institution, rather than administrative skills, background, or training. Dr. Garry Owens, music department chair at the time of this writing, at Texas Tech University, verified this phenomena in his very first remarks to the author during our interview: most administrators have no administrative training. According to Filan (1999), 70% of surveyed department chairs received no formalized training, with many chairs acknowledging this lack of training and expressing their needs for more advanced, formal training.

NASM, the National Association of Schools of Music, is a governing institution for music curriculum in higher education; it is composed of chairs and deans of NASM-accredited programs, and seeks to professionalize music administration. Nevertheless, more has been written about department chairs, in general, than about the concerns of department chairs of music schools, and the literature in this specific areas is relatively sparse, causing researchers in this area to rely on outdated materials. The literature regarding department chairs in general has significantly advanced, however.

The seminal book in the general area of department chairs is a 1981 publication by the American Council on Education by Allan Tucker, Chairing the Academic Department: Leadership Among Peers. This was a comprehensive text which was revised once before the author's death in 1992, and a third edition appeared in that year. In the 1990's a number of new volumes appeared, indicting that publishers were seeing the area as marketable. [3] Since the publication of Tucker's work, the responsibilities of department chairs have continued to undergo metamorphosis.

With one-third of the professorate in America retiring in 2010, chairs need to perceive themselves and other chairs as colleagues rather than rivals, with moral and legal responsibilities toward minorities. Current realities require new patterns of behavior; chairs must advocate not only for their own faculty, but respect the interests of other departments and of the university as a whole. Chairs set protocol: if a chair tends to dismiss the comments of a new female faculty, for example, this licenses other faculty to behave similarly. [4]

Currently, the average music department head is a 50 year old male, tenured professor with a doctorate in performance or music education, appointed to a 12 month position, with around a 7.5 year seniority. In our interview, Dr. Owens indicated that he really never dreamed that he would be doing administrative work, but was originally asked by his department in Flint, Michigan, to take on administrative work. All he ever wanted to do was to conduct and teach kids, which is why he got into music education. Educators generally chose this job because of a love of their discipline and a desire to promote their discipline to the coming generation; love of teaching, in other words.

Demographic changes have redefined the roles of department chairs. What once were mostly all-male student bodies are now characterized by a broad range of ages and colors, at least half of which are women. Postsecondary education once constituted a process of initiation into the ruling elite, but has developed into a lifetime learning environment and social good to which everyone has a right. In 1900, 30% of the U.S. population sought postsecondary education; by 1990, 50%. In 1950, 260% of postsecondary students were women; in 1990, more than 500%.

Current emphasis is on continuing education and lifetime learning, and thus in music departments, decisions have to be made regarding the management of non-traditional students, many of whom are avocational musicians, not necessarily preparing for careers in music. These students present budgetary concerns, since accommodating them necessarily changes the character of the curriculum. And they should be accommodated not merely based on the money they bring into the department, but artistically; the concern is that more flexible standards might weaken a department and dissipate effectiveness, based on financial exigencies. However, one perspective sees that non-majors present special opportunities to enhance the professional quality of teaching. Curriculum changes that attract a diverse student body are of great interest to chairs and faculty. This was one of Dr. Owens' primary interests/concerns. Curriculum tasks include scheduling courses, revising course titles and descriptions, and reviewing related matters (Brown, 2001).

Dr. Owens broke down his responsibilities to around 20% teaching, 55% administration, and the remaining, fund raising. His administrative duties are, in fact, much broader than that indicated in the one-page job description found in the faculty handbook, and have a much wider scope in the community outside the school of music. This broader environment often draws on music departments as talent pools for community orchestras, church music programs, and community theater and opera, and the chair may sponsor and house community programs for children, such as Suzuki programs, and also sponsor and house summer programs for young musicians in the community, youth orchestras, etc. All of this must be managed or delegated to others by the department chair. Dr. Owens was strong on delegating: "You hire good people and let them do their job, and don't try to do their jobs for them."

Responsibilities of the music department chair are both large and small, the small being in some ways just as significant, and calling for the "Mayor Daley" rule of governance, i.e., the recognition that what people want is their sidewalks free of snow and their garbage picked up. Nearly everything in the music department may end up coming to Dr. Owens' attention, directly or indirectly, even including parking issues. And all of this is done while maintaining, in the case of most chairs, a presence in the classroom. Dr. Owens currently teaches one class per term, supervises student teachers, and reads dissertations. Further, particularly in smaller, more collegial institutions, a chair must have some personal knowledge of the intimate concerns of faculty; their birthdays, their children's names, etc.

One of Dr. Owens' primary responsibilities, he said, is all faculty issues such as tenure and promotion, and annual review. Reviews occur in the third and finally, the sixth year, of every new faculty. Other chairs may have to deal with problems like how to handle an alcoholic staff member, or deal with a faculty member who won't retire. In dealing with faculty, the chair must be aware of the notion of two organizational identities: cosmopolitan and local (Merton, 1957). Cosmopolitan are those with higher outer reference group orientation and professional identification in the larger world outside their universities (more international connections, for example); locals have a keener loyalty to their employing universities and wish to, or are likely to, remain at their particular institutions. Naturally, there is controversy related to these categorizations, and tension does often exist between the need for expertise and loyalty; some empirical studies suggest the existence of mixed identities and some typologies include subgroups. Dr. Owens is very keen on recruiting faculty and students, both nationally and internationally, and is proud of the Tech music faculty, among which are some very exceptional individuals, both among those who have been at Tech for a long time, and the newer staff.

Above all, chairs must maintain effective working relationships with support staff, who generally know, after many years service, where, how and from whom, decisions actually come, and all the administrative details without which a department will fall into disarray and disunity. If support staff do not trust and feel appreciated by the chair, serious problems can occur; the staff can simply destroy the effectiveness of the chair by doing nothing, or by requiring his/her supervision on every detail, thus bogging down the whole operation to a standstill. Everyone knows, or should know, the importance of clerical and support staff, and act accordingly.

In the area of qualitative research, work has been done involving a study by NASM, using three-fourths of the accredited music programs. A paradigm was discovered respecting music department chairs, wherein eight separate characterological types were found from a survey of 48 questions using multidimensional scaling (MDS)(Miller, p. 72). These eight types include:

1. Dead on the Job: low role orientation. Little interest in students, university, professional standards, or colleagues. 2.9%
2. Scholarly Recluse: high regard for scholarship to the exclusion of institutional considerations. 5%
3. Administrator on the Make: little regard for standards, but orientated to outer reference group. 7.3%
4. Company Man: hoping to rise through the ranks. 2.5%
5. Professional in Residence: classic cosmopolitan orientation; keen interest in matters on a national basis. 33%
6. Isolated Idealist: idealized identity, somewhat dysfunctional; high orientation to profession and organization with no high reference orientation. One chair out of 314.
7. Theory X Professional Administrator: major concern is how organization is functioning. 6%
8. Virtuoso: balanced perspective among all elements (teaching, research, colleagues, students, the university). Over 41%

A demographic table (Miller, p. 55) indicates, as mentioned above, that most chairs are male, professors or associate professors with doctoral degrees in performance or music education, and tenured. With respect to gender, the 1993 figures are male, 88.20% and female, 11.80%. Brown's study (2001) revealed a slight increase in female chairs, with males currently at 84.60% Characteristics recommended for music department chairs (Jennerich, 1981) include:

Character/Integrity
Leadership Ability
Interpersonal Skills
Ability to communicate effectively
Decision making ability
Organizational ability

Planning skills
Professional competence
Evaluating faculty
Program/course innovation and development Budgetary skills
Ability to recruit new faculty
Fund raising ability

Other informal surveys have been done, the results of which are lists of department chairs' most recurrent problems (Miller, p. 81), and advice to first time chairs (Miller, p. 89). The top ten of the later include:

1. Integrate the department with the university
2. Recognize the inevitability of conflict (take the heat and not take things personally)
3. Solicit input from faculty on important issues (seek consensus)
4. Have courage to make decisions in the best interest of the music program
5. Work for faculty development
6. Take time to evaluate the existing situation before acting 7. Identify strengths and weaknesses and act upon them
8. Be honest and open
9. Work hard (do your homework, be prepared)
10. Be positive, don't get discouraged

Regarding specific duties of the music department chair, sets of similar tasks were organized in several ways by various researchers:

Samuel Jones (1959) arranged duties into ten broad categories:
1. Curriculum
2. Finances
3. Philosophy
4. Plant
5. Equipment and Supplies
6. Personnel Relations
7. Records and Reports
8. Scheduling
9. School Officers
10. Students

Mintzberg (1973) saw ten roles divided into three areas:
1. Three Interpersonal Roles: Figurehead, Leader, and Liaison; 2. Three Informational Roles: Monitor, Disseminator, Spokesman; 3. Four Decisional Roles: Entrepreneur, Disturbance Handler, Resource Allocator, and Negotiator

Tucker (1981) in his important seminal work, saw eight categories:

1. Department Governance
2. Instruction
3. Faculty Affairs
4. Student Affairs
5. External Communication
6. Budget and Resources
7. Office Management
8. Professional Development

Regarding preparation of music department chairs, Robert House recommends in "The Professional Preparation of Music Administrators" (1982) five possible methods:

1. Informal, on-the-job learning, by reading, studying, and attempting small assignments at first:
2. Supplemental training such as summer workshops specifically for music administrators (Westminster Choir College, Eastman School of Music), or four- or five-day clinics (NASM meetings);
3. Graduate courses designed for potential and current music administrators;
4. Full-fledged doctoral programs in music administration; and
5. Special schools, say, six month courses, which combine all of the above features.

As of this writing, there are currently no diplomas offered, anywhere, that certify individuals in this field, and despite various recommendations from higher education professionals, doctoral programs in music are not providing any coursework in this area. In 1973, Robert House wrote that the usual on-the-job training would probably prevail in most cases and that in the current context the "natural selection" of professional leadership actually works well enough at most schools, though more weight needs to be given to administrative expertise, rather than seniority and popularity. In the current context, musical eminence seems still to be the determining factor in job searches for music department chairs, even though the actual work in this position quite often has relatively little to do with the discipline of music itself. Musicianship, teaching skills and compatibility with the music faculty must be in place, but administrative ability should be a primary consideration.

According to Jennerich (1981), just because a music professional has a high skill level in their discipline, there is no reason to infer that they may have the skills necessary for administrative work without undergoing any training. Furthermore, the exceptionally demanding workload in these positions is expected to increase into the twenty-first century (Brown, 2001) with responsibilities continuing to expand in previously unexpected areas, such as sexual harassment issues, budgetary concerns of a high level of complication, personnel issues, and accountability.

* * *

The impetus to mass education is a notion born during the early beginnings of U.S. history—and at varying rates of speed, this notion of mass education is spreading throughout all the countries of the earth, and can be envisioned or pictorialized in terms of the photograph taken of our planet from the window of one of our first rickety spaceships. All of our notions of space and time have changed, inspired by the internet, email, and a technological upheaval not quite like anything in our past. The new music department chair must negotiate between tradition and innovation, walking a tightrope between serving their department, representing the administration, and developing perceptions of the larger environment. As education has shifted from being a privilege to a necessity, the U.S. moves towards mass education—an experiment unique to humanity, with global significance.

Endnotes

1. This document was initially presented for informal review to half a dozen professionally oriented listservs, including ASTA list (American String Teachers Association), OrchestraList, and a few others noted for their high activity and professional membership. Thanks in particular to Kellie Brown, who so generously sent me a pdf file of her recent Ed.D. dissertation (Brown, 2001).

2. The usual structure of power is represented by: Chair –Dean – Provost –Vice President – President – Chancellor – Board of Regents and/or legislature.

3. See: Cresswell, J.W. (1990). The academic chairperson's handbook; Hickson M. and Stacks, D.W. (1993). Effective communication for academic chairs; Gmelch, W.H. and Miskin, V.D. (1993). Leadership skills for department chairs; Lucas, A. (1994). Strengthening leadership: A teambuilding guide for chairs in colleges and universities; Green, M.F. and McDade, S. (1992). Investing in higher education: A handbook of leadership development; Higgerson, M.L. and Rehwaldt,

S.S. (1993). Complexities of higher education administration; Higgerson, M.L. (1996). Communication skills for department chairs; Charitable, P. (1996). Policy perspectives; Bennett, J.B. (1998). Collegial professionalism.

4. See Essays by Bernice Sandler.

Bibliography

Bisdorf, D. L. (1961). A study of administrative problems affecting the development of instrumental ensembles in selected small colleges. (Doctoral Dissertation, Michigan State University, 1961). Dissertation Abstracts International, (22)12.

Brookhart, E. (1988). Music in American Higher Education: Annotated Bibliography (Bibliographies in American Music, No 10). Warren, MI: Harmony Park Press.

Brown, K. D. (2001). The administrative preparation of music department chairs in NASM accredited programs. Unpublished doctoral dissertation, East Tennessee State University, Johnson City.

Clark, B.R. (1983). The Higher Education System: Academic Organization in Cross-National Perspective (Campus No 368). Berkeley, CA: University of California Press. Cowden, R. L. (1984). What makes a good music administrator. Music Educators Journal, 70(6), 46-47.

Dickinson, E. (1915). Music and higher education. NY: Scribners.

Filan, G. L. (1999). The need for leadership training: The evolution of the chair academy. In R. Gillet-Karam (Ed.), Preparing Department Chairs for their Leadership Roles (pp. 47-55). San Francisco: Jossey-Bass.

Goodman, A. H. (1975). Music administration in higher learning. Provo, Utah: Press Publishing.

Hecht, I. W. D., Higgerson, M.L., Gmelch, W. H., & Tucker, A. (1999). The Department Chair As Academic Leader: (American Council on Education Oryx Press Series on Higher Education). Phoenix, AZ: Oryx Press.

Hodgson, Walter H. (1951). Problems of music administration in colleges. Education 72(1): 12-18.

House, R. W. (1973). Administration in music education. Englewood Cliffs, NJ: Prentice-Hall.

House, R. W. (1982). The professional preparation of music administrators. In R. Colwell (Ed.), Symposium in music education: A festschrift for Charles Leonhard. (pp. 277-289). Urbana: University of Illinois.

Jennerich, E. J. (1981). Competencies for department chairpersons: Myths and realities, Liberal Education, 67(1), 46-65.

Jones, S. T. (1960). The development of desirable administrative practices for departments of music in institutions of higher education. (Doctoral Dissertation, New York University, 1959). Dissertation Abstracts International, (20)10.

Law, G. C. (1963). Music administration during transitional turmoil. Music Educators Journal. 21, 40-44, 52-55, 66-68.

Lucas, A. F. (1994). Strengthening Departmental Leadership : A TeamBuilding Guide for Chairs in Colleges and Universities. San Francisco: Jossey-Bass.

Merton, R. K. (1957). Social theory and social structure. Glencow, IL: Free Press.

Miller, R. E. (1993). Institutionalizing Music: The Administration of Music Programs in Higher Education. Springfield, IL: Charles Thomas Publisher.

Mintzberg, H. (1973). The nature of managerial work. New York: Harper and Row.

Monk, D. C. (1980). Power, politics, and the music executive. Proceedings of the 55th Annual Meeting of the National Association of Schools of Music 68: 143-151.

National Association of Schools of Music (1999). NASM 1999-2000 Handbook. Reston, VA: Author.

National Association of Schools of Music, Monographs on music in higher education (1973).

Trotter, M., The administrators's role in the reorientation and utilization of faculty; Bonelli, E., The role of the music administrator. Washington, DC.

Tucker, A. (1981). Chairing the academic department: Leadership among peers. Washington, DC: American Council on Education.

Wiesner, G. R. (1967). Preparation for music administration in higher education. Music Educators Journal. 54, 65-67.

Violin Pedagogy & the Adolescent Student

CONTENTS
* Background Information
* Reasons for Studying Adolescent Development
* Historical Perspective
* Freud
* Erickson
* Piaget
* Skinner
* Bronfenbrenner
* Kohlberg
* Maslow
* Family Values
* On-time and Off-time
* School, Peer Group Influences, Friendship
* Achievement
* Activity I
* Activity II
* SUMMARY
* ADDENDUM
* Issues of Discrimination
* Deana Baumrink, Role of Parents
* Conflict

Background Information

S.B., who is the subject of this paper, is a seventeen-year-old adolescent woman of South American ancestry (her parents are from Lima, Peru), who is currently a high school senior. She is a straight A student in the honors program in her school, involved in many community activities, and taking the hard sciences and math courses (she wants to go to med school), in addition to her responsibilities vis a vis her violin lessons, orchestra and string quartet rehearsals, and concerts. She participates in All-City, AllState, and private music festivals, and performs with her quartet for public events.

S.B. has studied the violin with me for about 18 months. During that time, she has progressed in her violin studies from the later books of the Suzuki method to pre-college level, professional repertoire. After a recent round of auditions and applications, several universities sent her offers of acceptance. She has won a President's Scholarship at a prominent university in the eastern part of the country. She won this through a combination of her good grades, good SAT scores, and extracurricular activities, among which is the music.

Reasons for Studying Adolescent Development

It is important for music teachers to understand their adolescent students in order to help guide their careers, if they're headed for careers in music, and what strategies to use to promote their highest level of development, whatever their goals may be. Due to the hardships and uncertainties involved in the artistic life, the majority of individuals who study music do so for a sense of personal enrichment and because of the way music study heightens the sensibilities. One of the most important precepts of Suzuki training is that the intent is not to produce professional musicians, but to produce "happy children."

Thus, there must be separate standards of evaluation for students headed toward artistic careers and those who probably are not. S.B. enjoys playing the violin and says that she could never give it up. She wants to play in the orchestra at her university and this experience will probably be very meaningful and pleasurable for her. What I would not say to her–because it might hurt her or discourage her–is the quite unnecessary observation (since she has no plans for a professional career in music), that people simply have varied levels of natural talent. While this is by no means always the case, sometimes the formal cognitive intellectual capacity is better than the raw musical talent in terms of tone production, phrasing, and especially intonation. Often, in fact, intellectual ability and musical talent may be askew, and very talented musicians will have no corresponding great abilities in other areas, while very able thinkers cannot produce a passable tone, no matter how hard they try or how very much they want to. These exquisite sensibilities are gifts; the ability to hear intervalic relationships or phrase in a meaningful way on a stringed instrument can only be taught up to a point; why some children have these gifts in abundance, while others are less gifted in this respect, is mostly unknown and mysterious.

This particular student has grades and standardized test scores indicating she is in the "gifted" range, which is sometimes defined by an IQ score of 120 or over. Her behavior and attitudes are characteristic of that group. She is very much in the category of other students who work with an intensity teachers really appreciate because so much may be accomplished. With this category of student, there is an underlying assumption that hard work will be the norm, and there is no rude or merely rebellious questioning of the teacher's authority. I think this underlying respect for the educational process is probably a result of matching parents' attitudes.

Historical Perspective
All of the changes which have occurred in society over the past several hundred years (the rise of the middle class, the emancipation of women, the developments in technology) affect the study of music among adolescents. One primary change is that women have more and more been allowed to pursue their studies seriously, given the necessary talent and opportunities. Hopes and expectations for daughters are now far less different than for sons: S.B.'s parents feel that she can succeed in medical school, and she gets plenty of emotional and financial support from them. There are really no operational beliefs that she can't do something because she is female, and this is a relatively new development. It was not so very long ago that women were not even allowed to read, and only the daughters of wealthy men were given the benefits of a classical education, though music has been one of the accomplishments a young lady might pursue, to a point. Having a professional career, however, requires years of arduous study beginning long before and progressing through adolescence.

Freud
The notion that biologically-based sexual instincts drive the personality would be fairly hard to dispute when one watches the psychosexual development of a young woman; it is a blossoming that is beautiful to observe. In terms of universal stages, S.B. is at a normal stage of development for someone her age, which Freud delineated as around ages 12-18, and called the genital stage. My own reservations with respect to the anti-female bias in Freud's theory makes me shudder to think that S.B. would ever be involved in any serious psychoanalytic investigation. I perceive her as being healthy and not in need of this method.

In terms of dating, I do think that S.B.'s parents, because of their culture, may be more strict with her than perhaps other parents are with their children. I know she goes to dances, because I see the stamps on the back of her hand. I asked her if she is getting ready to go to the prom, and she told me that she and a friend of hers - "they're just friends" - another violinist, are going to the prom together. It was at this point that she told me that she feels the most comfortable with other musicians or artists and perhaps this was because they have the most in common. Music study enculturates or socializes students to think in certain paradigmatic ways, and this is what she is referring to. Thus, this enculturation becomes an additional gatekeeping device for adolescent sexual impulses, through group identification.

Erikson

Psychological social conflicts as delineated by Erickson's eight stages-versus Freud's drive theory–can also be observed in this student. I would judge that S.B. is leaving the epigenetic "Identity vs. Role Confusion" stage and entering the "Intimacy vs. Isolation" stage. She is about to leave home for the first time in order to go to college; her mother told me in private, when S.B was in another room that she (S.B.'s mother) is experiencing some anxiety: S.B. has never been away from her–what if she gets sick? But there is in S.B. a strong sense of family, and of who she is, and I basically am not worried about her and I think her mother is not, either. S.B. on the other hand, is happy, excited, proud, and looking forward to living on her own for the first time.

The multicultural and social influences upon which Erikson based his theories can be traced in this student at that juncture between the "Identity vs. Role Confusion" stage and the "Intimacy vs. Isolation" stage. Over the last 18 months, I have observed S.B. moving between these two stages, and enduring the crisis attendant upon that development. I think she has handled it well. Perhaps because of the richness of her environment and the strength of family nurturing, S.B. has no problem with negative identity; the options she has are acceptable and achievable ones. She is able to preserve a consistency of self across time.

Piaget

This theory, with the four stages of cognitive development, has as its final level of development the period of formal operations – and S.B. is definitely at that level and has been for several years. There is a clear observable affect of this student's stretching her mental faculties to take into account environmentally imposed data –sociological, intellectual, and artistic. Her ability to think in the abstract is ubiquitous and well developed. She is well able to see others' point of view and has moved away from an egoistic purview.

There was both assimilation, where new experiences are incorporated into existing knowledge, and accommodation, where there is an adjustment to new knowledge. S.B. assimilated a higher level of performance practice with respect to her instrument, and she took in, or accommodated to, a great deal of brand new information, much of which contradicted the old assumptions she had as a less mature player. In order to incorporate this new information she had to change, and change educates the learner.

In terms of other characteristics of adolescents, S.B. is idealistic in the expected and normal ways that adolescents tend to be. (This notion of "is" versus "ought.") She saw "Shindler's List," for example, and she is now very clear that anti-Semitism is a horror. She feels very passionately about a number of people, things, ideas. She loves jazz, loves a number of specific musicians, love certain pieces–all with a youthful passion. There is a slight edge of hypercritically, but it is not extreme; she is mature enough to take her own passions with a grain of salt, I sense. And while she is still egocentric and self-conscious–she is very careful about her physical presentation–she does think about thinking. Above all, her approach to her schoolwork is systematic and purposeful. She does some divergent thinking: I would estimate her convergent/divergent ratio is 70/30. (Of course this is just a subjective guess on my part, unsubstantiated by any test or data).

Skinner
Observable, quantitative, cause-affect schemata are clearly observable in this student: the better she does at her lessons, the more musical experiences she enjoys in the company of other students, the more she performs in public–the more an enculturation or socialization toward the life of the mind becomes attractive. And this has occurred to the point that S.B. is wanting to "hang out" with student musicians or artists because, as mentioned above, she feels she has more in common with them. This is a huge benefit because she is going to want to stay in the company of the smartest and usually best behaved kids. You don't get into much trouble on a Friday night if you have rehearsals to attend on Saturday morning, and difficult music to prepare for your lesson. So her environmentally rich experiences in music reinforce the higher achievement goals; she is learning, based on the consequences of her behavior.

This student responds to learning enhancement techniques such as positive reinforcement and aversive cues. She is your basic "good student" and she wants to please me. Therefore, she is very sensitive to any slight criticism or less than happy remark (aversive cues), and conversely, does better the more she is rewarded with positive comments, e.g. "good" and "not bad." This "not bad" is something that is very rewarding to a student when a piece is particularly frustrating at the beginning. It gives hope and reinforces the notion that improvement is possible.

"That is a very difficult piece, and you have made a major effort." "I appreciate what you're trying to do here." "Every time I hear this, it sounds better." "Good work!" These remarks all improve the likelihood that positive efforts will be repeated. The paired association can be the teacher's smile and a positive comment. The teacher, following Skinner's precepts, must strive to be consistent, fair, regular in terms of frequency, and genuine. Thus, unwanted behaviors (not practicing, not being prepared, not playing the proscribed bowing, fingering, phrasing, etc.) can be extinguished and useful behaviors can be shaped into positive habits. These positive habits include a commitment to the work ethic, following directions and always being professional in the sense of being on time and prepared. These are strong, positive values, regardless of career path.

Bronfenbrenner
This theorist's ecological view of human development is based on a taxonomy of the environment, with ever widening circles of influences with the child at the center. The macro/micro dichotomy between those influences close to home and those in the wider world are demonstrable, in the case of this student, by observing her ventures out into, and speculation about, the larger worlds of college and professional life. She demonstrates a healthy balance between home and this larger world, and is looking forward to her life with joy and confidence.

Kohlberg
In terms of these levels of moral development, I would credit S.B. with a very high level, certainly Level II, Stage 4, and verging on Level III, Stage 5. The notion of "horizontal decollage" is appropriate to site at this point since a variety of behaviors cross categorical boundaries. I think S.B. cares about "the greatest good for the greatest number," and has feelings about "the way things ought to be," but she also still has a basic, age-appropriate, self-centeredness. It is typical of musicians and artistic people in general to take lofty concepts seriously, and she does this. However, I feel that she is more conformist, less given to storm and stress, than many, and also is more of a scientific, left-brain sort of person, than most right-brain types–the consequence of which is that

she is more practical and down to earth than many artists and therefore more stable. She is not, however, a rigid conformist, and she understands that some rules may need to be broken.

There is probably still some Level I behavior with respect to her desire to please her parents and her fear of not doing so. In some respects she is probably a selfish actor (this doesn't imply self-ishness, but an academic term); her parents have to be careful with finances and yet she wears very beautiful clothes all of the time. I think that she probably insists on this, and may get her way by the "deal is a deal" paradigm; if I make good grades an behave well, I must get nice clothes.

Maslow
This theorist postulates the notion of the self-actualized person and S.B. is moving in that direction. She has a set of high goals for herself, that of being a physician, and her development will take some time if she is to integrate all her different interests and aptitudes. As illustrated, below, each of the basic levels, moving from top to bottom, needs to be accomplished or fulfilled before the development of the next. S.B. has a solid base upon which to build her future life, since her physiological, safety, belonging and self-esteem needs are well taken care of. What remains is this long career development and ongoing development of personal maturity. Again, because of parental support and richness of environment, she has a chance to reach the highest level.

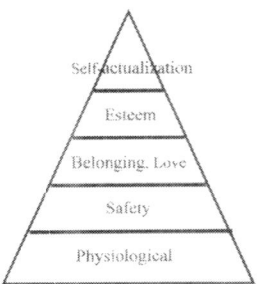

Family Values
S.B.'s family is Peruvian, but she grew up in the US and considers herself from here. I think that the relationship between S.B. and her mother is close; "daddy" is also an important figure in their

174

conversation. S.B. gets a lot of nurturing, and emotional and financial support. She is able to relate to others because her emotional needs are being met at home. Her mother adores her, to put it mildly. She can thus turn outward without fear and face the world with confidence. (Erikson). She is the only child, as her mother had to have a hysterectomy after S.B. was born. They attend church regularly and it appears to be important to them. Occasionally S.B. plays in church. Her faith appears to inform her moral choices.

On-time and Off-time

This is the notion of Bernice Neugarten's "social clock," which measures an adolescent's physical maturation in terms of the norm. I did not feel comfortable asking S.B. about when she started menses, but I feel that she is probably normal in this respect. She is rather thin, but not unhealthily so, or at least I hope not. I don't feel that there are any problems here.

School, Peer Group Influences, Friendship

Since S.B. goes to an optional school where good grades are the norm, she is not suffering from negative peer group pressure or the fear of being a "braniac," which is the pejorative term used for intellectual peers in schools. On the contrary, she seems to have carved out for herself a peer group of friends who are the best students, the most distinguished musicians, and the sorts of influences that best support her own interest in high achievement.

I substituted at S.B.'s school and met her two best friends; both are quite extraordinary musicians, one a violinist and one an oboist. They are both beautiful young women who get high grades and have adult level performance responsibilities in the community. They are both mature, likable persons. Her very best friend, Kara, is clearly loyal to her, cares about her and is very close to S.B. and her family. S.B. is no loner but is liked and admired by many people.

Achievement

James Marcia, an Erikson researcher, developed a status theory of identity which relates to achievement through crisis and commitment. Some examples of crisis, or points of decision making in S.B.'s history include: (1) When she was deciding how important music is to her; (2) when she was deciding what her college major might be; and (3) when she was deciding which schools to apply for and which one to accept. She has consistently stayed in the "Identity Achievement" stage, in that both crisis and commitment have been evident.

Activity I

S.B.'s quartet from the Youth Symphony performed at a local museum; S.B. played second violin very responsibly and seemed to enjoy herself. It was a very elegant concert and the quartet did well. S.B. is very proud to be in this group, and has worked hard on the music, which was rather difficult. She is gaining more and more self-confidence every time she performs. There was also a camaraderie among the young players and a sense of group unity which helped them perform at a higher level.

In terms of physical and cognitive changes, S.B. has changed from a scared insecure player who never wanted to be noticed and hid behind her instrument with her head down, to a calm and self-confident player who presents well, as well as sounds well. There is maturity and humor in her playing and overall presentation, rather than fear and an effort to hide.

Activity II

The local Youth Symphony performed with the local professional Symphony last week: S.B. worked very hard on the difficult contemporary piece that was performed by the two (united) orchestras. She was very excited about this concert and proud to be there in the hall with the other musicians, her friends, and her family. This experience seemed to have a profound affect on her cognitive processes; it was a step upward in terms of self-esteem and maturity.

In terms of development, the self-confident young woman I saw on stage this evening, sitting with professional players, was not the same scared little girl that played in the second violin section just a year ago. There was a look of elegance, a sense of humor, a confidence there. This was developed through many hundreds of hours of private lessons, group performances, travel and the up and downs of being involved in the musical life.

Summary

April 6, 1994
S.B. has three more lessons scheduled before the end of the term. She and her mother let me know last week that they valued and appreciated the work that we have done together. As a present, I gave her some music which is a computer generated print-out of the embellishments to a Corelli sonata which can be used to help students discover their improvisational abilities. This is kind of like baroque jazz, and S.B.

loves jazz. We also are doing some pieces for fun, like the Bach E Major Sonata with it's wild bariolage that students love so much. It is sad, her mother said, that these are our last lessons. I don't feel that sadness (though I may later) so much as the excitement of looking toward new things to do and new challenges to take on. I'm also used to students coming and going, and I try to maintain an objective, professional perspective. I think this is healthier for the student, too. S.B. has a lot to look forward to. Her development during these last two years of high school has been extraordinary. I will not be surprised if she continues with her medical studies and achieves her goal of becoming a physician. Whether or not she does this, or decides to go in a different direction, she is not afraid of risk and the prognosis of her finding her path in life is, I think, quite good.

ADDENDUM

S.B. had her final lesson with me last week and we took an hour to discuss her plans for the summer, her preparation for her audition when school starts (for chairs in the university orchestra), and some general topics. She and her mother hugged me when they left, and it was an emotional moment.

Ethnicity and Discrimination
One thing that S.B. shared with me is that she felt she had experienced discrimination because of her Latin America heritage and olive skin. She and her mother thanked me for working so hard with her these past two years, as if her being a minority were a consideration! I thought it was strange but apparently it is a big issue with them. It never occurred to me to think anything of that, since it has nothing to do with musical gifts. But S.B. and her mother apparently have suffered some rejection or discrimination because of their Hispanic ethnicity, which saddens (and angers) me.

It is generally thought that family loyalty, with the father as undisputed head, and religious beliefs (usually Catholic) play a large role in Hispanic culture. While the role of "daddy" seemed important, I did not discover if S.B. has a large extended family, as no mention of others was ever made. Their religion is important to them, though they are Protestants, which is something of an anomaly. They never elaborated about this to me.

Diana Baumrind: Role of Parents

Except for a brief conversation over the phone which yielded very little information, I have not had any interaction with S.B.'s father, though the opposite is true with respect to her mother, who, with the exception of one time, was always at the lesson. "Daddy" was mentioned, however, with love and respect. In terms of Baumrind's three parenting styles, my guess would be that S.B.'s parents come from an authoritarian background, but S.B. has seldom or never been spanked and that her parents' style is in the second, authoritative, style. This guess may have been influenced by a film I saw about South American immigrants, in which the old lifestyle with its brutal physical demands and sense of hopelessness, was contrasted with the newer style, when the family returned for a visit after many years in America. This switch in styles is probably a commonality in families where upward mobility is achieved through movement away from an agricultural lifestyle and its attendant survival-related fears, and movement into the middle classes. Thus, the love-orientated parenting style is possible, there is more symmetry of power, and more of a verbal orientation rather than just a punishment response. S.B.'s parents are by no means permissive, but the harsh, obedience-orientated style is not in evidence, either. There is a balance based on reasoning, rather than the parents' need to be in control.

This determination about the family's parenting style is based on (1) the interactions between S.B. and her mother, and (2) the results - S.B.'s behavior and attitudes. She is neither frightened or aggressive on the one hand, nor unclear about appropriate limitations, on the other. My feeling in general is that the love in S.B.'s family is too strong for her to turn to drugs, alcohol, cults, or other aberrant behavior.

Conflict

At this last lesson S.B.'s mother requested that I talk to S.B. about a conflict S.B. was having with one of her teachers. Apparently the teacher was being assertive about having some specific assignment completed for her class, and S.B. was balking a little because of her extra-curricula duties, and not understanding the teacher's position. My guess is that this assertiveness on S.B.'s part is related to her recent accomplishments–playing with the Symphony, getting a scholarship to college, preparing to leave home–and her efforts to move into adulthood.

What I had to offer were my memories of the sort of adolescent I was, and the contrast between those memories and the feelings I have in the classroom as an adult, which of course are very different. I told S.B. that I would be very proud of her if she would make an effort to learn from my mistakes, and to consider the teacher's point of view as an adult. No fortyplus year old person wants to take direction from a 17 year old kid, no matter how bright or promising. Public school teaching is difficult, at best, and the wisest path is that of respectful agreeableness–her time of authority would come one day. S.B.'s mother thanked me for presenting this point of view, and S.B. seemed to be taking it into consideration. This little nontumultuous tiff she had with her teacher is not serious, but was probably inevitable, due to the cognitive and social changes focusing on independence and identity that this adolescent is undergoing currently.

Elitism versus Popularism in Music Education

Prior to the first thirty years of the 20th century, music education retained an elitist view; at around that point a more egalitarian attitude gained acceptance, influenced by writers such as Whitman, Emerson, William James and John Dewey. These newer attitudes were predicated on the notion that the culture which enriched the upper classes had little significance if it did not serve a function for all. Progressive thinkers felt that too much attention had been given to the education of the bright, that social cohesion suffered as a result, and that education for all would be more appropriate for a democratic society.

If education has a two-fold aim, that of instruction and that of training in good conduct, then an enlightened educator may well have to hold simultaneously two rather contradictory views in order to best serve all their students. Like it or not, herd instinct is an important element in democracy, but contradicts on many levels the personal development of the individual student. This range of possibility is illustrated by the great violin pedagogue, Ivan Galamian, who cautioned that a music teacher must be wary of judging students as incapable of development, since some students are slow developers, and yet, on the other hand, remarked that it was impossible to start a fire "where no flammable material exists." [1]

A primary conflict in education is that between those who feel that education should serve the aims of the individual psyche versus those who wish education to serve the needs of the community–the question of whether education should train good individuals or good citizens. In the Hegelian sense, there is no conflict, since there is no antithesis, but in practice the cultivation of the individual mind is not the same as the production of a useful citizen. Dispassionate searching for truth may lead down avenues that contradict an indoctrination aimed at producing future tax payers:

Absence of finality is of the essence of the scientific spirit. The beliefs of the man of science are, therefore, tentative and undogmatic. But in so far as they result from his own researches they are personal, not social. They depend, that is to say, upon what he himself has ascertained by observation and inference, not upon what society considers it prudent for the good citizen to believe. [2]

This dichotomy is mirrored in the conundrum of an elitist academic view as opposed to the methodology and philosophy of Shinichi Suzuki, who developed and founded a school for talent education that teaches violin to very young children. Talent education is based on the mother tongue method wherein infants are exposed to music in the home, consistently and progressively. At age three the child enters the world of the music school, and mother and child begin together to learn the instrument, in the company of a group of children and Suzuki parents. A carefully developed system of group lessons, literature, recordings, and violin pedagogical methods moves the child swiftly to fine violin literature at a very high level. These methods have been Americanized with some success, and are often the basis of string programs in public school, though far from faithful to the original, and thus far less successful.

I cannot emphasize firmly enough and often enough how wrong it is to judge an already trained child and to say that its abilities are due to superiority or inferiority at birth. This kind of thinking should be abandoned. We must put an end to this misconception. There is no telling to what heights children can attain if we educate them properly right after birth. Should we not investigate the possibilities? Good environmental conditions and a fine education cannot help but bring children genuine welfare and happiness, as well as promising light and hope for the future of mankind. [3]

Dr. Suzuki's methods are child centered, and based on the notion that all children are capable of a high level of development, given significant personal attention and intensive training at an early age. This practice works very well, though less so in America where children are far less obedient and parents have far less time to devote to them. This methodology contradicts the notion that certain individuals are gifted from birth; environment, not heredity, is the key focus. Gardner's theory of multiple intelligences is a midpoint, somewhat, between these two views, but does not take into account the great accomplishments that can be garnered by early childhood immersion in an art.

An older, elitist view, is that education based on a desire to create good citizens, if it wisely designed, can retain what is best of individual culture, yet has an inherent danger in that the result might be merely to make the students convenient tools of the prevailing orthodoxy: There is an idea that rubbing up against all and sundry in youth is a good preparation for life. This appears to me to be rubbish. No one, in later life, associates with all and sundry....In later life a man's occupation and status give an indication of his interests and capacities. I have, in my day, lived in various different social strata; diplomatists, dons, pacifists, gaolbirds and politicians; but nowhere have I found the higgledy-piggledy ruthlessness of a set of boys....If you walk through a farmyard, you may observe cows and sheep and pigs and goats and geese...all behaving in their several ways: no one thinks that a duck should acquire social adaptability by learning to behave like a pig. Yet this is exactly what is thought so valuable for boys at school, where the pigs tend to be the aristocracy. [4]

According to this position, clever children would be spared a lot of pain if they are not compelled to associate with stupid contemporaries. The advantages of schools for clever children are great: exceptional children can be spared social persecution and emotional fatigue, they can be taught much faster, avoiding the boredom of having to listen to materials which they already understand. Their interactions with one another are likely to be fruitful; clever children often feel odd in the general populace.

Thus the contrast between a focus on all children and their inherent capacities and on those few who have, by environment, heredity, or fortuitous birth, developed at different rates than the norm. Children who read a great deal tend to be in this later group, and sympathy for them is expressed by Russell:

The man who holds concentrated and sparkling within his own mind, as within a camera obscura, the depth of space, the evolution of the sun and planets, the geological ages of the earth, and the brief history of humanity, appears to me to be doing what is distinctly human and what adds most to the diversified spectacle of nature. [5]

Thus a cultured and enlightened educator must tread a path between the needs of a democratic society and a devotion to the best in art, science, literature and human thought. Certainly this is not an easy task, but worthy of effort, since the happiness and welfare of children, of all abilities and from all backgrounds, is at stake.

Footnotes

1. Ivan Galamian. *Principles of Violin Playing and Teaching*. Prentice-Hall, New Jersey. 1962. p. 8.
2. Bertrand Russell. *Education and the Modern World*. W.W. Norton, New York. 1932. p. 22.

3. Shinichi Suzuki. *Nurtured by Love.* Exposition Press, New York. 1969. p.
4. Russell, *ibid.* p. 166-67.
5. Russell, *ibid.* p. 11.

Book Review: George Leonard's Education and Ecstasy

Review: Leonard, George B. (1968). *Education and Ecstasy*. New York: Delta Books.

The Suppression of Genius and Sensibility
in the Public School System

This is a work which in a very interesting way, answers the question, what is the goal, what is the purpose of education? George Leonard's answer is: "the achievement of moments of ecstasy." (p. 17), and he quotes Einstein: "It is in fact nothing short of a miracle that the modern methods of instruction have not yet entirely strangled the holy curiosity of inquiry." (p. 231). According to Leonard, "the master teacher is one who pursues delight." (p. 232); "to follow ecstasy in learning in spite of injustice, suffering, confusion and disappointment is to move easily toward an education, a society that would free the enormous potential of man." (p. 234)

The author quotes the work of a University of North Carolina researcher, Dr. Harold G. McCurdy, who studied the childhoods of 20 historical geniuses. He found three common factors:

1. a high degree of attention focused upon the child by parents and other adults, expressed in intensive educational measures and, usually, abundant love;
2. isolation from other children, especially outside the family; and
3. a rich efflorescence of fantasy, as a reaction to the two preceding emotions.

McCurdy concludes that "the mass education of our public school system is, in its way, a vast experiment on the effect of reducing all three of the above factors to minimal values, and should, accordingly, tend to suppress the occurrence of genius." (p. 113) Thus, the underlying thesis of George Leonard"s book is that the public schools in their present form suppress human genius and produce students who are "usable components in the social machine" but "just about finished" as learners. "Only the inefficiency of the present school system and the obdurance of certain individuals can account for the creativity, the learning ability that survive after age twentyfive." (p. 113).
Given that compulsive mass education is an "experiment," educators may well be indicted for breaking the principles outlined in the

Nuremberg Code for research involving human subjects:
1. The voluntary consent of the human subject is absolutely essential.
2. The experiment should be such as to yield fruitful results for the good of society, unprocurable by other means of study, and not random and unnecessary in nature.
3. The experiment should be designed and based on the results of animal experimentation and a knowledge of the natural history of the disease or other problem under study, so that the anticipated results will justify the performance of the experiment.
4. The experiment should be so constructed as to avoid all unnecessary physical and mental suffering and injury.
5. During the course of the experiment, the human subject should be at liberty to bring the experiment to an end if he has reached the physical or mental state where continuation of the experiment seems to him impossible. (p. 114)

This is a book from the '60's era, a time when free schools were being developed; it was published during the same year of the Berkeley "summer of love." George Leonard is an interesting person; he is currently an Aikido master with a school on the west coast. (Aikido is a martial arts discipline). He also continues to lecture and write books. He is associated with Esalen Institute and Michael Murphy.

This is a remarkable, magical book in many ways; the introductory materials tell the story of the author's visit to a traditional, public school, and his psychic interaction with the students there. 'It is an exacting and exhausting business, this damming up the flood of human potentialities.' (p. 1). He talks about teachers being actors:

> Retiring behind a psychic proscenium arch, the actor-teacher is forever safe from the perils of education. His performance flourishes. He plays for laughs and outraged looked. Phantom applause accompanies his trip home to his wife and he cannot wait to go on stage again. Assured of a full house and a long run, he knows he critics will be kind. Those who give him a bad review will get a failing grade. (p. 2).

The principal gives him a "little tour around the plant" until, finally, they arrive at a classroom where a "stout maiden" presides, and suddenly

There is a witch in the room. I see her near the back of the fourth row. Dark eyes and dilated pupils are fixed on me now, bold and direct, telling me that she knows, without words, everything that needs to be known about me. I return her stare, feeling that this girl, with an education she is not likely to get, might foretell the future, read signs, converse with spirits. In Salem she eventually would suffer the ordeal of fire and water. In our society she will be adjusted.(p. 4).

Leonard offers alternatives to traditional schools: "Visiting Day, 2001 A.D." and the following chapter, "We Find Johnny," describe a sort of free school on the Montessori model, with computerized learning systems and interactive learning modules. The children at the proposed school are gathered in a grassy area, reading Thucydides' *The History of the Peloponnesian Wars*, acting out the parts of the Athenians and the Melians. At one point, the children break down crying, several of them sobbing audibly, because they don't understand war. "Don't worry about it," one of their parents tell them, "Anyone who can relive the Peloponnesian War or any war without crying is somehow defective. Something's lacking." (p. 172).

Emotionally, this chapter is the heart of the book. Unfortunately, that date (2001) has arrived, without the changes in pedagogical technique and human sensibilities the author envisioned. Once again, the world has refused to conform to the wishes of some thinker's conception of what the world should be and will become. Leonard's predictions were wrong, I'm sorry to say, though one hopes that some day, the idea of war will become so foreign that young children are overcome with sadness and incomprehension at its reading. Unfortunately, contemporary children are so immune to violence that it is quite unlikely that a reading of any such book would bring tears.

Rather than being an ecstatic, joyous, and lifetime quest, education primarily continues to serve the needs of a society for "reliable, predictable components." (p. 120) The principle purpose is "narrow competition and eager acquisition." (p. 121) Leonard writes of the male bias of education [and how] in order for young men to bear the conditions of war or colonization, it was necessary that they reduce their imagination and self-awareness to a minimum. Stereotyped behaviors were trained by close-order drill in the classroom. Slogans justified the behaviors. "To die for Rome is noble" said more for Rome than for the Roman soldier's. If it is true that the battle of Watterloo was won on the playing fields of Eton, it is also true that some of the players' sensibilities were lost there. (p. 123).

The author postulates that this competition, acquisition and aggression is increasingly inappropriate, given current socioeconomic conditions on the planet, and can be reduced by the schools. I've had this book for many years, and always return to it, in hope and wonder; one can only read or reread a book of this sort as a sort of brace to one's underlying theoretical position regarding education. Whether future pedagogues will manage to replace aggression with ecstatic learning, I would not venture to predict, but I profoundly hope that it will happen

Music Pre/Post Test

1. What is the difference between a major and a minor scale?
2. Which composer was deaf by the time he wrote his 9th symphony?
3. Name the four sections of the orchestra.
4. The piano is considered to be a percussion instrument (rather than a stringed instrument); aside from the harp, name the four stringed instruments of the orchestra and their respective five groups, which comprise the String section.
5. To what section of the orchestra does the oboe belong?
6. What is a concertmaster, and what are his/her duties?
7. What is A440?
8. What does thorough-composed mean?
9. Give an example of duple meter. (A time signature).
10. Draw a 3/4 conducting pattern.
11. Draw a staff and put a half rest on it.
12. Draw a bass clef on a staff.
13. Draw an eighth note with the flag up and one with the flag down.
14. What is the definition of a measure?
15. Name the five major periods in music history. Do you enjoy the music of one period more than another?
16. What is the major difference between the violin and the viola?
17. Name a famous conductor.
18. What is a concerto?
19. What is an opera? Name one.
20. Give at least one reason for studying music. (Hint: the wrong answer is--because I have to for school).
21. What is chamber music?
22. Who wrote "The Messiah?"
23. In what work can you find "The Halleluja Chorus?"
24. What relation was Leopold Mozart to Amadeus?
25. What is a reason that Amadeus Mozart died in poverty?
26. Where did classical ballet originate?
27. In what century did Stravinsky live? And where did he live toward the end of his life?
28. What does polyphony mean?
29. Contrast classical and romantic: do you think of yourself as more one or the other?
30. What composer is the main link between the classical and

romantic periods?

31. What is art music?
32. Give an example of ethnic music.
33. Draw five accidentals. Tell what they do.
34. What are the two basic scales in western art music?
35. What are ledger lines. Draw examples above and below a staff.
36. Draw all the sharps in the proper order.
37. What is the typical arrangement of a score with respect to the instrument groups?
38. Name some characteristics of Romantic music.
39. Has it been proven that Pope Gregory wrote the Gregorian chants?
40. Name some duties of a conductor.
41. In what ways have 20th century composers experimented with music?
42. Name some electronic instruments.
43. Define melody, harmony, and rhythm.
44. What is Grove's dictionary of music?
45. What does a musical anthology contain?
46. What is a metronome?
47. Name four percussion instruments.
48. Clarinets, oboes, bassoons, and English horns have what in common?
49. Name five brass instruments. Where do they sit in the orchestra and why?
50. How many players are in the following groups? Write the number above the name:

    Duet Trio Quartet, Quintet, Sextet, Octet, Nonet

51. Name a composer famous for his piano compositions.
52. Name five careers in music.
53. Draw a staff and illustrate: perfect 5th, major 3rd, octave, minor second.
54. What does the term Forte-Piano mean? (With respect to the history of a certain musical instrument).
55. Name five characteristics of a professional musician.
56. Define: Allegro, Largo, Piano, Fortissimo, Decrescendo. (Turn page over).
57. What does projection mean?
58. What is a trill?
59. What is rubato?

60. Define perfect and relative pitch.
61. Define noise versus sound.
62. What is the science of sound?
63. What is serial music?
64. What is a tritone?
65. What are lieder?
66. What is a V-I cadence called?
67. What is the Mannheim Rocket?
68. What is vibrato?
69. What is ethnomusicology?
70. Name ten composers of art music.
71. In C Major, name the notes do, mi, sol, do.
72. Draw a quarter note, a duplet and a triplet.
73. What is the difference between a tie and a slur?
74. Name a jazz musician.

String Teachers Questionnaire

Thanks to everyone who responded to this informal survey. I found the responses to be touching and thoughtful, and I hope they will be of interest to string teachers.

1. Most professional musicians experience orchestras as being fairly authoritarian, or at least authoritative. Do you agree or disagree? How does this affect the way you teach? (Competency 4; how learning occurs)

This doesn't affect the way I teach. My primary goal is to instill love of music into my students. Orchestras help them see the value of discipline, working with others, pulse...

Having been a professional violinist, I did experience orchestras as being somewhat authoritatian therefore, I have created a powersharing setup in the HS orchestra which I conduct. While I am still in charge of many things, students have a considerable voice. They "earn" this by being senior in the organization and by making various significant contributions.

We should learn to distinguish between discipline and authority. If there is collective discipline in an orchestra, no authoritarian approach is required. This has to be made clear to students from the outset. During individual or collective instrumental classes this must be explained, and must be well understood by students. One must try to get a team spirit installed.

I agree that most orchestras function in an authoritative way. The conductor tells the orchestra what he/she wants and/or how to achieve his/her desires. Depending on my precise teaching situation, I vary how authoritative I am. For instance, in a high school orchestra rehearsal with approximately 100 students, I am fairly authoritarian. In an elementary orchestra rehearsal with 20 students I am much less authoritarian, although I become more authoritarian as concerts approach. In my private teaching, I am far less authoritative as I view myself in the role of coach or helper rather than director.
No. well - perhaps -ie the music director chooses the music, but he tries to give the children some input- what scale shall we warm up with, what piece shall we play to end the rehearsal and so on. But the overall direction is in the hands of the director.After all, that's their function

I agree that orchestra, by its very nature is authoritarian because it has to be. The difference between an autocrat and a "benevolent dictator" is a matter of approach. In my orchestra at the university I like to think that my approach is the second one. I expect attention while rehearsing, but also know when to take a breath, smile and crack a dumb joke (I do dumb jokes well, just ask my students) ;-)

I agree that most orchestras and directors are not only authoritarian, but also have their "favorites" within the sections. It does not affect the way I teach at all. I teach what I think is most beneficial for a student to progress technically and musically

I agree, but I think they have to be. After all, if they weren't, you would have chaos.

I try to give the students some input, and to listen to their concerns and suggestions. I encourage the students to teach one another–work together to solve problems, write fingerings or bowings in their music for their stand partner, etc.

I am not aure I would agree. In the best orchestras there is a sense of teamwork. A good conductor is like a jockey - encouraging each player to give of their best. Authoritative seems to me like the kind of orchestra I would avoid, and advise my student to also!

Yes, I agree. Composer and conductor are ordaining. "Classical" music has this structure.So we have to subordinate to the prescript. We have to accept this when we play music of the last two centuries.

Agree.I feel that students must learn to respect and listen to the conductor but may also give suggestions or ideas within a controlled format.

Agree. No.

Yes, usually. I would have to admit "yes" to second question. Agree. In order to have a successfull orchestra, you must establish authority. The teacher is to be in charge. (Note: That does not mean that the authoritarianship should be malignant. You have to have cooperation from your students to be successful.)

My professional experiences have been much the same. I prefer to teach as a coach, butwith large, young group that do not have large group experience, I find that theauthori-tarian/tative approach works well. Smaller groups are a different story

2. Everyone knows that fairly strict discipline is necessary in order to accomplishanything during rehearsals. Do you agree or

disagree? How do you think this attitude has changed, or has it? Should it? (Competency #4; how learning occurs)

Rehearsals are a process. I am in a small chamber orchestra and the conductor is a "newbie", straight out of university. It is interesting to see how things work themselves out. We often suggest procedure, such as who tunes first, what tempi suits our group, bowings...I like it when the process is more democratic. That is also true of the Toronto Symphony Orchestra here. We had one conductor who was very autocratic and the orchestral members did not work well with him. There must be mutual respect.

I disagree somewhat. I think it's possible to have rehearsals with fun & a sense of humor so long as there is a boundary line to prevent chaos.

Absolutely agreed. When this attitude changes, a great effort should be made to point towards the trouble-makers, underline the injustice done to those who wish to get the work done, and to enjoy the results.

I tend to agree with this statement, although as above, I believe that the exact strictness needed varies with the size and level of the group. In general, I think this attitude has stayed the same, although at the elementary rehearsal level, discipline may be less emphasized than in the past. I think that with smaller groups discipline can be a little more lax than with larger groups, and younger groups take a different type of strictness than olde r groups.

Yes, discipline is important. we must bow uniformly on most pasages, must play in tune, must sit up in good position and so on. "No, you can't chew gum and play the bass at the same time"'Yes Ronda, you can go to the bathroom.' (What will happen if you say NO?)It has to be FUN, rewarding, disciplined - but FUN too.

Strict discipline is necessary, but again the discipline can be friendly or unfriendly. There should never be an adversarial attitude in any rehearsal.

I agree and do not think that it has changed much, nor do I think it should.

My discipline is fairly lax because my classes are 14-16 people at a time, and I can afford to be lax.

I agree, if you didn't have strict discipline, again, you would have chaos. I don't think this attitude has changed in the orchestras I am familiar with, but they are very high quality, serious organizations, so discipline is usually not a problem. In my son's youth orchestra, there is one young man who is somewhat disruptive. He is being dealt with, and I suspect may either be moved in the back for the next year or asked not to return because it is not fair to everyone else to have him disrupting the rehearsals.

I agree. But there is nothing more time wasting than not being prepared be it conductor or player.
Today dictatorial conductors aren't anymore acceptible.

Agree.Discipline has become an increasing problem in our schools. A short attention span promoted and "TV" mentality has made it difficult for students to listen. Much time iswasted on repeated instructions.

Disagree

Yes. A more humane approach by many conductors has come about, and I like that

Agree. I believe the more stricter, the better. However. one must be flexible to outside forces that the teacher has no control over. (Try teaching class if there right after a fire drill and you'll get my point)

As above. Other factors include how often you see them. If you see a group of kids everyday, you can afford to develop a working rapport. With rehearsals once a week, it is most important that everyone be very attentive to what is going on

3. What is your general sense of how children respond to the revered composers of the past such as Vivaldi, Bach, Mozart? What methods do you use to inspire interest inthese traditionally revered composers? (Competency #9; materials andresources)

I have one student, who just turned 9 years old and he just adores Beethoven. There is a video called "Beethoven Lives Upstairs" and he watches it often. We intuitively talk about the composers, showing him pictures and telling him a summary of their lives or looking them up in a music dictionary.

My students seem to love these historically famed composers. Often by senior year they purchase Cds and listen for fun. My only method is to select beautifully crafted and tuneful compositions by these composers. I always choose works in the original editions, by the way, as my students tend to find the "student editions" prepared by some companies to be condescending and poorly written (therefore less fun to play).

I see three distinct reactions. Vivaldi is generally good - when you're talking of Spring or the Seasons, they already know it and want to play it right away. We did a string arrangement of Gloria, and I think they liked the repeated 16th notes. Bach: generally speaking, they like the instrumental challenge and that drives their interest. Mozart: I find that besides the inherent quality of the music, the students need to understand sonata form in the simplest sense for them to really enjoy his music (esp other than melody.)

The best way to get children to admire the works of great composers is to obtain a fair version of their music. The pleasure they derive from this is far stronger than words. The method is repetition, but with a new little details added each time, such as: In repeats,more P; certain accents; shorter notes here, longer there, etc. The: "Let us try this" approach works nicely–and one should consult students afterwards, how they liked this, or whether another solution was preferable.

I think some students really enjoy and are fascinated by the music of the revered composers of the past. In general, I think younger students tend to have a more open mind and are quite willing to play music of all styles, while older students have developed their own personalized preferences concerning what music they enjoy. At all levels, I try to expose students to a wide variety of musical styles and hlep them realize that they share many characteristics. Specifically for the revered composers, I try to link them and their music to things that the students may know similarities (in their music), historical stories about the music or composer, show pictures of the composers, etc.

Our orchestra loves chorales and thinks fugues are trey trey cool. And they like Vivaldi because they know the pieces (by and large)were written for children their age to play.

They seem to love these composers without my having to impose their music on them. They seem to get this sense either through the school orchestra setting, family background, friends, or from playing something by those composers. I usually pick pieces that I think will be interesting to the student regardless of the composer–and many times it will be Bach or Vivaldi; and then Mozart.

Generally speaking, the great composers touch something "eternal" in all of us. I realize this is a somewhat biased statement coming from a private teacher, as students who study privately tend to be those who have already responded in some personal way to the great composers.

My students are excited, and proud to be performing the masters

I think they respond beautifully. I suggest reading Catherine Wolfe Kendall's books–Stories of Composers for Young Musicians and More Stories of Composers for Young Musicians. I also require my students to complete a "listening" assignment each week–They listen to a classical recording or go to a concert. The recording must be listened to at least 3 times and then they report back, telling me the name of the piece, composer, performer/conductor/ensemble. My son did this for a number of years and is often able to tell the composer and performer just from listening to something on the radio.

Mostly they respond positively to the works of these composers. I try to explain background, linking in to their history lessons at school. I explain the reasons why the music was written and the type of performances it would be given. I make this music as accessible to them as players, as possible by teaching them to interpret written music accurately.

A question of age. Teenagers become interest in music with high esteem thyself.

My students respond very well to this music. They generally don't like what they have not had a chance to hear or play. I feel it is my job to encourage them to try "new/classical" music. Once they have learned it, they like it.I also let them know that it is OK not to like every piece of music. Each person will have personal preferences.

Kids don't connect to them. I learn as much about the composer as I can, and relate that information in as interesting a way as I can Rhythm alone, perhaps. Or the color of the orchestra.

As much as I Love those guys, the kids will tune out if you force it upon them. I choose fun pieces arranged from great composers to gain their interests. Note: Kids prefer the faster numbers.

4. How much verbal interaction among students do you allow during rehearsals or lessons? Does this depend on the group or the individual(s)? How do you decide how much talking is okay? (Competency #7; communication)

Talking is discouraged, especially when it is not related to music. When it is, it is brief. Otherwise it interferes with making music. That's what it is all about.

I have to work all the time to keep the talking constructive and the more playing we do, the less extraneous talking there is. If I spend too much time and energy repressing talk, rehearsal time gets wasted, so I have to find ways to keep us playing while dispensing quick instructions. If I need to talk alot, I call sectionals.

Depends. Talking for the purposes of fixing mistakes and peer instruction is great and encouraged. The "hey, how's it going" happens before and after. This depends on whether you have leaders of each group (1st V. 2nd V, Va. C. and Bass) which have worked with you before the rehearsals to get the bowings right, etc They may of course communicate with their group members, at certain moments of the rehearsal, for an established time. Once you judge they got their job done, order is reestablished and the playing continues.

The amount of verbal interaction I allow among students in rehearsals and lessons depends on the following: size of group, age of group, material being covered.I tend to allow more talking in smaller groups and less in larger groups. I also tend to allow more talking when we first look at new skills or pieces (letting the students share their discoveries with their neighbors) but allow less talking when we are focused on preparing for a concert. I guess my general rule concerning talking is that it is okay up until it interferes with my teaching or the learning of other students and that this covers most situations in my rehearsals and lessons.

We allow no talking between players other than 'business' "Can I borrow your rosin, use your extra mute' and so on.But the director asks the children for their ideas about the music, what images it brings, and so on, so there is talking, but related to the music.

Section leaders may talk to their sections and I will wait for them to finish. I don't allow any distracting banter.In my master class I encourage students to respond to me and each other since they are all partially responsible for teaching the class. Each student performs in the class after which the others critique

I am pretty straight forward in lessons. There is usually so much material to cover that there is only time for talking about the music. Social life or how it is going in their personal life comes at the beginning of the lesson as they are setting up and preparing to begin the lesson or a little bit at the end unless there is a personal or musical crisis.

I view the lesson as a collaboration between student and teacher. Thus, the talking is a conversation and not a lecture.

Students are encouraged to teach each other, but not to mess around or visit about other things besides orchestra. I can allow this because my groups are very small (14-16 per hour).

I teach fairly young children, but I am training them to be polite and talking is not polite when someone is playing, or talking to the group.

I try not to lose sight of what is actually being achieved. I have a plan in my head of what I expect each student to be able to learn and at what rate, and if this is being held up by too much chat, I will take steps to remedy the situation. Often this will be through cheerful exhortations to get on and play the next tune, or a light hearted 'Yes, but what about this piece here?' if they start talking too much. It very much depends on the age and standard, and attitude of, the pupil. I probably allow more 'chat' than some teachers because music reflects life, and to ignore their perspective on life will also be to inhibit the ideas they may pass to the music. Very 'chatty' children are often the most imaginitive, musically and generally.I always make time to answer questions about music or string playing, as thoroughly as possible - and encourage them to ask these questions.

Musical work has priority. I do not accept disturbances. But small comments are OK.

I try to allow talking only between different pieces of music but it definately varies with the group. The more disciplined they are, the more freedom I will give them.

Young musicians may talk when I am not on the podium. i invite discussion during rehearsal related to the performance of the piece being played. Kids are kids and one must be ready to steer the q/a to a meaningful significant question.

Very little interaction.

If I am able to get my goals accomplished, soft talking is appropriate. Once the talking disrupts the learning, however, I put a halt to it

5. What do you do if the student(s) is disrespectful to you personally? What if they're clearly upset? Do you continue with the rehearsal or lesson, or take time out? How understanding are you, in general? What are your limits? (Competency #2, 11, 15; self-esteem, classroom management, ethical/legal/professional standards)

If someone is disrespectful, which rarely happens (but it's not unheard of), I speak firmly with them after class. This has always worked in the past (I'm told I have "fierce eyes" when displeased).

In general, I think I'm too understanding. I always assume that the student's intent is not to be disrespectful–that it just came out that way. I usually ask if they intended to be disrespectful if something strikes me wrong. Then I take the opportunity to tell them a story about how I once said something that came out wrong . . .

The way you act will either cause respect, or will cause trouble. If students show disrespect, I start blaming me, to start with, and only on mature reflection would I take issue with one or some of them. In extreme cases, you might ask them to leave the rehearsal, for, say, 10 minutes, to think their grief over, and come back afterwards. As stated in 2), one should have a majority on one's side and let them put their troublemaking pals to collaborate peacefully. If nothing works, the rehearsal is interrupted, I sit there to read a book, and wait for the group to get bored from inactivity. Then the rehearsal is resumed.

If a student is disrespectful to me, I try to address it either at that time or later. If the student is clearly upset or the situation requires it, I may have the student take a time out while I work with the rest of the group. At some point, even if it is at the end of the rehearsal or class, I will talk to the student one-on-one about the disrespect and follow it with appropriate action. If on the other hand, the situation demands more immediate attention, I will give the other students something to do (practice your part on your own or check with your neighbor that you both are playing this part correctly, etc.) and immediately talk with the disrespectful student. I view myself at rather understanding and try to be responsive to the needs of my students. I want to know why the student is being disrespectful and find a way to eliminate that behavior. At the same time, I will not tolerate continued disrespectful behavior towards me or any of the other students.

We have had some children with attention problems. I told one student to go out and run around the church ten times to use up energy (he did)The other children are understanding, but not tolerant. They have spoken to the problem children, as the others perceive them as obstacles to the group progressing.

When I've taught in public school, I have usually solved this problem by first speaking to the student privately about the incident (away from other students so as not to embarrass the student). If that doesn't work, the next step is calling the parent and explaining what is going on and asking for support. I do not interrupt the rehearsal or lesson. I ask that they see me after class. It rarely, if ever, happens during a private lesson. At that point, then I'mlikely to say that perhaps our personalities are not a match and that they should search for another teacher. Sometimes clearly these eruptions could be caused by something that really has nothing to do with the class or lesson. In that case, I try to understand why it came out in my class or the lesson. I don't have specific limits because it rarely comes up, if ever. My limits are pretty narrow. Find out the problem. Solve it. If I can't solve it, then it is time for the student to move on. No point in senseless confrontations. Besides, the student is the immature one or should be. The teacher shouldn't respond as if on the same maturity level as the student.

I try to keep up at least on a superficial level with my students' personal lives. Though problems of this nature are rare in my studio, the occasional one can usually be traced to some hardship the student is having personally. I have at times, under these circumstances, stopped the lesson to discuss whatever the student may wish to disclose or have cancelled the lesson entirely in order to allow the student to take care of whatever the situation required.

I am very understanding. I assume the best about my students.

I am very understanding. I do not tolerate blatant disrespect, but try to handle it quietly. If a child is clearly unprepared emotionally or behaviorally to have a lesson, the best thing to do is to stop the lesson immediately, but kindly. It works like a charm and does not usually have to be repeated. With very young children, I only teach them the amount of time they can handle without fidgeting. Then I instruct the parents so that they will understand the small lessons they need to help their children with at home.

Disrespect to me personally - I take GREAT exception, in the same way that I would not disrespect them. I will make it clear to them, quietly but firmly, if I find their behaviour disrespectful.If they are clearly upset, I will take time to establish firstly if they want / need an adult's help and then offer them help, consolation, or whatever. I am conscious that I may be the only adult besides their parents with whom they have one-to-one contact. What are my limits ? I am paid to teach them violin - I can be flexible, but if the upset takes much time away from actual learning, I will discuss with their academic teachers and a parent. A joke may be OK. Then I invoke for concentration.

I ask them to see me after class. I'm generally tolerate for awhile and then come down hard on the individual.

Interpersonal relationships are extremely important to young artist development. If anartist cannot express feelings and emotions that they are feeling they are invited to take a moment to reflect on the difficulty at hand. It is then the possible to communicate on a break in the rehearsel. I do not stop rehearsel.Many times the difficulty that a student is working thru can be a positive experience betweeen the members of the group. The teacher/conductor must model compassionate understanding behavior and steer the ensuing conversation to a satisfactory end.Students that are physically threatening orrefuse to engage in presenting their difficulty calmly are asked to leave and parents are called.

Require that they leave the room. Do NOT interrupt the learning of others!

Not enough room to answer...Every situation is different. I take the appropriate steps necessary in accordance to school district policy and where that particular student is on his/her step. Since I am provided with a cell phone by the school, there will be immediatecontact with parent.If I am unable to make parental contact, I remove student from room (either sit outside door or refer to office.)If I am very upset, I wait 24 hours before the student gets his/her consequence. That way the child has a reasonable consequence instead of the euthanasia that I would like to administer.

6. Do you have any particular stories you like to share about composers to make them more human and immediate and real to the students? If you have time, please share those with us? How do the students usually respond? (Competency #9; materials and resources)

I tell some stories I've read in the composer bios I'm always reading. I also tell stories about conductors who've inspired me. Am too tired to pass any on, but I'd advise reading the latest bios!

I told that one student about Paganini and how innovative he was and how people thought he was the devil...When it was his sister's turn for her lesson, he drew a picture of what he thought Pagannini should look like. He explained to us (his mother, sister and I) that he has a big head because he needs it for all his violin ideas. So charming!

While doing overture to Rienzi, I usually tell some fiction about Wagner and his penchant for over-the-top opera roductions

Stories belong into the music class, not into the rehearsal–unless it is a short joke or pun. And only, if the rehearsal goes well.

I like to share some of the "traditional" stories about composers. For instance, I share the story about Haydn composing the "Surprise" Symphony to wake up his guests and one about Haydn's servant who would get Haydn out of bed in the morning by playing all but the last note of the Surprise Symphony theme which Haydn felt compelled to end. I also share the story of Beethoven being unable to hear while conducting the 9th Symphony and not knowing that the audience was applauding at the end. I tend to use these stories when playing themes from these pieces in method books or other pieces. In addition, I have a couple books about composers from which I will relate some historical facts about the composers we are studying. The students usually are interested in the "human" side of these composers.

Well, I think that there will always be a need for traditional teaching methods until the student has enough knowledge so begin giving opinions. And if the opinion is worthwhile and works, fine with me. If I think that the opinion on say bowing of fingering doesn't work, then I am pretty dictatorial. In instrumental music courses, it depends on the level. Is it elementary, junior high, high school, or college. It depends also on the situation and the level of the students in the class.

We just generally talk about the composers. The students are usually interested.

I will, of course, discuss Mozart the child with younger students, will describe Vivaldi, the Red-Haired Priest and headmaster of an orphanage, tell of Haydn's life as a royal composer and if nothing else, help the students to categorize the composers whose works they have played into the four major style periods. Students are usually interested in these things. I can't say that they particularly "relate," but they enjoy knowing about the different lives and times of the composers whose works have survived to their time.

In general, I try to show how composers were just normal human beings with a whole range of emotional responses, and that their skill lies in reflecting this by writing music.
I generally pass out material about the composers that we are playing.

I study composers from a variety of sources. Ex. Composer and Critic by Max Graf. Young artists are always eager to understand that composers were people too. They had everyday concerns like the students. Relating amusing anecdotes from the lives of the composers and their contemporaries is just one way to give access to the life of any composer. Telling why a composition was written and the story of it's creation is oftenfascinating. Young artists are willing to know more about a composer if they can relate his life to theirs. The student should know why we revere a composer and must bestow their own measure of his/her greatness.

Not really, because many are irrelevant or like gossip.

Yes. (Don't have time to share.)

7. What are your feelings toward traditional teaching methods versus a response-centered approach, where the burden of learning is placed on the student? Howdoes this apply in instrumental music courses? Does it apply? (Competency #8; instructional strategies)

I think that in most instrumental courses we need to rely on a traditional approach, though not lockstep and rigid and inhuman. Response is necessary too.

I relially feel that ultimately, it is the children that learn. I try to find out how they learn, model it, and give them the opportunities to experience what they need to teach themselves.

In string instruments, the burden of learning lies necessarily on the student. It is important that the students gets it right–if only once–in class, and then he has to get used to this right way on his own.

Teachers need to find the approach that works best for them in each particular teaching situation that will best help the students learn. I think that some situations call for a more traditional approach while others may work better with student exploration. When dealing with new skills or concepts, I use a mixture of methods from direct instruction ("Do this to achieve this sound") to exploratory ("What different sounds can you achieve?" and then "How did you get that sound", etc.). While I know some teachers who feel quite strongly that instrumental music needs to be traditional (and authoritarian), I feel free to include response-centered approaches to try to meet the diverse learning styles of my students.

It seems to me that in today's world (and perhaps earlier as well) the burden oflearning orchestral music is the students AND parents. (Mr. S' triangle!) I have no students who are succesful without the parents involvement as well as their own interest.

Students need to be taught by example and continually corrected. It is up to the teacher to teach students to teach themselves. In this sense some of the burden of learning is placed on the teacher. Still I have to emphasize that this can only be accomplished if the teacher teaches teaching.

Not too much. It doesn't come up much. It happens only if I feel a student needs to think about a bow position first before playing, or a certain musical thought before beginning a piece. I guess I do more thinking than I thought. One has to always be prepared mentally to play as piece or whatever. And sometimes that demands a short period of quiet ahead of time to prepare mentally for a performance, audition, a lesson, or whatever.

Of course, in the private lesson, the responsibility is placed on the student to practice daily and to become one's own teacher during those practice sessions. It is up to the private teacher to teach the student to teach himself.

I think it does apply. It helps the less advanced students catch up, and it gives the more advanced students the chance to be teachers and solidify their learning through teaching.

I teach Suzuki violin, so I am very biased towards the Suzuki philosophy. Lots of listening, parental involvement, I encourage them to start very young, because the philosophy works better.Response-centred - does this mean, you teach what the student asks ? I am almost certainly in the traditional sector, but determined to be flexible and sensitive to each individual.

In the last 20 years i leaved the trad. methods more and more. Now the music itself gives the direction the way to go either technically as musically too.

I don't think that it applies very well.

the learner is always in charge of learning. The teacher facilitates the acquisition of knowledge by sharing technical and artistic info and holding the student accountable to the student established benchmark of quality.

Children ALWAYS need instruction.

Traditional? verses Response-Centered?The only way to have a succesfful music program is to demonstrate to the kids and to have them mimmic back. (short answer)I place theburden on the student to learn the material. It's my job to teach them how to play and read music. It's their job to do it.Musician/Teachers have the unique position of trying to learn the current trends in what the edu gurus think will work. I refuse to mold what we do into an English class setting. We are hands on therefore, the student must experience it for him/herself.

8. Do you find the notion of metacognition (thinking about thinking) useful in your teaching? If not, why not? If so, give example(s)? (Competency #8; instructional strategies)

Yes, but I can't give examples because it's the end of the school year, I am tired, and this questionnaire is going on forever:)
I am prone to teaching this way, but find that only a few students appreciate this approach. If the student learns this way, I tend toward it.

Planning movements beforehand, knowing what you want to feel before playing, is very important. Therefore metacognition is always useful, and the more difficult things become, the more it will help to overcome. There are talented youngsters, artistically minded, but very slow mentally. You can see how slow they make progress, even if what they have learned sounds stunning. This proves that mental activity is paramount.

I think metacognition is useful in my teaching. For myself, I like to think about how I thinkabout new situations and approaching new skills and techniques. For my students, I like to get them to think about what they are doing and why which leads some of them to thinking about how they think about skills and concepts in music.

Well I think a lot about PLAYING. What di I do to make this sound? Why does it work (or not) Howcan I explain this to Raoul whose English is rudimentary.Think about thinking? I think not.

Definitely. If I understand the term correctly you are talking about thinking about what tothink as you practice and as you analyze your playing. This saves time in practice and in lessons.

One of my "avocations" is neurophysiology thus, I am always thinking about thinking. Currently, I am exploring the "oganism-environment system" theory put forth by Finnish Professor Timo Jarvahlet. My philosophy in life is "go to the source." If one knows how the brain thinks, one has a better chance of preparing information for learning in the mostpalatable ways.

Yes, it's very useful. It helps the students develop evaluation skills which are critical for good practice.

Not particularly.

Yes, it is important to know what we do.

No.

Yes. Helping a student understand their individual learning style is essentiol to the success of that student.

No. Better to train for CONCENTRATION.

No. I have tried it in the past and am willing to try it in the future. It has been my experience that I simply define what I expect in a skill and why we have to do it that way. Then I have the students reinforce that.When you are teaching a 45 minute class with many performance deadlines criscrossing each other, one teaches in the most efficient manner possible. There, again, strings is different that math and english. Maybe if we giveup performing....

9. Share some of the most successful methods you have in handling disciplinary problems? Define what you perceive as a discipline problem? Why do you think they usually occur? (Competency #2, 11; self-esteem, classroom management)

Discipline... I think if the student has had not enough sleep, or ate the wrong foods (as children having too much sugar), can affect their moods. I ask them what they ate, what they have been doing, or they tell me (or their parents) Every day is different.

I believe that concepts of behaviour and discipline are a deeply embedded part of western culture, especially in our attitude to education and child rearing, to the point where it is difficult to see other ways of teaching. Focussing on "getting behaviour right" results in lessons about behaviour focussing on the music results in education about music.

If students aren't paying attention and miss a cue or play badly, I have to address the issue. Usually I address it by talking to the student. This often works. If it doesn't I have to come up with some other solution.

Discipline problems result from needs not being met. Usually I can solve them by meeting the musical needs of the student other needs are beyond my scope.

Inspire respect–the students must know that you are really good at what you do. If you can do this naturally, without affectation, you have won the disciplinary battle before it starts. Accidents will occur–try and dismiss them as fast as possible. If indiscipline persists, get disciplined students to help you. The causes for indiscipline are various: Boredom, frustration of not getting it right. If the teacher is clever, he'll make a note and correct the situation before the next rehearsal. Indiscipline in a collective class depends on the number and age of students. The best way is to mix collective with individual classes–where you can have it out with the usual troublemakers.

In general, I try to be proactive and prevent potential problems. I try to move around the group and use eye contact to make sure students know that I am aware of what they are doing. I think minor discipline problems (such as excessive talking, not following directions, etc.) are usually caused by the student wanting attention (usually prevented by my proactive approach) or by the student who is confused and needs help to figure out what is expected. More serious problems tend to come from outside concerns or minor problems that have not been solved. I tend to handle these with a disciplinary plan that includes a warning and then consequences (talk to me after class, phone call home, etc.).

Usually, I try to stop any before they start. A discipline problem is anything that interferes with the learning problem, a disruption to a class or lesson.They can occur for any number of reasons. The student can be bored; they can be tired; the room can be too cold or hot; something at home has gone wrong; they've had a right with a boyfriend or girlfriend; there was a fire drill just ahead of class. I usually take it in stride and try to move the class at a quick pace to get their minds back on the task. And I might not get accomplished my goals for the day, but I have kept order and they are playing.

In a class situation, it usually happens through peer pressure. If you're a good string teacher, you probably are teaching to the highest level of student in your class. That's always a motivator. But, every situation is different. What works in one class might not work in another.Sometimes I've used practice charts; holding a grade over their heads can work; an upcoming performance to prepare for can work.I try to keep this low key, but let them know that their success and improvement on the instrument lies with the amount of time they spend on the instrument in personal practice time. Some students take longer than others to get this idea.

See #5 above.

My classroom rules are simple. When infractions occur, my corrections are very short, and then I return to the music. I criticize the action and not the student. I point out what is good for the whole group.

I am not a disciplinarian, but if a child oversteps the bounds, usually I have the parent in the room. I feel it is their job to discipline, not mine. If the parent doesn't do his job, I have, on occasion dismissed the student from the lesson, or I very firmly, but kindly tell the student that the behavior is not acceptable–that I have rules in my studio. Usually it involves getting into things which I use as teaching tools. If I explain that those things are off limits, I don't normally have a problem. A discipline problem is where learning is interrupted through inappropriate behaviour. My first line of defence is to explain why their behnaviour is unacceptable and unfair to others trying to learn. I have sent children out of the lesson for short periods. With serious cases, I will use other adults in authority to me, or to the child, as support.

Problems occur when the student doesn't understand the teacher or when the basic motivation is absent. Speaking about is the only way. Try to keep the class moving with as little down time as possible.Play challenging music.

Somone who is not ready to be part of the TEAM is a problem. Put the student on the spot to respond to that point.

My class rules are posted clearly in rehearsal room and all students sign a behaviorcontract. A discipline problem is anything that keeps a student from learning (including nonparticipation). Each student gets a warning and then they follow the consequence steps for each infraction.All discipline problems occur when students have down time. I find that if they are busy the entire class period,

10. Share some of the most successful ways you have found to motivate string students to practice, focus, try their best. What motivations do you seek to inspire in your students? (Competency #5; motivation)

Positive feedback is so essential. Not to be too critical. If they make a mistake, I say "oops" but if they play something well, they get a heartfelt bravo from me. The students, old and young alike, enjoy getting stickers to indicate they completed a piece.

The best motivation, in my experience, is love of the music we play.

That's why I try to choose works the students like that's why I give them a vote in what we rehearse and play that's why I encourage them to suggest music to me (last year, kids suggested Holst's Planets, Bizet's Carmen Suite, and other pieces in the past, they've suggested Mendelssohn Symphonies, works by Mozart and Bach that they heard on the radio or elsewhere etc.)

I'm still working on this.

Self-realisation is probably the most important motivation. The "you can do it" approach is positive, encouraging and stimulating. Don't ask too much, but also not too little. Actually, the best motivation is that you tell the student clearly how difficult his task is, not to underestimate what he is trying to achieve, and ask him to bring at least a "small sample" of what he is out to master. (He'll probably bring a generous sample–a typical reaction).

I try to build a good working relationship with my students where we have a common goal of learning, making music, and doing the best we can. I use frequent positive reinforcement and try to frame my comments in a positive manner (such as, "That piece made progress from last week. It still has some rough spots...."). On very rare occasions, I may use a piece of candy or sticker as motivation, but I really try not to use external motivators. I try to get students to want to improve on their own. Some specific ways include: using a practice journal for a week where students record what and how they practiced so I can help them practice more effectively presenting a new idea or technique and asking the students to see if they can work out the technique on their own a few times a year letting my students play a piece they select on their own for the rest of the group (I've done this in combined rehearsals as a "Recital Day" or in regular rehearsals as a "Pick your own song" day).

I motivate my students to practice by setting a good example, by being excited when I teach, by making use of audio/visual aides in the lesson, and by serving as a performance role model. I learned early on that you can't motivate students with grade threats. My students are also motivated by performance expectations. They must perform constantly in various recitals and master class situations, even when they are not music majors.

I like to let my students know that I care about them as a whole person. What they are doing in the rest of their learning life has a direct effect on what inspires them in strings. Also, what is going on in the home effects all aspects of learning, including strings. I simply try to push them in the lessons and get them going to the next level as quickly as their minds can absorb it. If they aren't challenged, then they tend to slack off or lose interest.

See #22 below.

Practice charts, music that they are excited to play, hearing older students play.

I ask them to bring in various sticker charts to show me that they have done something. For example, one child was resisting having her mother help her, so I had her keep a star chart with a start and end point. Every time she graciously allowed her mom to help, then she put a sticker on the chart and they both got to do something together when the chart was completed.One student had been ill a lot this year and for one reason or the other, practicing on a regular basis had come to a halt. The child told her mother she hated violin (the mother is a piano teacher and should have known what was causing the problem). I asked the child to practice every day for two weeks, charting her practice. When she successfully completed her chart, she was to get a prize. By the end of the first week wehad a complete turn around in attitude. By the end of the 2nd week, we were completely back on track, enjoing violin again. The lesson for the parent was that consistent practice was essential to keeping a child motivated.

Motivation to practice - by eliminating those things which de-motivate ie, lack of specific things to do during practice (so I fill out a practice sheet which has separate sections eg exercises and things to remember, pieces to play, things to sing, games to play), uncertainty about how much practice is expected (on my practice sheets there are 5 boxes to tick, I usually note how long each practice should take, and for younger students, parent signature is asked for, and there is a space for parent to comment - many use thisquite fully), lack of understanding of what is right or wrong and how to get things right (my teaching is based around training the ear through singing and rhythm games, and explaining theory as it becomes relevant eg tones & semitones)Specific problems might also exist eg child expected to practice in the living room with distractions arguments arise over practice because the child is always asked to practice when it is in the middle of something more interesting the solution is to make a timetable when you will practise,and the stick to it.I NEVER tell my students that "I always wanted to practice because I was so dedicated and I can't understand their attitude" - it is not true (there were plenty of arguments over practice and it didn't mean I wasn't keen on music) and it does not help pupils to have a paragon of virtue to have to emulate ! Even Maxim Vengerov hated practising, so he says.

Often a problem. Idees: Performances, concerts, working and playing together. No dry exercices.

Pass out music with different levels and have them audition on the advanced part. Most students will learn it.I play for the students. Decide what goals they can actually reach, and how to reach them. Fun music, practice sheets, candy for taking instruments home (only those who comeby after school know I do it)

11. Share some of the most successful ways you have found to inspire string students, emotionally and intellectually. (Competency #5; motivation)

Reading about composers or topics in the Grove's Dictionary at school.

Again, great music makes kids want to play it over and over again hearing CDs and live professional groups makes kids aware of the best sounds they can aspire to making recordings of kids (on CD and Video) lets kids see and hear how they really sound, and motivates them to make improvements.

Praise when due is a powerful tool. For instance "Very good, but try this –don't you think you'll gain by that?" Convincing is the word–not instructing –and the convincing should be done in such a way that the student feels h e actually discovered the better solution.

As above, I try to challenge my students to do the best they can. I have had students critique a performance they heard or describe what they felt when they heard a piece of music. In addition, while I have not done this that frequently, I have had students work on special projects such as creating a variation for a short melody, creating a story and the musical effects that could help tell the story, and research a composer or piece.

Take time to talk to them. A couple of minutes discussing life and how things are going makes a good emotional bond.
Since I teach mostly privately, I use whatever method works to fit a students' needs. It could be songs from the Suzuki method or sometimes it could be some basic information as presented in All for Strings or Essentials for Strings. And I always, always supplement with

music that I think they will enjoy! They need to like what they are playing. I have never had too much problem with this and most of my students are happy and successful with what they are playing or learning. I rarely have a student who quits lessons. And by the time they are ready to go on to college, they usually plan to continue cello as either a major, a minor, or as a strong avocation in their lives (school orchestra, community orchestra).

The most important is to establish an understanding with the students that no matter what, they as human beings are accepted and understood. Once this is established, honest and constant feedback in constructive ways about their accomplishment of the lesson material, and aid in the development of their approach to practice are the most beneficial to their success.

Praise their progress.

Group lessons twice a month. Workshops and festivals. My teenage son works from time to time with some of my more advanced students during group lessons and then they come back in the group lesson and "perform". He is very motivating. I use my son to mentor one of my young boy students. He helps him with his orchestra music and sometimes with a piece prior to his lesson.I think if you are teaching consistently, the child is progressing, that provides the inspiration. I educate the parents.

The only true way is to examine why I think music really matters and why I love stringed instruments so much. Then I can speak genuinely to students, and always they are caught up by my genuine enthusiasm.

Inspiring by the music itself (incl. analysis): Different styles: Baroque Classic - Romantic - Modern - Folk - Jazz - Improvisation / Playing together (+violin, +piano)

With advanced students, work on a piece such as the Bach Adagion and focus on musical line.

Get excited over the music.

PRAISE THEM!

12. How do you feel students respond to various teaching methods (traditional methods, student-centered methods); have you tried different methods and what were the results? (Competency #4, 8; how learning occurs, instructional strategies)

Kids seem to respond well to my traditional directive style so long as I (a) know what I'm talking about (2) don't talk too much (3) give them a voice whenever possible and (4) listen actively when they voice their opinions

Every student is a world by his own. You have to adjust tuition individually. No one is equal, fortunately. Otherwise string teaching would be boring. Some students want more technique before trying to make music, others want it the other way around. You have to learn how the student reacts and behaves, and give him what is best for him, at a given moment. Time cures defects, if there is interest to get better.

I think different students learn in different ways and that it is important that I try to find ways to meet the needs of every student. Most students have been enthusiastic about at least some of the methods I have used, although some students have had definite preferences for one way and not another. For instance, a student who plays extremely well, reads music pretty well, and started in the Suzuki method, excelled in traditional methods where I told him what to play or how to play it. However, he was resistant to a more student-centered method when I had each student create a variation to a short melody. On the other hand, another student who played well in more traditional methods, also excelled in the variation creation. She really enjoyed the freedom to create and work on what she wanted. By using these methods, I think I did help every student

I have tried may different approaches to teaching in the last 30 years and probably will continue to evolve until I quit teaching. I think students respond to any method you use as long as you are consistent and do it well.

I think I must somehow apply this method. However, I don't sit down and think about it before each student walks in the door. I do, however, keep notes and a folder on each student that tells what went on in the previous lesson, what they were to work on, what was new, and what was a review. Then I always review, review, review. And I always have a plan for the lesson. What I want to hear and work on first, etc. based on the past week's work.

As a private teacher, my approach is essentially "student-centered." This method has worked very well for me and to be honest, I don't believe I have tried another one (unless I am doing so unintentionally).

I have seen traditional methods, and Suzuki. Suzuki, if done properly is in my opinion the way to go. I think that the listening skills are developed, the ear training is wonderful, and the social interaction in group is very stimulating and inspiring.

The best results I have had are with teaching solfa and rhythm alongside so that students know what sounds to expect.(Sorry, no time for a fuller answer!)

Each student has an individual approach. I must employ different methods.

Each student is different.

Better not to change methods

Student-centered methods have to be extremely structured. It is time inefficient with the performance deadlines. (I do use it in tutoring situations or if I have a hotshot kid.)Some Fridays I have 3 students teach class (10-15 min. each) and give them feedback.

13. How do you apply the notion of scaffolding, or building on prior knowledge, in your teaching? Do you apply this method? (Competency #4, 8; how learning occurs, instructional strategies)

Yes I do. Am too tired to tell how except to say that I might rehearse a difficult sixteenth-note passage, for instance, in one-measure segments, slowly at first, gradually increasing speed.

I attempt to do this, but it is not natural for me. I am a hyper-linked learner, and I enjoy students that get a bunch of information in their heads and start putting it all together without my help.

Yes. The advancing by small steps is particularly indicated in string teaching. It is essentialthat the foregoing step is well assimilated, before proceeding to the next one.

I always try to link new technique or ideas to past knowledge, because I think that this helps many students make important connections. I do not always verbalize the connections right away as I sometimes see if the students can make the connections on their own and then I confirm the connections. I think that almost all the skills and ideas we teach in music connect to other skills and ideas. For instance, rhythm and meters aredirectly related to math. Music reading skills, music improvisation, and composition are all parallel skills to reading and writing skills. I try to use these types of connections in addition to the obvious linking of musical skills with one another.

I use analogies a lot to explain physical concepts. We also fire up the kids with TEAM ORCHESTRA rallies.Attendanceat rehearsals is like attendance at soccer!

All teaching is built on this model. Careful choice of etude and solo progression is the key.

Speaking from a private teacher standpoint, I base everything on what has been accomplished and what needs to be accomplished in the upcoming year. I have a mental plan of where I think each student ought to be in their development and act upon that inmy mental planning. Everything I do is customized to fit the needs of the student. Do I need to work the bow arm? Is bow distribution a problem? Can the student successfully play extensions? Choice of technical studies and pieces are built around the specific needs of the student.

As described in 15 below, I use essentially a "spiral curriculum." Every concept is revisitedagain and again at ever-deepening levels of understanding.

The Suzuki method provides an ingenious set of building blocks. Book 1 is the foundation, by providing a proper set up and then each book builds on different skills. Ido supplement with scales and etude books later on.

Essential. I hate teaching students who have insecure basic knowledge. I make sure my beginners understand everything so they can build on secure foundations.

This is extremely important. It is difficult to go on to a new level until one has confidence with the basics.
Point that out whenever you can

Yep. I constantly remind them when they learn the concept... 5th Grade, 6th Grade, 7th Grade, Last week and etc. Sometimes I have to reteach, but usually not.

14. What sort of non-traditional methods have you used which you have found to be successful in teaching strings? (Competency # 4, 8; how learning occurs, instruction:lstrategies)

Singing, dancing, painting. Get the students to express themselves creatively in as many ways as possible.

Can't think of any, offhand.

If a method works, it becomes traditional. Therefore, I am not using nontraditional methods.

I have mentioned some of these above. I have found the following methods or activities to be quite successful:student exploration, student composition/improvisation, linking writing and composition students create a story and then compose music or sound effects to correspond to the story which is an idea based on a conference presentation by Shirley Mullins), providing students with choices some of the times concerning exactly what we work on or how we work on it, etc.

I don't really think I do anything that is non-traditional.

I assign students a "scalemap" for each key. This is a (albeit hand-drawn) blank map of the fingerboard with all of the possible chromatic pitches notated in finger-tip-sized circles in their appropriate "geographical" locations on the strings. (At the top left corner of the page, the student writes the name of the key, the number of sharps or flats in the key, and the names of the notes which are sharp or flat.) For each key, the student must "color in" with a highlighter pen the appropriate notes for the given scale. Once the scale is "mapped," the arrangement of half- and wholesteps becomes visually obvious to the student.

Suzuki

Improvisation, variation and experimentation as a method to cope technical problems an questions of interpretation. Playing together with the student: familiarisation with musical behavior

Using improvisation.Having a pops ensemble.Having special chamber music sessions.

Can't think of any

None so to speak. More edu guru bull.

15. On what do you base your lesson plans: pieces to be learned, technical studies, some other criteria? How, in other words, do you plan your week, the term, the year? Are your plans based on concerts? (Competency #6; planning)

We have conservatory exams and a syllabus as a guideline. I ask them their goals and try to find material suitable.If they are performing a concert, I try to find related material.

Pieces to be learned. Scales and studies kill orchestra for kids. Great music contains enough scale-work, passagework and technical challenges to use as educational material without further supplement.

Our plans are ideally based on exit competencies:what we want the students to learn before they get to the next level. We try to coordinate what is being learned in the content lessons with the music we will perform.

The overall plan depends of the pupil. If they want to pass an examination, everything is directed towards that goal–not necessarily playing only the examination pieces, but acquiring technique towards facilitating the job. If they just want to have fun, or play for their pleasure, a piece is chosen, and the necessary technical exercise suggested to get that right. If concerts are programmed, the material should be ripe at least 3 months before, letting to rest, and taken up again a fortnight before the event.

My general response is that I try to focus my plans on helping students meet their needsand show improvement in their playing.In school rehearsals and group lessons, I base my plans on the outcomes I need to meet by the end of the year. I try to make sure that at least some of these outcomes are met directly or indirectly by the pieces the groups play and usually perform. My normal yearly break down would include starting the year with a focus on outcomes related to technique needed for later pieces (based on method books or other exercises). When ready, I introduce the concert pieces and continue work on the techniques or skills needed to play the pieces and the related outcomes. Prior to the concert, I focus more specifically on concert preparation and getting the pieces in as goodshape as possible. The cycle continues throughout the year depending on the number of concerts. Obviously there will be times when concert demands dictate certain aspects of my plans. There are also times when the concert preparation will be interrupted to provide a more student-centered activity (student run sect!ional rehearsals, group practice time where I can help those who need it, a complete break with students playing pieces they have been working on alone, etc).In my private studio, I base my plans on a combination of pieces to be learned as well as skills that need additional work. For instance, we mightbe working on a piece, on reading 5th position notes, and reinforcing a relaxed vibrato at the same time.

Each semester I discuss goals for the semester with each student. Then I choose the études and repertoire which will realistically allow those goals to be accomplished.

I generally follow a type of "spiral curriculum" which addresses varying levels of technique, style periods and practices, theory, musicality, etc. I accomplish this throughuse of scales, études and a gradual order of piece material.

My plans are based partially on concerts, and partly around the method book and thescales we cover during the year.

My plans are based on the next step for each individual child, technique building.

For older pupils, I use one of the three exam systems here in the UK. Pupils perform in concerts when such opportunities arise but I don't (yet ?!) have specific termly pupil concerts. They do a mixture of scalework, studies and pieces. I have long term plans of what is achievable in a year, combined with what speed the student is learning. I don't write specific lesson plans.

Fischer BASICSA fundus of violin pieces. Weekly a folk-piece as prima vista exercice. No year planning, but planning of concerts, performances, Class-teaching a.s.o.

The plans are based on learning music for a concert but I try to focus on specific items in the music like a particular bowing or rhythm. Better to think where successes can be achieved, instead of inviting failure.

We meet as a cluster (1 high school, 3 middle schools and a ton of elementaries) anddecide what skill we want learned by 6th, 7th, and 9th grade. It is our job to make it happen.I would like to say it is based on the TEKS... but anyone who has read them know it is not specific. (No difference for Band, Choir, Strings, or General Music.) Our curriculum guide is 20 years out of date and we exceed its standard anyway.

16. About how much time do you spend on non-instrumental, verbal instruction in music theory and music history? (Competency #7; communications)

Almost none. My kids won't have it. Plus, I speak more effectively in short, metaphor-laden, humorous bursts in rehearsal. They remember those much longer than they'd remember a lecture.

Very little and not enough. I would like to instruct the entire orchestra on a weekly basis on such things as scales, finger patterns, practice techniques, etc., but there is not enough time.

As little as possible. It is preferable to have the student assist to theory lessons with another specialised teacher, if this becomes necessary.

For me , thisvaries depending on the age of the student and the setting. In my elementary school groups, I spend an average of 5 minutes out of 40 on theory and history usually related to the material for the day (linked to idea in method book or pieces). With older groups, the amount of time would vary with more than that percentage when introducing new ideas and skills in pieces or books and less time when focusing on preparing for a concert. With my private students, I usually strive for a couple minutes out of a 30 minute lesson to betheory or history linked to what we are doing. For instance, I have students play a sight-reading piece every lesson and will tend to question them about the piece (key and how do they know, form, etc.). I also tend to introduce the historical ideas when first starting a piece or when needed throughout the work on a piece.

About 10 to 20%. In Canada, most serious students take theory courses through the Royal Conservatory separately from the instrument lessons. The RC courses are offered in our school at two different sessions each week, and we have about 60 theory students at any one time.

Not much. Most of my students are in good orchestra progams or study piano. I may ask them to listen to recordings of several different performers of a piece that they are working on. Or I may have them look up the style of the music orcomposer they are playing. It is all done in the context of the regular instruction. I, of course, teach scales and arpeggios. And if, for some reason, they don't seem to understand how these are constructed, I take time and show them.

I talk about the pieces we are doing in light of chord structure with demonstration at the keyboard as well. I always ask the student to analyze the music within limits of their knowledge. Historical perspective is touched on as necessary for a better understanding of performance practice.

I play piano with all students....the accompaniments as soon as I can so they can hear the piece as a complete work. I also play with them on cello, particularly at the beginning of learning of a piece. Mostly to establish fingerings, bowing style, rhythm, key, etc. And I am speaking as a private teacher.In a classroom setting I have used a student's instrument or brought my own to class to demonstrate and then I verbalize what I want. Usually it has to do with bow distribution and style.

Again, this is simply part of the "conversation." If a new concept comes up in the piece or the etude, I discuss it with the student.
not enough

Incidental time as it applies to a piece a student is learning. For example, the May Strad had an article on Minuets with pictures of people dancing the minuet. I brought in the article and shared the pictures with some of my young students and then had them play gracefully so that the women with tight dresses and men with tight pants wouldn't split their teams.

Theory: I get pupils to work through theory workbooks in their own time and I mark them in my own time - we only discuss problems which arise. Music history: I give as much introduction to new pieces as possible. Very rarely I might get them to look something up or find out about a composer.

0 - 30 %

About 25% of class time.

Very little

Not enough. We are going to double blocked scheduling next year. (Orchestra 90 minutes every day!!!)I plan to really work it in.Again, when you have 45 minute classes, there is only cram time for all the activities associated with strings.

17. Do you use a piano to demonstrate ideas during rehearsals, or your own instrument, or borrow a student's instrument? (Competency 9; materials and resources)

Yes, a piano especially for scales. My instrument is they are having problems with intonation or bowing.Their instrument if they don't like their sound.

I demonstrate on one of the violinists' instruments, or I ask a senior musician to "show me what I mean" (puts a smile on the senior's face and earns additional respect from the younger ones).

Borrow, or bring my own.

I show certain details on my own instrument. If the student doubts he can get this out of his instrument, or he produces unsatisfactory sound, I show him on his instrument that it can be done.

In my school groups, I tend to demonstrate ideas with my own instrument (I will sometimes use my own violin or viola or one of the extra cellos or basses at my schools depending what is available and what I think will work best for the situation) or with my voice. I will use the piano for some other demonstrations or to play multiple parts when I want students to hear multiple things at once. I think I have borrowed a student's instrument at most twice in 10 years of teaching, because I really do not want them to feel like I am taking advantage of them or that I don't care enough to have my own materials ready for my use.

All of the above. I find for tone production itis best to use the students instrument, as you may otherwise ask for something that the instrument cannot do. Also this allows the student to hear that their instrument CAN make a richer sound, ring on pizz. and so on.

I don't take my viola to rehearsals so my bad habit is occasionally using my principal violist's viola to demonstrate a technique. I will then run an impromptu master class teaching methods of mastering certain techniques required in the music.

Yes, I've done that when I felt it was of value–both as a private teacher and as a class teacher.

I usually demonstrate on my own violin or viola. As students begin preparing for recitals, I often will play a "violin reduction" of the piano score along with them to help reinforce style and "vertical" listening.

I use the piano and I borrow a student's instrument. I use a piano, my own instrument andborrow a student's instrument

I always teach with a piano. I have my owninstrument to hand to demonstrate, or I might use theirs if I want to see what sort of sound they could get, or prove to them that their violin will sound ok. Actually I try to play their violins regularly to check for set-up problems (bridge leaning or moved over, strings sinking into the bridge, rattles and squeaks, and amount of rosin on the bow etc.)

Piano and my own violin

I use a small keyboard and my violin.

No

I demonstrate on my instrument or a student's instrument.

18. Do you spend time listening to recordings during class time? (Competency #9; mateirals and resources)

Yes.

No.

No.

Sometimes yes, but just for some particular detail, i.e., for a few minutes.

I will have students listen to recordings during class time if I think that the recording will be a useful tool to help the students play better, but I don't spend much time with them. I tend to use recordings to help students hear how parts fit together in pieces they are working on, to help them get an idea of ONE interpretation of a piece, or as a demonstration of a particular skill, style, or technique.

No

Generally we don't listen to recordings during the lesson time, but I do try to provide students with (at least loaner) copies of the pieces on which they are working. I also encourage them to listen to the local classical radio station and to begin to develop personal classical music CD libraries.

Yes, but only parts of most recordings.

No

Sometimes - not often

Not often

Infrequently - I wish we had time to do more.

No

Very little, but yes.

19. How do you feel about your students' parents? The administration at your school? Supported? How important is that? (Competency #11, 13, 14; professionalism, school-home relationships, school-community relationships)

Parents of children need to be involved.

I love the support I get from my parents and administrators couldn't do my work without it! And, seeing how some colleagues elsewhere struggle, I feel fortunate in my situation.

A very complex question. Good about the parents, but with a price—☐ they want a big, top-notch quality performance, which sometimes comes at the cost of meaningful, long-term instruction. The administration does not support us with staff, but says that it is important. Our program has grown, and we need more staff. .

Without parent support, nothing can be done. Learning a string instrument is like a music stand, i.e., a tripod. The three legs are the student, his parents, and the teacher. If one of these fail, the tripod falls down.

I think it is pretty important for a teacher's sanity to feel supported by the parents and administration. I think that the parents of mystudents realize that I am a professional who is working to help their children achieve success in playing a stringed instrument and more broadly in music. They know that I am open to communication with them whenever they have a question or a comment (even if not all of them take advantage of my willingness to communicate). Likewise, I think that the administration at my schools respects me and supports me due to my professionalism, high expectations for myself and my students, and my willingness to help my students improve. I think that these are important areas and that many beginning teachers don'trealize just how important parental and administrative support can be for a teacher of any type.

I teach at a private music school. The school pays the coaches (three of us), supplies the room, the stands and the music. Orchestra is free to ALL students, not just ones at our school. Its the parents who make it work on top of this. They all come to rehearsal, they all stay through, they put the stands together, mark the younger children'smusic, take Ronda to the bathroom and bring the teacher's coffee.

My administration is very supportive of my program. Administrative support is an absolute necessity for any successful program. Parental support at the university level is relatively less obvious due to the circumstances. They have already shown their support by virture of the fact that their children are now university students and still involved in music.

In my private studio, most of my students' parents are highly supportive. And it is crucialto the success of the student that they are supportive.In a school setting, if your administrator is not backing your orchestra, then you've got recruitment problems and possibly other problems.

Most of my students come to me through referral from their school music teacher.I believe that in our schools here, they have a published list of the private instructors in the area.

As a private teacher, I feel that regular contact with the students' parents is necessary for mutual support and for the support of the child. Parents are more likely to help the child achieve musical goals if they are aware of what those goals are.

My parents and the administration are supportive. Very supported. It is extremely important

It is very important for teacher and pupil to feel they have parents' support and equallyessential for the support of the school.Parental support for my current pupils is above average - nearly all seem to have supportive parents. Support of schools is sometimes good, more often average because the director of music does not know enough to know

Administration OK, Support OK, Organisation: in my own hands
It is very important to have parent and administrative support. I have been very fortunate to be in a system with excellent support.
It most important to keep in contact with the parents.

I am at a low socioeconomic school. Historically, parents are noninvolved in these situations. I really haven't gotten to know them.The administration is great and supportive.It is vitally important to be supported. Otherwise, you'll feel like you're all alone.

20. Do you have any specific methods to encourage parents to provide private teachers for your string students? (Competency #13)
I am only a private teacher.

No. They either do or they don't sometimes it's an economic problem and sometimes the student doesn't want lessons. The most brilliant clarinetist I've ever worked with spent four years in orchestra without lessons and by senior year he played more musically and at a higher technical level than any of the lessoned clarinetists I've had in 16 years. Not all students can accomplish that, but lessons aren't the key factor in all aspects of student growth (many people don't want to hear this, yet I say it as a longtime violin teacher too).

Lists of teachers, making our own contacts and hooking them up, HS students to help younger beginners.

Explaining that string instruments are the most difficult to master, and therefore private tuition is mandatory if frustration or impotence is not to cause havoc.

I try to provide parents with a list of area private teachers (or of music stores that have private teachers who teach at their stores) with a note early in the year discussing the benefits of private lessons. I think this helps parents because they have a list of names without having to do any extra work.

All our string students are private students. The wind players, with a few exceptins, like our Tanglewood kid, don't. And we (at our school) who rent hundreds of band instruments a year are totally stumped on how to convince parents that private lessons would help maximise the investment on that $3500 sax.

When I taught public school, I encouraged students to study with someone else....felt 5 days a week was enough for one teacher. Study privately with another person for other musical and technical ideas.

No, I need to develop this.

My students are all private. UK system - largely private tuition in any case.

I try to call the parents of students when they are starting to really make progess and show interest.I send home a form letter about the importance of private lessons.I have a private lesson teacher list ready at all times.

Point out where the stident needs individual attention.
I talk to them 1 on 1. Mostly its a dead issue.... no money and no realistic opportunity for scholarships.

21. Do you teach private lessons? Are there ever any conflicts with your private teaching and your public school teaching responsibilities, if you have private students in your classes? How do you handle that? (Competency #12; professionalism)

I teach, but avoid conflicts.

Yes. No. But I've seen conflicts arise elsewhere where the public school elementary teacher was not a string teacher.
I never had that problem. The German Government ran the public school I taught at, and string lessons were private, although they lent the premises.

In my current situation, my private students are not in my public school classes. In a previous situation, I did have a few students who I taught privately also in my school classes but did not really have problems with conflicts. I have had a few school students who have studied with private teachers with whom I have not completely agreed. In general, I have told the student that as they know teachers don't always agree. We sometimes have different ways we do things just like we are different people. Depending on the specific cause of the conflict, I either try to find a way to make both ways work (sometimes contacting the private teacher to work on this) or have the student follow the private teacher's advice (since they see the

See above. In all of British Columbia there are only 4 string programmes in the public school system.

I am strictly a private teacher.

I teach privately. I teach some of my students and no problems have developed.
I only teach private lessons.
Yes, I teach all of my current pupils privately.
No
No.
Yes. No.

It is a violation of the Texas Code of Ethics for Teachers (or whatever it is called) that allteachers sign before receiving their employee contract.I charge $100.00 an hour for private lessons if they're willing to pay it, I'm willing to teach them. (Not my own students, of coarse!)

22. What characteristics do your "best" students possess? How does this relate to their parents, these students' other activities, their grades, or other factors? (Competency #3, 13)

Love of music high intelligence or quickness of mind. Not sure this relates in any measurable way to factors you listed above.
Focussed, respectful, work at home to learn what they need to know, listen, never give up. Their parents are the ones that you know.

My best students had either outstanding intelligence, or an extraordinary charisma. The ideal would be to have both, but that doesn't happen so often. In both instances, parents collaborated generously, the intelligent students sometimes went for other professions (law, architecture, and medicine) and the charismatic went after music, since they were not that brilliant in other fields.

My best students are ones who listen, follow directions, work hard, give their best effort,and in general do what I expect them to do. I'm sure that these same characteristics are ones that their parents also support and encourage. I would also think that these characteristics would yield success in other activities and high grades.

Desire and a good attitude. Talent is a requirement in my situation.

Best students are usually self motivated and with terrific parental support at home. And they usually are excellent students in all other subjects besides. Choice of friends revolves around this too!

The best students are the ones who have goals of their own. These students, then, are motivated to do the work required to achieve those goals. My best strategy for encouraging students to practice is in helping them to set those goals. (Of course those with strong family support are generally more confident people and tend to believe that they will achieve.)

Intelligence and musicality are their best characteristics.
I don't have a "best" student. I try to look at each one as special.

REALLY interesting question ! Mostly, enthusiasm and readiness to apply their minds to problem solving. Bright children often make good string players. The very best students also have larger than life personalities (often, are good at drama and are not shy,or handle shyness well) and good co-ordination (often, are good at sport)

Motivation, intelligence, curiousness, broad general education, ambition

Determination, Willingness to learn, Respectful, Adept
TALENT(quick learners)

Two words: Self Motivated!These students are usually very active in many school and nonschool organizations. Their parents take an active interest in their child. These students usually make all "A"s.

23. What is your view and philosophy about seating? How do you handle auditions? (Competency #10; assessment)

I try to rotate seating unless there is a player who everyone acknowledges is strongest. I don't have auditions I watch and determine the level of my players. I also ask people to play out in rehearsal (alone or in groups of two). I avoid asking the weaker students to do this alone, but the strongest get asked to play out alone all the time, to increase pride (I praise their strengths, or else we all just applaud).

Rotate within sections until two weeks prior to the concert. I like to keep a core of strong players at the first two desks.

If you know all the students well, it is a good idea to pair rhythmically strong ones with weaker ones, good readers with worse readers, etc If you form an orchestra by auditioning, watch out for strengths and weaknesses, and pair those.

I think that seating and auditions vary based on the age of the student. In my elementary groups, I vary the seating frequently. I have students make a name tag to hang over their stand on the first day (while I learn their names and for substitutes) and then each time they come in, they find their seats based on where I have put their name tags. Sometimes I set them up with weaker players next to stronger ones while other times I put the stronger ones together. Usually I keep the sections separate, but sometimes I sprinkle the violas, cellos, and basses, in with the violins. My seating plan is based on what I want to accomplish that day. When the concerts get close, I use the same basic seating over and over but do not put them in a "ranked" order. With older groups, I try to vary them somewhat or at least do some type of rotation (sometimes with the first stand or two not moving) and I try not to have them sitting best to worse. I don't hold real audit!ions, but rather I find out how students play at all school levels through my regular assessments (playing tests alone or in groups, playing a piece of their own choice, etc.) Another teacher I heard say something similar to this with which I agree: At school we are a team and we need to work together to help us sound the best and learn the most. We are not trying to compete with one another but are trying to help everyone succeed and do the best they can. Outside of school, at contests or festivals, is where you may try to compete with others and get a feelfor the very competitive nature of some musicians.

They have supportive parents or grandparents. They're interested and participate in other things - soccer, Odyssey of the Mind, Scouts, church groups

One of my favorite topics. I hold auditions only for the principal chairs in the orchestras. Then I place students in with partners to assure pretty even strength throughout each section and rotate stands each week, except the first stand. I also rotate violins in and out of the different sections for each concert, keeping thefirst violins just a bit stronger than the seconds. I am very fortunate to have excellent string players, especially violinists and violists, so both violin sections are very strong.I find that students are very happy with this type of arrangement since all the students know they will get equal treatment.

Many thoughts on this. My past philosophy was to have the best players in the front, but also to rotate the sections so that all had the opportunity to sit up under the directors' nose. I never had auditions. I placed the students where I felt they belonged. Very few complaints. They all know where they stand, pretty much.

As a private teacher, I deal with auditions from the standpoint of preparing the students for them. I try to help them prepare as though they will take a professional audition. When the results are in, I am proud of them regardless of specific placement.

At the middle school level, I seat students as partners, a strong student with a less advanced students. There are as many strong students in the second violin section as in the first. This allows us to play more difficult music, and it doesn't leave the least advanced players stranded in the back of the section, not knowing what is going on.

I don't teach orchestra, but I think that seating should not only be based on audition performance, but leadership skills as well. A couple of students–one very talented boy quit the youth orchestra I work with this year because he wasn't placed in a principal position. He clearly played rings around anyone in the orchestra. But I understand the director's decision. This student had missed/left early a number of rehearsals the prior year and a principal needs to be there. So it is not just on how well someone plays.

If the expectation is that it is done on standard & ability, then this must be adhered to and objective decisions made - this is not easy. If standard & ability do not apply, for instance if older children are asked to support a younger ensemble, it should be made clear that it does not matter where you sit

I need good musicians in the second v. too. They alternate. (No auditions)

I do not have auditions for seats in school. There are opportunities for competitive seating in our region and area orchestras.
Look for a variety of factors in the playing.

I've always tried to seat a strong player with a weak player. This year I am changing it we will be in chair order. All auditions are live during class. My students learn quickly that we are a performing ensemble which means everyone must play in front of each other. Also, it squashes any rumors of favoritism when I do grades. Students who had a bad audition may come in before/after schoo and make up the grade.

24. How do you support the exceptionally talented students without inspiring jealousy or a sense of injustice from the ones who will probably go into other fields? (Competency #1, 3)

Each person has their strengths and weaknesses. Make sure they focus on their strengths.Encourage love for music and to cooperate with each other. We learn from each other. Discourage competition.

I give exceptionally talented students solo opportunities and leadership opportunities. I also quietly ask their opinion all the time (trying not to arouse public jealousy, tho it has happened). As for other fields, everyone in my orchestra goes in to other fields except the one girl who just went off to Juilliard, and many who go into other fields are exceptionally talented as musicians.

Provide for the needs of the others as well. Orchestras need to be viewed as a team the fabulous violinist at the front of the section would be nothing if it weren't for the other 13 that support during FF sections, sweeping melodies, tremolos, etc. we need them all.

The fact that some students will become musicians and others wont, helps to solve this: The future pros play to survive, the others don't. This is usually understood, and a certain protagonism is allowed for those who will become professionals. I have had no problems with this.

I try to stress that we all have our own strengths and weaknesses and that we need to work to develop our strengths and improve as we can our weak areas. I also stress that we, as a group, need to work together so that we are all getting a chance to do our best. This may mean that some students will play a special part in a piece or participate in special activities related to orchestra just as other students may have special activities for academics, sports, theater, or any other area. Most students seem to find this reasonable especially if I don't over-emphasize how wonderful or what special things the very talented students have achieved.

I ask them to play in my chamber music programmes. On July 8 I have three violins and two voice students performing in From My Garden, with music by Ursula Mamlok, stephen paulus, Gershwin etc.

I just try to instill the idea that everyone has talent. And that these talents can be choices as to which direction a student wants to go. Just because it may or may not be music is no reason not to do the best they can do.Also, I try to have the students focus on themselves and their strengths and goals rather than on what another student may or may not be doing.

Generally, I give extra time and extra opportunities for performance. I keep these "extras" very low-key and I also let every student be assured that I am 100% behind him/her.

Many learn to play a second instrument in orchestra.

I feel that all students are talented. Talent Although some students have an easier time, I look for areas in which that student is talented and try to develop that. I have no sense of jealousy or injustice in my studio because I appreciate each student individually.

I haven't found instances of such jealousy yet, perhaps because I remind people why they are playing in the first place, also that everyone has different strengths, and simply encourage people to give of their best that is all that is required.

All students are taken individually and become the same devotion. (At least, I hope so...)

I give them solos to play and use them as role models. We have a cadet teaching system in my school.
Keep them IN the group.

I get them in the local youth orchestra and involve them in outside school orchestra activities. In class, they are treated as an equal with the other students.

CPSIA information can be obtained at www.ICGtesting.com
Printed in the USA
BVOW03s1017230714

360217BV00027B/571/P